Shiva Charitra
Narratives of Shiva

BIHAR SCHOOL OF YOGA

50 years

1963–2013
GOLDEN JUBILEE

WORLD YOGA CONVENTION 2013
GANGA DARSHAN, MUNGER, BIHAR, INDIA
23rd–27th October 2013

Shiva Charitra
Narratives of Shiva

Swami Niranjanananda Saraswati

Yoga Publications Trust, Munger, Bihar, India

Printed by Yoga Publications Trust
    First edition 2013

ISBN: 978-93-81620-71-7

Publisher and distributor: Yoga Publications Trust, Ganga Darshan, Munger, Bihar, India.

Website: www.biharyoga.net
        www.rikhiapeeth.net

Printed at Thomson Press (India) Limited, New Delhi, 110001

Dedication

*In humility we offer this dedication to
Swami Sivananda Saraswati, who initiated
Swami Satyananda Saraswati into the secrets of yoga.*

Contents

Introduction

In 2008, the children of Bal Yoga Mitra Mandal, Children's Yoga Fellowship, a yoga movement of children established by Swami Niranjanananda Saraswati, approached Swamiji and asked him to tell the stories of Shiva. Swamiji assured them that he would do so. Accordingly, from 14th to 19th February 2009, Swamiji conducted a unique program in Munger consisting of discourses on Shiva and worship of Shiva, one of the most prominent figures of Indian culture, philosophy and history.

Held at Baidyanath Shankarbag, an ancient temple dedicated to Shiva, adjacent to the old ashram where the Bihar School of Yoga first came into being, it was an ideal location for invoking the 'auspicious one'. The satsangs were held in Hindi; however, devotees and guests from all over the world sat transfixed through the program, as if transported to another realm. This was no ordinary storytelling; every word that Swamiji spoke became a mantra, radiating a power that lifted everyone present out of their ordinary selves, irrespective of whether or not they understood the meaning.

All through the satsangs, an extraordinary brilliance seemed to emanate from Swamiji, as if Shiva himself had come to reside in him. Interspersed with powerful chants from ancient texts, rituals of Shiva worship, joyous kirtans and short enactments of Shiva's life by children, each session was a vibrant invocation of the Shiva tattwa. Shiva no longer remained an idea, but became an experiential truth for every participant.

Puranic tales

Titled *Shiva Charitra*, 'Narratives of Shiva', the satsangs distilled the essence of *Shiva Purana*, one of the eighteen major Puranas of Indian literature. The word *purana* means 'once upon a time'. Often interpreted as mythology, the Puranas are actually documented history of the earliest days of creation, sometimes written in coded language, sometimes in stories and parables.

The facts stated in the Puranas are now being corroborated by modern science. Swamiji talks about the Big Bang theory clearly referred to in the Puranas, saying: "When this fact of science is compared with the events described in our *itihasa* or history and the Puranas, we come to realize that what is written in the Puranas is true. They are not flights of imagination from somebody's fertile mind. Scientific truths, the eternal truths, have been inscribed in the Puranas. If you think that the scriptures contain random speculation, you should revise your opinion."

Yogic katha

Narration of stories from ancient texts and scriptures is an enduring tradition of India, and is known as *katha*. Specialized *kathakars*, storytellers, who may be householders or sannyasins, travel from place to place conducting days of storytelling in which the young and the old alike participate. Swamiji's satsangs were based along the lines of this tradition, but conducted in his distinct style. His approach was deeply yogic and spiritual.

Swamiji's central question was: 'Who is Shiva?' Is he to be accepted just as a Godhead or can we really access him? For an answer to this question, said Swamiji, we have to look at the basis of creation. The universe with its galaxies, stars and planets is constantly expanding. This is the literal meaning of *Brahman*, the term used for the ultimate reality or Shiva. If we apply this concept to the past, it means that the creation began at some point of time and since then it has been expanding continuously. The question therefore

2

arises, 'What was there in the beginning?' Swamiji says, "It is said that before creation there was neither *sat*, existence, nor *asat*, non-existence; there was no sky, no space, no infinite expanse of water. Were they hidden somewhere? Who could have hidden them? Who was the creator? Is there a creator, or is there not a creator?"

The answer follows, "There was total darkness in all the directions and in that darkness there was only the one existent reality, *Tatsat Brahman*, and there was nothing else beside that. In the Shaiva agamas, the tantric scriptures of Shiva, that existent reality has been called Paramshiva. This reality is immanent in creation; is responsible for creation, preservation and dissolution, yet is not bound by it. Paramshiva is the eternal witness or *drashta* of this play of creation."

After detailing the different events related to the evolution of creation, Swamiji says, "The word 'Shiva' points towards both Shiva and Shakti, and it is the most benevolent and auspicious element in creation. Shiva is jnana and Shiva is the ultimate experience. If Shiva is the goal, then bhakti is the means. Once again, ask yourself, 'Who was there before creation and who will be here afterwards?' You will receive the answer, 'Before creation, Shiva was there and he will be there after creation, and Shiva and Shakti are not different from each other.'"

Shiva lila

Shiva is the transcendental reality of this creation and the stories in this book are connected with his *lila* or divine play throughout the different ages. Some of the stories depict his transcendence, while others are symbolic. For example, it is said that the moon god had twenty-seven daughters. The gods represent the different forms of the energies that pervaded creation after the Big Bang. These energies eventually solidified into the planets and constellations as we know them today.

The stories related to Kartikeya and Ganesha, the sons of Shiva and Parvati, represent different aspects of this transcendental reality. Kartikeya, the first born, is essentially the offspring of Shiva. He was born from Shiva's third eye, the eye of wisdom, and he represents the pure jnana aspect of being. It is said that six mothers, the six krittikas, nursed him. The individual journeys through the six chakras and evolves to the state of wisdom in sahasrara. This state of jnana is accompanied by non-attachment or *vairagya*. This is what is conveyed in the story of Kartikeya, when he leaves behind his parents in Kailash and settles in the South.

The other son is Ganesha, who is born of Parvati and later accepted by Shiva. Ganesha represents the higher mind and is the first evolute of Shakti. We can say that the manifest creation begins with his birth. In human existence, it is said that Ganesha stands for the lower brain, which includes all the autonomic functions. One has to develop awareness of these functions before one can have access to the higher functions of the brain. As one progresses on the path of evolution, one will be able to piece together more insights into this symbology.

These stories are not only symbolic; they are also factual. However, they speak of a transcendental reality not readily comprehensible to the human intellect. All the elements of the internal creation are there in the external creation. If Shiva, as the pure consciousness, exists inside, then it is equally acceptable that he resides in more than one place in the external world, for example, in Kailash and in the Shivalingams. Similarly, as Shakti is responsible for the entire creation, she is present in Kailash and in the sixty-four Shakti peeths.

The path of evolution
Shiva is the formless reality, and it is through the agency of Shakti, who came forth from him, that this entire creation takes form. To understand the mystery of this creation one has to follow the path of vidya, as detailed by Shiva in his discourses with Shakti. The science of tantra, which deals

with the expansion of consciousness and the release of energy, was also detailed by Shiva to Parvati.

The final question posed by Swamiji is, "When the creation is destroyed, what happens to the earth, the moon, the planets, the stars, the constellations? Where do they go? Has anyone thought about this? This creation is not eternal; it is the creation cycle that is eternal, and that cycle involves creation and destruction. The creation that is born is certain to be destroyed. Where does it go? Where is it dissolved? Science is presently trying to investigate this. At the time of dissolution, there is not even a ray of light in existence, let alone the planets. What happens? Where does everything go? Is the entire creation burnt to ashes?"

It has been said in the Shaiva agamas that at the time of dissolution, everything merges in the lingam. The lingam is of three different kinds: gross, subtle and transcendental. Shiva and the lingam are one and the same. The lingam is the symbol of the formless reality. In deeper states of meditation, the causal body is perceived in the form of the lingam. The lingam is also an integral part of the chakras. The entire creation, the microcosmic and macrocosmic, merges in the effulgent lingam.

In Shivaloka

Over the course of the five days of Swamiji's satsangs, the entire place transformed. It was no longer Shivalaya, but Shivaloka, as Swamiji called it. From *laya* to *aloka* or from *alaya* to *loka*: from dissolution to brilliance, from temple to eternal spheres, the very axis of one's existence was shifted. What Swamiji spoke of was not myth, or mysterious, unknowable precepts, but became a living experience.

As you read this translation of the satsangs, drop all your conditionings, and move through the pages with an open and alert mind; you will undoubtedly receive invaluable insights in this journey of consciousness. It will open up the inner world of your own true nature, and teach how to live fully in the here and now.

5

Prātaḥ smarāmi bhavabhīti haraṃ sureśaṃ
Gaṅgādharaṃ vṛṣabhavāhanamambikeśam.
Khaṭvāṅgaśūla-varadābhayahastamīśaṃ
Saṃsāra roga haramauṣadhamadvitīyam.

Prātarnamāmigiriśaṃ girijārddhadehaṃ
Sarga-sthiti-pralaya-kāraṇamādidevam.
Viśveśvaraṃ vijita viśvamano'bhirāmaṃ
Saṃsāra roga haramauṣadhamadvitīyam.

Prātarbhajāmi śivamekamanantamādyaṃ
Vedānta-vedyamanaghaṃ puruṣaṃ mahāntam.
Nāmādibhedarahitaṃ ṣaḍbhāvaśūnyaṃ
Samsāra roga haramauṣadhamadvitīyam.

6

Satsang 1

14 February 2009

The great dissolution

In this universe, numerous ages, aeons or *yugas* have gone by. Creation has happened a number of times and dissolution also. Now there is darkness everywhere, there is no sign of any life. The last age has ended and the atmosphere is still; the space is empty and there is nothing in that still, empty space. There is no life, death, gunas, negative qualities, light, matter or objects: everything has dissolved into an unmanifest, supreme element. This state has been described in the *Nasadiya Sukta* of the Vedas:

> *Naasadaaseenno sadaaseet tadaaneem*
> *naaseedrajo no vyomaa paro yat;*
> *Kimaavareevah kuha kasya sharmannambhah*
> *kimaaseedgahanam gabheeram.*

> *Na mrityuraaseedamritam na tarhi na*
> *raatryaa ahna aaseet praketah;*
> *Aaneedavaatam svadhayaa tadekam*
> *tasmaaddhaanyanna parah kim chanaasa.*

> *Tama aaseet tamasaa goollahanagre'praketam*
> *salilam sarvamaa idam;*
> *Tuchchhyenaabhvapihitam yadaaseet*
> *tapasastanmahinaajaayataikam.*

Kaamastadage samavartataadhi
manaso retah prathamam yadaseet;
Sato bandhumsati niravindan hridi
prateepyaa kavayo maneeshaa.

Tirashcheeno vitato rashmireshaa
madhah svidaasee'dupari svidaasee't;
Retodhaa aasan mahimaana aasantsvadhaa
avastaat prayatih parastaat.

Ko addhaa veda ka iha pravochat kuta
aajaataa kuta iyam visrishtih;
Arvaargdavaa asya visarjanenaa'thaa
ko veda yata aababhoova.

Iyam visrishtiryata aababhoova yadi
vaa dadhe yadi vaa na;
Yo asyaadhyakshah parame vyomantso
anga veda yadi vaa na veda.

The *Nasadiya Sukta* says that before creation there was neither *sat*, existence, nor *asat*, non-existence; there was no sky, no space, no infinite expanse of water. Were they hidden somewhere? Who could have hidden them? Who was the creator? Is there a creator, or is it not a creator? Maybe He stays high up in the sky, invisible. Perhaps He alone knows, or maybe He also does not know. No one knows, no one knows, no one knows . . .

Paramshiva

There was total darkness in all the directions, and in that darkness there was only the one existent reality, *Tatsat Brahman,* and nothing else beside that. In the Shaiva agamas, the tantric scriptures of Shiva, that existent reality has been called Paramshiva. This reality is immanent in creation; it is responsible for creation, preservation and dissolution, yet is not bound by it. Paramshiva is the eternal witness or *drashta* of this play of creation.

8

In that endless void, a vibration spontaneously came forth in the Paramshiva tattwa. In that dark expanse there appeared a glimmer of light, and slowly that wide expanse became a playground of light and darkness. At that moment there arose a desire, a sankalpa in the Paramshiva tattwa to enact a *lila*, a play, and to become 'many' from that 'one'. At that moment, the Shiva tattwa brought forth from within itself the Shakti tattwa, called *Shivaa*.

Shiva and Shivaa

Shiva and Shakti are not separate from each other. Shiva is not the male gender and neither is Shakti the female gender. On the basis of language, Shiva is identified with the male gender and Shakti with the female gender, but in that Paramshiva tattwa, the universal truth, there is no male gender, nor any indication of masculinity; similarly, there is no female gender, nor is there any indication of feminity. Fire is hidden in the wood; it is not seen. Nonetheless, we can say that the fire resides in the wood. Wood and fire are two different elements: one is visible and the other invisible. You have to follow a process to bring the fire out from the wood. Similarly, Shakti is always existent in Shiva. Shakti is an integral part of Shiva, who, as the element of consciousness, becomes the witness of everything. It is said in the Shaiva agamas that both Shiva and Shakti are jointly responsible for the evolution of the world and take part together in this lila, and in the end they absorb the creation into themselves.

Manifestation of Vishnu

When the sankalpa of *Eko'ham bahusyamah* – "I am one, let me become many" arose in the Paramshiva tattwa, Paramshiva rubbed the *amrita* or nectar on his left side. A very handsome masculine figure then emerged from his left side. That person had a predominance of sattwa; he was peaceful, good-looking, endowed with brilliance, and was an ocean of serenity.

9

Avimukta kshetra

Paramshiva told that person, "You are born from my left side and you have an extensive role to play in the ensuing creation. Therefore, your name will be Vishnu. Vishnu, undergo some austerities, some *tapas*, and do sadhana to bring forth the new creation." Vishnu said, "Lord, where do I undergo this tapas? All around I can see nothing but an empty sky without any support. Where do I sit? Where do I contemplate? Where do I work?"

Paramshiva then built a city in the sky which was five *kosa* (about two miles) wide and he placed that city beside Vishnu. Vishnu established himself there and with the resolve to bring about a new creation, he began doing tapas. During the tapas, streams of water gushed out from Vishnu's body; so much sweat welled from his body that it engulfed the entire sky and space. Nothing but water was visible and the city started drowning in that deluge of water.

When the water level started rising, Vishnu's meditation was interrupted. He found himself surrounded by water. He was astonished to see so much water and wondered how it had gathered. He moved his head to look around and in the process dropped one of his earrings in one part the city. The place where he dropped his earring is known as *Manikarnika* (the name of the sacred ghat in Kashi, modern-day Varanasi). As the city was now drowning in water, Vishnu prayed to Paramshiva and said, "Lord you asked me do tapas here, but this city is now drowning in water."

Paramshiva placed the city on top of his trident and kept it there. This city became known as *Avimukta Kshetra*, the realm of liberation. It is said in the Shaiva agamas that even during the time of *pralaya*, dissolution of creation, this city is not destroyed as it is placed on the tip of Shiva's trident. The entire creation is destroyed, everything is dissolved in the one ultimate reality, yet that city of five kosas remains intact at the tip of Paramshiva's trident. Later, when the world is again created, Paramshiva places the city back on the earth and starts living there. That city is known as Kashi, and also as Anandavana and Avimukta Kshetra.

Creation of the elements

Vishnu then resumed his tapasya. In the process of doing tapasya and meditation, he entered the state of yoga nidra and lay down on his bed of water. Thus, Vishnu's second name is Narayana, as water is also called *nara*. Vishnu stayed in the water in the state of yoga nidra for a long time, and during that time all the elements appeared from his body. First came the *Mahat tattwa* or 'the great element', and from the Mahat tattwa arose the three gunas. The threefold *ahamkara* or ego arose from the gunas, the five *tanmatras* or the five subtle elements from ahamkara, and the *pancha mahabhootas* or the five gross elements from the tanmatras. The five organs of perception, or *jnanendriyas,* and the five organs of action, or *karmendriyas*, also manifested. Adorned by these elements, Narayana reposed into yoga nidra in the water. All the twenty-four elements became permeated by Vishnu.

Emergence of Brahma

Time passed without any indication of its measure. It is possible that it was only a moment, or it might have been an infinity. When Paramshiva saw Vishnu lying down in the water, he realized that creation would not proceed through him, so he rubbed the nectar on his right side and Brahma manifested. Brahma did not see Paramshiva, who is invisible and *nirguna*, without any qualities. Brahma found himself alone and saw only his own self. Paramshiva deluded Brahma and brought him near Vishnu. Through the will of Paramshiva, a lotus now appeared on the navel of Vishnu and that nirguna, unmanifest, invisible Paramshiva put the deluded Brahma on that lotus.

When Brahma opened his eyes, he found himself seated on the lotus. He wondered, 'All around is darkness, void; there is nothing, neither existence nor non-existence, sat or asat, and I am sitting alone here. Who gave birth to me? From where have I come? From the time I opened my eyes, I have seen only myself. There must be some person who has given birth to me. Where is he? I should find out.' With this intention, Brahma then entered the stalk of the lotus and travelled downwards.

Brahma wandered around inside the lotus stalk. It is unknown how much time passed in infinity, yet he did not find anything. Brahma then started to ascend towards the lotus flower. Possibly he had forgotten the way out, as he stayed in the stem for thousands of years. When he could not find the way out, Brahma became frightened. However, because of Paramshiva's grace he heard, "Brahma, you will not find your creator by searching for him. If you want to know him you have to do *tapasya*, undergo austerities." Then Paramshiva once again deluded Brahma through his *shakti*, energy, and *maya*, power of illusion, and put him back on the lotus. Brahma was wonderstruck. There was no one visible, yet he had received a clear instruction, "Do tapas."

Param linga

Brahma started doing tapasya. After an infinitely long duration of tapasya, Narayana appeared before him. Brahma asked him, "Who are you?" Narayana said, "I am your creator. You are born from my navel lotus." Now Paramshiva wanted to do his lila, so he planted a seed of mischief in Brahma's mind. Brahma said, "How is it possible that I have appeared from your navel lotus? You are just like me. Our height is the same, our bodies are similar. If I had really appeared from your navel lotus, then you should have come when I was looking for you. You are not my creator. You are just like me; somebody has given birth to you just like me."

Narayana said, "No, I am your creator; I am responsible for your birth." In this manner, both of them started arguing. When the arguments reached a peak, a tremendous sound or *nada* was heard and a pillar of fire appeared between Narayana and Brahma. That pillar of fire enveloped the entire sky and nobody could see either its top or bottom. That massive pillar of fire made both the gods speechless with wonder.

Brahma and Vishnu were now curious to know the source of the sound and fire. Brahma said, "I will go to the top of the fire and find out from where it has originated." Vishnu said, "I will go down to find the end of this fire. Whosoever amongst us comes back with this knowledge will be the winner." Vishnu put this challenge to Brahma: "Find out what this pillar of fire is; where does it begin and end?" Brahma took the form of a swan and flew upwards, while Vishnu took the form of a boar and went downwards in search of the source of the pillar of fire. However, both of them came back without finding the end or the beginning, and they stood in a state of surrender with their hands folded in prayer saying, "We have not been able to find the beginning or the end."

Pranava

At that moment, the nada of *Aum* was heard from the pillar of fire. This sound was heard clearly in all the directions and was heard first by Narayana and Brahma. They heard the eternal, primordial and original sound of 'A' on the southern side of the pillar, 'U' on the northern side and 'M' in the centre. When they heard the combination of these three sounds as *Aum*, they again became curious to know what was happening.

According to the Shaiva agamas, at that point of time a person with the divine splendour of a rishi appeared before Brahma and Narayana and said, "The sound of *Aum* which you just heard and the pillar of fire which you see is the form of Paramshiva. Paramshiva is the source, the ultimate element through whom all creatures and matter are created, sustained and destroyed. The nada of *Aum* is the sound body of Paramshiva. Paramshiva himself appeared between you as the pillar of fire and the sound of *Aum*." Saying thus, the rishi disappeared.

Brahma and Vishnu bowed down to that pillar of fire and stood quietly on their respective sides, right and left. At that moment, Paramshiva manifested himself in a visible form.

The form of Shiva

The five-faced Shiva is the manifest form of Paramshiva. He has ten hands, in which he holds a *kalasha* or pot, a half-moon shaped sword, a bow and arrow, a spear, a *trishula* or trident, a *shankha* or conch, a discus, a *damaru* or small drum, a lotus, and his last hand is held in *abhaya mudra*, the gesture of benediction. His body is white like camphor and all the faces have three eyes, matted locks and snakes garlanding the throat.

Paramshiva manifested himself in this form to Vishnu and Brahma and said, "I am Paramshiva. I have two manifestations: one is called *sakala*, complete, which implies being with form, and other is called *nishkala*, which implies being without form."

Paramshiva further said, "The lunar day upon which I have manifested myself will be known as *Sivaratri*. On this day, whosoever worships my sakala manifestation in the form of an image of Shiva, or my nishkala manifestation in the form of a lingam, will surely attain me and be liberated."

Shivalingam

Paramshiva is formless, unmanifest, eternal, without a beginning, and is consciousness itself. Paramshiva is not visible to anybody, nor cognizable by any sense organ, and cannot be touched by the mind, nor reached through any emotion. The symbol of this ultimate reality is the Shivalingam; it is the symbol of the formless existence of Paramshiva. Paramshiva says, "As I am formless, this Shivalingam is also beyond form." Therefore, the worship of the formless is achieved through the Shivalingam.

The form of Paramshiva

The form through which Paramshiva manifested himself before Brahma and Narayana is the form of Sadashiva. Five-faced, three-eyed, ten-handed, complexion white as camphor, Paramshiva manifested himself in his sakala form to Narayana and Brahma in that empty sky through his own effulgent light. The other manifestation of Paramshiva is his mantra body. *Aum*, which is composed of A, U, M, has been accepted as the *shabdabrahman* form or the sound body of nishkala Paramshiva. Five sounds come forth from the five mouths of Sadashiva to create the sound body of sakala Shiva. The five sounds are Na, Ma, Shi, Va, Ya, which form the mantra *Namah Shivaya*, which is also known as the *panchakshari* mantra or the five-lettered mantra.

Through divine coincidence, we also encounter the number five in the mantra *AUM*. A is the first vowel. U comes next; U is the fifth vowel in the group of Sanskrit vowels. Then comes M; M is the fifth letter in fifth group of Sanskrit consonants: 'pa, pha, ba, bha, ma'. The combination of A-U-M forms *Aum*, which is the mantra of the formless, nishkala Paramshiva. The aradhana of the Shivalingam should be done with the *Aum* mantra only. When *Aum* is added to the panchakshari mantra, forming *Aum Namah Shivaya*, then it becomes a medium for both formless or nishkala worship and worship with form, sakala. The letters of the mantra are eulogized in the *Shiva Shadakshara Stotram*:

Omkaaram bindu samyuktam nityam dhyaayanti yoginah;
Kaamadam mokshadam chaiva omkaaraaya namo namah.
Namanti rishayo devaah namantyapsarasaanganaah;
Naraah namanti devesham nakaaraaya namo namah.
Mahaadevam mahaatmaanam mahaadhyaanaparaayanam;
Mahaapaapaharam devam makaaraaya namo namah.
Shivam shaantam jagannaatham lokaanugrahakaarakam;
Shivamekapadam nityam shikaaraaya namo namah.
Vaahanam vrishabho yasya vaasukee kanthabhooshanam;
Vaame shaktidharam devam vakaaraaya namo namah.
Yatra yatra sthito devaah sarvavyaapee maheshvarah;
Yo guruh sarvadevaanaam yakaaraaya namo namah.

Namah shivaaya namo namah, Namah shivaaya namo namah.

Five faces of Shiva

The five faces of Shiva are called *sadakhya* in the Shaiva agamas. The sadakhya manifestation is sakala, with form. The five faces are known as Shiva sadakhya, amurta sadakhya, murta sadakhya, kartri sadakhya and karma sadakhya.

The first face, *Shiva sadakhya*, is the state of purity, where there is no mark, blotch or darkness. He is always complete and pure by himself, and there is no change. The pure Shiva sadakhya is also the form of Sadashiva.

The second is *amurta sadakhya*, who is facing north. Its brilliance is said to be equivalent to that of one million suns. Its shape is that of a luminous pillar and it is responsible for the creation of the world and also for its dissolution. Just as Shiva sadakhya is the symbol of purity and divinity, amurta sadakhya is the symbol or form of creation and its dissolution.

The third is *murta sadakhya*. Its shape is like a blazing fire and it is endowed with beautiful attributes. This face is facing west and *icchashakti*, or the divine will, is its manifestation.

The fourth is *kartri sadakhya*, whose form is like the aura of pure crystal. Its nature is *jnana* or knowledge. When you work, the intellect is applied and that intellect is jnana. Kartri sadakhya is seen as jnana, as a definite method or system.

The fifth is *karma sadakhya*, which connects the *jivatma*, individual soul, with the objects of the world and makes one lose oneself in those objects until, through karma sadakhya's grace, the jivatma is liberated from the bondage of the worldly objects.

Paramshiva's Shakti manifests herself in the world through these five faces. That Paramshakti, also known as Paramshivaa, manifests herself as *kalaas*, expressions, through the five faces of Paramshiva. This is the reason why the story of Shiva and Shivaa always goes together.

Five actions of Shiva

Brahma then told Shiva, "Lord, we are blessed to have your darshan. Please tell us now what it is you do. What is your role? We have come to know that your body, which is composed of mantras, is of the nature of *Aum*. We have also seen your form in the shape of the five-faced Sadashiva, and you have told us about the roles of those five faces. Now please tell us, what are your actions or *karmas*?"

Shiva said, "I have five basic actions which are known as the *panchakrityas*. First is *srishti* or creation, second is *palana* or sustenance, third is *samhara* or destruction, fourth is *tirobhava* or veiling, and fifth is *anugraha* or grace. These actions are eternally perfect and there is never any change. I have performed these actions since time immemorial. From time to time, I send others also to carry out some other actions. They complete these actions according to my will.

"The creation of the world is srishti. It is also known as *sarga*. Maintaining that creation in an orderly state is *sthiti* or palana, and destruction of that creation is samhara. Reversing the tendency of the pranas so that one engages one's attention in the world is tirobhava, while going beyond that or release from that is anugraha. Srishti takes place on earth or *bhutala*, sthiti in water or *jala*, samhara in fire or *agni*, tirobhava in air or *vayu* and anugraha in space or *akasha*. My five faces shoulder these five tasks.

"Brahma, you have undergone tapasya, therefore I am giving you the job of creation, srishti. I am giving to you one of my actions, which means that now I have one less job. Vishnu has also done tapasya. I am giving him the job of sustenance, sthiti, which is my second action or *kritya*. Two more beings have also manifested from me. To the form of Sadashiva, the form in which I am standing before you, I give the job of tirobhava or veiling, and after some time I will incarnate as Rudra, who will take care of my kritya of samhara or destruction. I myself will continue with my task of anugraha in my unmanifest, beginningless and infinite form, as Paramshiva."

Srishti, sthiti, samhara, tirobhava and anugraha: these five actions are his *lila* or play of creation. A lila is not a drama; rather, it is this panchakritya or five actions. These five tasks are accomplished through the will or sankalpa of Paramshiva who, as a result of this sankalpa, enacts a lila. Paramshiva himself, through his totally independent shakti, sometimes involves himself in creation, sometimes in sustenance and sometimes in destruction. He withdraws everything into himself and projects and expands the entire creation from himself. From time to time, he binds the created beings through his power of tirobhava and he also releases them through his power of anugraha. This whole world is, in essence, a lila of Paramshiva, and we all live our lives within his panchakritya.

Instructions to Brahma and Vishnu for creation

Paramashiva, in the form of Sadashiva, gave the teachings of the Vedas to Brahma and Vishnu through the medium of breath. After giving the teachings of the Vedas, he commanded Brahma, "You have been born from my right side for the purpose of creation, so carry on with your work." He then told Vishnu, "You have been born from my left side. You sustain the creation, and Rudra, who is also a part of me, will carry out destruction. This trinity of gods will look after the gross aspects of creation. As Sadashiva and Paramshiva, I will look after tirobhava and anugraha, which are the subtle aspects.

"My inseparable Parashakti will help Brahma in the form of Vagdevi Saraswati, the goddess of learning; she will take shelter with Vishnu in the form of Lakshmi, the goddess of prosperity; and in the form of Kali she will come to my other incarnation, Rudra. My Parashakti will go to Brahma as Vagdevi Saraswati, because for creation one needs *jnana* or knowledge, *buddhi* or intelligence, *vani* or the power of speech, *chintan* or contemplation, and *kalaa* or the creative arts and their expression. My Parashakti as Lakshmi will come to Vishnu. Her nature is that of *samriddhi* or prosperity and *poornata*, fulfilment, which is something everyone looks for in life. Kali will help my other incarnation, Rudra, in his job of destruction, and thus the work of creation will continue.

18

Equality of Paramshiva and Vishnu

Paramshiva said, "Vishnu is in my heart and I am in his; whoever sees both as the same, who sees no difference, that being is dear to me." Paramshiva never said, "Brahma is in my heart and I am in his." He mentioned only Vishnu's name. Why not Brahma's; after all, Brahma is also born from the same body of Paramshiva ?

Brahma is the creator, and you will recall that he had all sorts of doubts about Shiva and Vishnu. He started thinking that he was greater than Paramshiva and Vishnu. He is the symbol of a rajoguna-dominated person. Vishnu had a predominance of sattwaguna and Brahma, of rajoguna. Brahma would not obey anybody. He would say forthright, "I am the creator, I am great, I have produced everybody." He had a fight with Vishnu and also with Shiva. Paramshiva said, "Whosoever has a simple and straightforward nature and is pure and pious, I reside within him. If somebody's mind is full of crookedness, hypocrisy, cleverness and ignorance, how can I stay in him? Vishnu is peaceful, sober, serene, pure, permanent, eternal and beautiful. He resides in me and I reside in him."

Paramshiva then told Vishnu, "You will be respected and worshipped in all the worlds. In the worlds created by Brahma, whenever there is a crisis, you will have to make an effort to resolve that situation. You have to constantly strive to eliminate all forms of suffering, and in an incognito form I will keep on helping you in all difficult situations. I will eliminate all your invincible enemies. In Brahma's creation, you will incarnate in different forms to keep up your good work and you will always strive to release people from the bondage of the world."

Paramshiva further told Vishnu, "You will meditate on Rudra and Rudra will meditate on you."

Rudradhyeyo bhavaamshchaiva bhavaddhyeyo harastathaa;
Yuvayorantaram naiva tava rudrasya kinchana.
Rudrabhakto naro yastu tava nindaam karishyati;
Tasya punyam cha nikhilam drutam bhasma bhavishyati.

19

There is no difference between you and Rudra. If any person who is a devotee of Rudra and Shiva criticizes you, all his accumulated merits will come to nothing. That person who bears ill-will towards you must go to hell in accordance to my laws, disciplines and system.

When Paramshiva had finished, Vishnu and Brahma praised him thus:

Namo nishkalaroopaaya namo nishkalatejase;
Namah sakalanaathaayaa namo sakalaatmane.
Namah pranavavaachyaaya namah pranaavalingine;
Namah srishthyaadikartre cha namah panchamukhaaya.
Panchabrahmaswaroopaaya panchakrityaaya te namah;
Aatmane brahmane tubhyamanantagunashaktaye.
Sakalaakalaroopaaya shambhavi guruve namah.

Paramshiva gave them his blessings and disappeared as they were looking at him. From that time, the ritual worship of the Shivalingam started.

Lingam worship
The worship of the lingam predates the worship of the image of Shiva. The Shivalingam is the first manifest symbol of Paramshiva. When there was nothing in existence, the formless manifested itself as the lingam. Thus, the Shivalingam has been accepted as the first symbol of divinity, of God.

Do not forget that Shiva and Shivaa, his shakti, are the same. Just as fire is hidden in wood, Shivaa is concealed in Shiva. As water has fluidity inherent in it, similarly Shivaa is inherent in Shiva. They are not different from each other. There is strength hidden in the body and when it is needed, it comes out. If a glass of water is to be lifted from the table then that much strength will manifest. If the whole table is to be lifted then a corresponding amount of strength will become manifest in the muscles. If you have to move the cupboard then that amount of strength will come forth

20

from within. *Shakti* or power remains in the body in a subtle form. Similarly, the Shivaa element remains in Shiva in a subtle form.

The Shivalingam is the expression of the nature of Shiva and Shakti. The part where the lingam is placed is called the *argha* or *peeth*. This argha is of the nature of Shakti. Why is it called a lingam? The lingam is the symbol of Paramshiva himself and it is derived from the world *laya*, dissolution. As it is the support for dissolution, it is called lingam. When the entire creation ends and merges into the formless, then everything dissolves into that lingam.

The lingam is the symbol of Paramshiva and the peeth or argha is that of Paramshakti. There is no life without Shakti. There is no srishti, stithi, samhara, tirobhava or anugraha without Shakti. Shakti exists in all ages. Argha is the form of Shakti that has taken the past, present and the future into her fold. The Shivalingam is the symbol of consciousness and thus faces upwards, and is uplifting. That which wants to know and understand itself, to achieve something, to go beyond the worldly existence and try to evolve, that consciousness has the form of the Shivalingam. The Shakti or energy that expands into the three temporal dimensions of past, present and future has the shape of the argha. Therefore, the Shivalingam has both Shiva and Shakti established in it.

Argha is also the symbol of the *yoni*, the female reproductive organ. The lingam is placed in the yoni; the creation proceeds through the union of the male and female elements, and the Shivalingam is the symbol of that union.

Creation

After giving the command, "Proceed with creation", Paramshiva disappeared and Vishnu and Brahma went back to their respective places. Brahma went back to the lotus and sat there contemplating creation. While he contemplated, an egg manifested out of his will. That egg was the insentient form of the twenty-four tattwas or elements that had

21

come forth during Narayana's tapasya. That egg which was composed of the twenty-four elements is known as hiranyagarbha. *Garbha*, meaning womb, is that place where a being grows and is nourished. *Hiranyagarbha* is the golden womb.

Vishnu in creation

From Vishnu, Brahma took the twenty-four elements, which were in an insentient form, and put them into the golden womb. Vishnu himself entered into this egg created by Brahma, and the twenty-four elements started becoming conscious as soon as Vishnu entered the egg. Vishnu entered that cosmic egg in different forms. That *Parampurusha*, Ultimate Person, has thousands of heads, eyes and legs. He surrounded the earth in all directions and enveloped the whole egg. He is described in the *Purusha Suktam*:

*Om sahasrasheershaa purushah. Sahasraakshah
sahasrapaat. Sa bhoomim vishvato vritvaa.
Atyatishthaddashaangulam. Purusha evedagvam sarvam.
Yadbhootam yachcha bhavyam. Utaamritatvasyeshaanah.
Yadannenaatirohati. Etaavaanasya mahimaa. Ato
jyaayaagvamshcha pooorushah.*

*Paado'sya vishvaa bhootaani. Tripaadasyaamritam
divi. Tripaadoordhva udaitpurushah. Paado'syehaa
bhavaatpunah. Tato vishvanvyakraamat.
Saashanaanashane abhi. Tasmaadviraadajaayata.
Viraajo adhi poorushah. Sa jaato atyarichyata.
Pashchaadbhoomimatho purah.*

*Yatpurushena havishaa. Devaa yajnamatanvata. Vasanto
asyaaseedaajyam. Greeshma idhmashsharaddhavih
saptaasyaasanparidhayah. Trih sapta samidhah kritaah.
Devaa yadyajnam tanvaanaah. Abadhnanpurusham
pashum. Tam yajnam barhishi praukshan. Purusham
jaatamagratah.*

22

Tena devaa ayajanta. Saadhyaa rishayashcha ye.
Tasmaadyajnaatsarvahutah. Sambhritam prishadaajyam.
Pashoogvamstaagvamshchakre vaayavyaan.
Aaranyaangraamyaashcha ye. Tasmaadyajnaatsarvahutah.
Richah saamaani jajnire. Chhandaagvamsi jajnire
tasmaat. Yajustasmaadajaayata.

Tasmaadashvaa ajaayanta. Ye ke chobhayaadatah. Gaavo
ha jajnire tasmaat. Tasmaajjaataa ajaavayah. Yatpurusham
vyadadhuh. Katidhaa vyakalpayan. Mukham kimasya
kau baahoo. Kaa vooroo paadaavuchyete. Braahmano'sya
mukhamaaseet. Baahoo raajanyah kritah.

Ooroo tadasya yadvaishyah. Padbhyaagvam shoodro
ajaayata. Chandramaa manaso jaatah. Chakshoh
sooryo ajaayata. Mukhaadindrashchaagnishcha.
Praanaadvaayurajaayata. Naabhyaa aaseedantariksham.
Sheershno dyauh samavartata. Padbhyaam bhoomirdishah
shrotraat. Tathaa lokaagvam akalpayan.

Vedaahametam purusham mahaantam. Aadityavarnam
tamasastupaare. Sarvaani roopaani vichitya
dheerah. Naamaani kritvaa'bhivadan yadaaste.
Dhaataa purastaadyamudaajahaara. Shakrah
pravidvaanpradishashchatasrah. Tamevam vidvaanamrita
iha bhavati. Naanyah panthaa ayanaaya vidyate.
Yajnenaya jnamayajanta devaah. Taani dharmaani
prathamaanyaasan. Te ha naakam mahimaanah sachante.
Yatra poorve saadhyaah santi devaah.

Adbhyah sambhootah prithivyai rasaachcha.
Vishvakarmanah samavartataadhi. Tasya tvashtaa
vidadhadroopameti. Tatpurushasya vishvamaajaanamagre.
Vedaahametam purusham mahaantam. Aadityavarnam
tamasah parastaat. Tamevam vidvaanamrita iha bhavati.
Naanyah panthaa vidyate'yanaaya. Prajaapatishcharati
garbhe antah. Ajaayamaano bahudhaa vijaayate.

23

Tasya dheeraah parijaananti yonim. Mareecheenaam
padamichchhanti vedhasah. Yo devebhya aatapati. Yo
devaanaam purohitah. Poorvo yo devebhyo jaatah. Namo
ruchaaya braahmaye. Rucham braahmam janayantah.
Devaa agre tadabruvan. Yastvaivam braahmano vidyaat.
Tasya devaa asan vashe.

Hreeshcha te lakshmeeshcha patnyau. Ahoraatre paarshve.
Nakshatraani roopam. Ashvinau vyaattam. Ishtam
manishaana. Amum manishaana. Sarvam manishaana.

When Vishnu enveloped the golden egg, the elements that
were previously in an insentient state became conscious, and
in that cosmic egg Vishnu was called *Virat Purusha,* or the
Cosmic Self.

Creation of the different planes of existence
During creation, Brahma created fourteen *lokas,* or planes
of existence, from *Patala,* or the nether world, to *Satya Loka,*
or the divine world of truth. These are called Brahma's
lokas. From Satya Loka upwards to *Kshama Loka,* the realm
of forgiveness, there are fourteen other lokas, also called
bhuvana, which are the empire of Vishnu. Higher up, from
Kshama Loka upwards to *Shuchi Loka,* the realm of purity,
there are twenty-eight other lokas whose emperor is Rudra.
In this way, Brahma and Vishnu each have fourteen lokas
and Rudra has twenty-eight lokas. From Shuchi Loka
upwards to *Ahimsa Loka,* the realm of non-violence, there
are fifty-six other bhuvanas. Situated on Ahimsa Loka is the
city of Jnana Kailasha, where Sadashiva resides. This Jnana
Kailasha where Sadashiva lives is thus at the upper end of
the fifty-six bhuvanas.

After Ahimsa Loka is *Kaalachakra,* wheel of time, where
the Virat Purusha or Cosmic Self presides. The lokas go into
laya or dissolution up to this point only, not beyond. The
fourteen bhuvanas of Brahma, the fourteen of Vishnu, the
twenty-eight of Rudra, and the fifty-six of Sadashiva all go
into dissolution. Upwards from that is the state of *Mahakaala,*

literally 'the great time'. Beyond Mahakaala is the eternal and permanent life.

Where there is enjoyment of the karmas, there is laya or dissolution. Where there is enjoyment of the karmas, people experience happiness and suffering, tensions, frustrations and crises, and desire the good. Laya works on this enjoyment of karmas and it takes place up to Jnana Kailasha. After Ahimsa Loka is Kaalachakra, and beyond that is enjoyment of jnana. Here a person merges into the ultimate truth, thereby eliminating the necessity of the repetitious cycle of birth and death. The lower bhuvanas are subject to *karma maya* or delusion, and beyond Kaalachakra is jnana maya.

Human life evolves from karma maya to jnana maya. Maya is present in both. *Vidya* or right knowledge is propelled by maya, and *avidya* or ignorance is also a result of maya. *Buddhi* or discriminative knowledge is directed by maya, as are indiscriminate actions. Nobody is free from maya. Maya is spread through all the bhuvanas. Wherever there is destruction or dissolution, the maya is known as *karma maya*. When an individual faces his *ishta*, his personal deity, or God, that same maya becomes *jnana maya*.

Liṅgāṣṭakam

1. Brahma murāri surārchita liṅgam
   Nirmala bhāsita śobhita liṅgam.
   Janmaja duḥkha vināśana liṅgam
   Tatpraṇamāmi sadāśiva liṅgam.

2. Deva muni pravarārchita liṅgam
   Kāma-dahana karuṇākara liṅgam.
   Rāvaṇa darpa vināśana liṅgam
   Tatpraṇamāmi sadāśiva liṅgam.

3. Sarva sugandhi sulepita liṅgam
   Buddhi-vivarddhana kāraṇa liṅgam.
   Siddhasurāsura vandita liṅgam
   Tatpraṇamāmi sadāśiva liṅgam.

4. Kanaka mahāmaṇi bhūṣita liṅgam
   Phaṇipati-veṣṭita śobhita liṅgam.
   Dakṣa suyajña vināśana liṅgam
   Tatpraṇamāmi sadāśiva liṅgam.

5. Kuṅkuma chandana lepita liṅgam
   Paṅkaja hāra suśobhita liṅgam.
   Sañchita pāpa vināśana liṅgam
   Tatpraṇamāmi sadāśiva liṅgam.

6. Devagaṇārchita sevita liṅgam
   Bhāvairbhaktibhireva cha liṅgam.
   Dinakara koṭi prabhākara liṅgam
   Tatpraṇamāmi sadāśiva liṅgam.

7. Aṣṭadalo pariveṣṭita liṅgam
   Sarva samudbhava kāraṇa liṅgam.
   Aṣṭa daridra vināśana liṅgam
   Tatpraṇamāmi sadāśiva liṅgam.

8. Suraguru suravara pūjita liṅgam
   Surataru puṣpa sadārchita liṅgam.
   Parātparaṃ paramātmaka liṅgam
   Tatpraṇamāmi sadāśiva liṅgam.

Om śāntiḥ śāntiḥ śāntiḥ. Hariḥ om

Satsang 2

15 February 2009

Eleven Rudras

First of all, Brahma built the lokas, the bhuvanas, which then needed to be populated, so the creation of beings became necessary. Thus, Brahma again did tapasya, sadhana, and gave birth to his *manas putras*, or sons born through his will or sankalpa. All his manas putras were yogis, devoid of attachment and beyond likes and dislikes. Brahma asked his sons to help him in his work of creation. The sons replied, "Father, why are you involving us? We have no inclination to do the work of creation. We would like to immerse ourselves in contemplation of God, practise yoga and meet God." In this way, all these saints and evolved beings who were mind-born sons of Brahma went off to do tapasya.

How could the work of creation proceed now? Brahma himself was manifested from Paramshiva's right side through the lila of Paramshiva. Vishnu was born from his left side. These two gods were born through the sankalpa of Paramshiva. Paramshiva and Parashakti, or Shivaa, exist together, without any difference, in the same element of Paramshiva. However, Brahma was a lone person, without a corresponding shakti. Vishnu was also male, without any shakti.

Earlier, Paramshiva had indicated that in the work of creation, Shivaa shakti, in the form of *vak*, speech or sound, would help Brahma. In the work of sustenance, Shivaa shakti in the form of Lakshmi would help Vishnu. "And when I take

27

the form of Rudra, I will invoke Shivaa shakti Kali in the form of Sati. She will do her lila in the form of Sati and then leave." All this Paramshiva had told Brahma and Vishnu. Brahma was born through sankalpa, thus he knew only that method of creation and he brought forth his sons in that manner. Remember that the noose of maya or the world cannot bind beings who have come into existence through sankalpa. Sankalpa is a very powerful concentrated energy of the mind. Sankalpa shakti is the integrated, dense form of shakti.

All the sons of Brahma refused to go ahead with the work of creation and said that they would rather spend their time doing tapasya, sadhana and aradhana. When they went off to do tapasya, Brahma was very disturbed. This was only natural; if your sons do not listen to you and leave the house, of course you become unhappy. Brahma was very upset. In the Shaiva agamas, it is said that this pain, this suffering, led to a heart attack! When he saw his sons leave, he fainted and fell down, and the pranas left his body.

At this point, Paramshiva manifested from Brahma's forehead in the form of Rudra. It is believed that Rudra is the full manifestation of Paramshiva and this is why he is also called Shiva. The trinity of Gods includes Brahma, Vishnu and Rudra. Rudra was endowed with all the qualities of Paramshiva and he was given the work of destruction. After manifesting, Rudra created eleven more beings similar to him from the body of Brahma. These were known as the *Ekadasha Rudra* or the eleven Rudras. Paramshiva, as Rudra, addressed these eleven Rudras: "Look, the pranas of Brahma have left and I have brought all of you here so that you may grace the lokas. You establish the lokas and increase the population of these lokas."

When Shiva addressed the Rudras in this manner, they became nervous and started running helter-skelter, not really knowing what to do. They were immortal and disease-free. How does an immortal and disease-free being give rise to a mortal creation? He does not have that knowledge.

According to the commentary, it is said that since they started running around nervously, literally in tears, they were called 'Rudra'. Some say that the word *rudra* comes from the root *rud*, which means to cry. In the Shaiva agamas, the word is explained in terms of *Ruta dravana*. *Dravana* means 'one who disposes of'. Therefore, the one who disposes of sorrow and pain is called Rudra.

The group of eleven then told Shiva, "Lord, we will not be able to do this job as we do not have the necessary training. We are soldiers, we cannot manage creation; we can only destroy." Shiva said, "All of you enter Brahma's body and from today you will take the form of pranas inside the body." Accordingly, the eleven Rudras entered Brahma's body and revived him. To this day, these eleven Rudras exist in our physical body as pranas. The pranas are eleven in number. There are five main pranas: prana, apana, samana, udana and vyana; there are five *upapranas* or sub-pranas: kurma, krikara, naga, devadatta and dhananjaya; and there is also one master of them all, mahaprana, who enters the womb before birth, and when he leaves, the body dies. Therefore, the five pranas, the five sub-pranas and mahaprana are the eleven forms of Rudra. These Rudras are always running around inside our body; they are never still. The pranas are always active.

When these Rudras entered Brahma's body, he revived and saw a person standing in front of him. He asked him, "Who are you?" Paramshiva, in the form of Rudra, said, "Brahma, I have manifested from your forehead and Paramshiva has commanded me to do the work of destruction. I am the ultimate reality who has manifested as your son. Eleven Rudras, who have manifested from me, have come for your protection, and to uphold the entire creation. Get rid of your depression and get back to your work of creation."

Blessing of Ardhanarishwara

Brahma had tried hard to expand the creation, yet failed, as all his sons were his mind-born sons. One day, while sitting on the lotus flower, Brahma was wondering what could be the reason that the creation was not progressing. He heard a voice from the heavens say, "Brahma, start creation through sexual union. Only then will the beings multiply, otherwise not. Any creature born through sexual union will not be immortal or disease-free. That being will live for some time and then die. In this way, creation will be balanced and it will become an organized system. A wicked person will not be able to tyrannize the world forever, as he will not be immortal. Likewise, a saint will not be able to forever inspire the world to advance on the path of liberation, as he will also not be immortal. There has to be a balance on both sides. If there is fifty percent sorrow in the world, there should also be fifty percent happiness, and vice versa. If there is fifty percent darkness, there should be fifty percent light. There has to be balance everywhere. Therefore, go ahead with creation through sexual union."

Brahma started wondering how to initiate the creation through sexual union. 'Until now, there has been no increase in the female creation. So far, only *devatas* or gods, saints, rishis and munis have come, and they have all been divine and mind-born. How do I increase the female population? The only option is to go to Paramshiva and Shivaa and pray to them for help.'

Brahma started his tapasya. Paramshiva was pleased with his tapasya and appeared before him in his form of *Ardhanarishwara*, the androgynous or half-male, half-female form that is both Shiva and Shivaa combined. Paramshiva told Brahma, "I know the intention with which you have performed tapasya." Saying this, he separated Shivaa from his body and manifested himself in two separate bodies: one completely male and the other completely female. When Brahma saw Shivaa standing separately, he prayed to her, "Please give me the power to create the female species." Shivaa said, "So be it. Paramshiva desires that the creatures in creation multiply. Whoever lives in the world will be under the control of *Prakriti*, Nature."

When Shivaa separated from Shiva and manifested, her form at that time was of an eight-armed goddess; she had one head, but eight hands. The eight hands represent the eight dimensions of Prakriti. In the *Bhagavad Gita* we come across the reference to this form of Prakriti (7:4).

Bhoomiraapo'nalo vaayuh kham mano buddhireva cha;
Ahamkaara iteeyam me bhinnaa prakritirashtadhaa.

Earth, water, fire, air, ether, mind, intellect and egoism, thus is My Nature divided eightfold.

The eight-handed goddess gave her blessings to Brahma and said, "I will help you in this work. With my blessing, go ahead with the creation of the female species." Brahma said, "Mother, I have a request. I will carry out your instructions; however, since you are now standing in front of me, I am asking for this boon from you. When the creation expands through sexual union and my sons are born, I want you to be born as my son's daughter. This will purify my entire lineage."

Shivaa smiled and said, "Okay, but this is something that will come later. Now, I am giving you the power to create through sexual union." After granting this boon, Shivaa merged back into Shiva's body, and both Shiva and Shivaa disappeared.

Creation through sexual union

Through the blessings of Shivaa, a female form now manifested from the left side of Brahma and a male form from the right side. The female became known as Shatarupa and the male as Swayambhu Manu. Swayambhu was a sadhaka of the highest order and Shatarupa was a tapasvini, a yogini. Brahma told them to try for mortal creation through union.

According to that instruction, Swayambhu Manu and Shatarupa involved themselves in the work of expanding the creation. They had two sons called Priyavrata and

Uttanapada, and three daughters called Akuti, Devahuti and Prasuti. Akuti was married to Prajapati Ruchi, Devahuti to Prajapati Kardama and Prasuti to Prajapati Daksha, and their lineage stared growing. Daksha had ten daughters, whom he married off to Dharma. Daksha then had twenty-seven more daughters, whom he married off to the moon god, Chandradeva. Yet again, Daksha had another thirteen daughters, whom he married off to Maharshi Kashyapa. Four daughters were given to Aristanemi, and two each to Bhrigu, Angira and Krishashva.

Today, the entire population of the world stems from the lineage of Maharshi Kashyapa's daughters. Maharshi Kashyapa had married thirteen daughters of Daksha and through him came all the demons, all the gods, and all the different races. All the creatures of the entire world owe their origin to him. His various wives started the lineage of different races and species. The *devatas* or gods came from Aditi, the demons or *daityas* from Diti, and the other demons or *danavas* from Danu. Each wife created a different race or species.

As the races increased, conflicts ensued, jealousy and envy arose between them and trouble brewed. You all know more than me in this respect, as all of you run families. As long as there were two of you, there was no worry. Then the third comes and you have to take care of him. The fourth comes, and tension brews between them. When the fifth comes, fights and conflicts start among all three of them. Wherever there are children, they will be involved in mischief and create trouble. The daityas, danavas, devatas, and the other species will indulge in various activities, giving happiness to some and pain to others.

Vishnu's discus
There were some species who were involved in spreading suffering. They would create a disturbance somewhere, harass everybody, hit somebody, steal something, murder someone, commit dacoity, burn down someone's house, and so on. All

32

the harassed beings of the world approached Vishnu with a desperate plea for help. They told him, "You are supposed to be responsible for the maintenance of creation and you are not doing your job properly." Vishnu said, "What can I do? I do not have any weapons with which I can destroy these wicked beings. Paramshiva gave birth to me and said that I have to take care of the creation, but he has not given me any weapons: no stick, no rope, no handcuffs, no chains." Brahma told him, "You should tell this to Paramshiva."

As advised by Brahma, Vishnu started doing aradhana of Paramshiva in *Vaikuntha*, the heavenly realm. In order to please Shiva, Narayana decided to offer one lotus flower for each name of Shiva and commenced the worship with the *sahasranama* or the thousand names of Shiva. In order to test Vishnu's devotion, Paramshiva took away one flower from the bunch of one thousand. Vishnu did not realize this and he went on performing his worship. At the end, when he found that he was one flower short, he was very upset. He said to himself, "I am sure that I counted the flowers correctly; this is just not possible. How could this happen? Anyway, what do I do now? I cannot go and get another flower now; I have to complete the pooja first."

Vishnu then remembered that people fondly referred to him as 'lotus-eyed' because his eyes were like the petals of a lotus flower. "Eureka! I got it. I have two eyes; I need only one. Let me pluck one out and offer that to Shiva." As Vishnu brought out his knife to take out one of his eyes, Paramshiva appeared before him in the form of Sadashiva and said, "Mahavishnu, I took away one flower in order to test your devotion. What do you want?"

Vishnu said, "Since the population of the world began to multiply, two types of beings, good and bad, are being born. The wicked ones have been harassing and torturing the good and making them suffer. The good have come to me for help, but what do I do? I do not have any weapons."

Sadashiva told him, "I will give you my weapon." He took his discus, the *sudarshan chakra*, in his hands and said,

"Vishnu, from today this discus is yours; it will be your symbol and will be under your control. You will control the situation in the world and maintain order with this sudarshan chakra." Sadashiva gave his divine sudarshan chakra to Vishnu, who killed all the terrorists and murderers with its help.

Departure to Kailash

After giving the sudarshan chakra to Vishnu, Paramshiva disappeared and manifested in front of another sadhaka named Kubera. Kubera had been doing tapasya to obtain the grace of Shiva. Earlier, Kubera was a very poor man, yet a great devotee of Shiva. Paramshiva was pleased with his sadhana and appeared before him as Sadashiva and asked him the reason for his tapasya. Kubera said, "The reason was to have your darshan, just to see you. When your darshan fulfils all the desires of life, what need is there for any other reason?" Shiva was pleased with this devotee and made him the treasurer of the gods and gave him Alakanagari, a region situated close to Kailash, as his residence. After that Paramshiva disappeared.

A thought then came to his mind, "As Rudra, I will become friendly with Kubera and live with my close followers on Mount Kailash." Thus, as Rudra, Paramshiva started living in Kailash with his assistants. They spent their lives immersed in yoga and meditation.

Shiva as Avadhuteshwara

One day the king of gods, Indra, told his guru, Brihaspati, "Paramshiva is living in Kailash as Rudra. Why don't we go and meet him?" He started out for Kailash accompanied by Brihaspati. Rudra is omniscient, so he knew that they were coming, and he wanted to test them both. He took his clothes off and stood on the road winding towards Kailash, behaving like a madman. Not a stitch of clothing on his body, hair loose, moving about like a lunatic, sometimes crying, sometimes laughing, sometimes shouting: that was Rudra's behaviour on the road to Kailash.

Sometime later, Indra and Brihaspati reached the point where Rudra was waiting. Indra was proud of being the king of the devatas and when he saw this avadhuta behaving like this, he asked him, "Who are you, mad fellow? You are standing here absolutely naked and behaving like a lunatic. What is your name?" Indra repeatedly asked him this question and, getting no response from him, he prepared to use his *vajra* or thunderbolt. The moment Indra took the vajra in his hand, the avadhuta just looked at him and his hand froze.

The avadhuta went on enacting the drama. Brihaspati saw that Indra's hand was stilled in mid-air and realized that the madman dancing about naked was none other than Rudra. He then started praising Mahadeva with a stuti, a hymn of praise:

Jaya shankara shaanta shashaankaruche
ruchiraarthada sarvada sarvashuche;
Shuchidattagriheetamahopahrite
hritabhaktajanoddhatataapatate.

Tatasarvahridambara varada nate
natavrijinamahaavanadaahakrite;
Kritavividha-charitratano sutano
tanuvishikha-vishoshanadhairyanidhe.

Nidhanaadi-vivarjita kritanatikrit
kritivihita-manorathapannagabhrit;
Nagabhartrisutaarpitavaamavapuh
svavapuh paripooritasarvajagat.

Trijaganmayaroopa viroopa sudrig
drigudanchana kunchanakritahutabhuk;
Bhava bhootapate pramathaikapate
patiteshvapi dattakaraprasrite.

Prasritaakhila-bhootalasamvarana
pranavadhvanisaudhasudhaamshudhara;
Dhararaajakumaarikayaa parayaa
paritah paritushta nato'smi shiva.

Shiva deva gireesha mahesha vibho
vibhavaprada girisha shivesha mrida;
Mridayodupatidhra jagat tritayam
kritayantranabhakti-vighaatakritaam.

Na kritaantata esha vibhemi hara
praharaashu mahaaghamamoghamate;
Na mataantaramanyadavaimi shivam
shivapaadanateh pranato'smi tatah.

Vitate'tra jagatyakhile'ghaharam
haratoshanameva param gunavat;
Gunaheenamaheena-mahaavalayam
pralayaantakameesha nato'smi tatah.

Iti stutvaa mahaadevam viraraamaangirah sutah;
Vyatarachchamaheshaanah stutyaa tushto varaan bahoon.

Brihataa tapasaa'nena brihataam patiredhyaho;
Naamnaa brihaspatiriti graheshvarchyo bhava dvija.

While Brihaspati was eulogizing Rudra, Rudra's body was burning with anger and Indra was being roasted in that fire. However, through this stuti, Brihaspati placated Rudra.

Brihaspati told Indra, "Indra, recognize who stands before you. He is none other than Paramshiva, Rudra." Indra fell down in obeisance to Rudra. Brihaspati then pleaded with Rudra, "Lord, I beseech you to take back this *tejas*, this fire, which has emanated from you, and release your devotee." Rudra said, "I cannot take this fire back inside me. The fire has to be doused. Do one thing: go and put this fire in the ocean."

Brihaspati took the fire and put it in the ocean. A being emerged out of this doused fire. His name was Jalandhara, son of Sindhu, the ocean, and he was ultimately killed by Rudra. After performing the *aradhana* or worship of Paramshiva, Indra went back to heaven.

Eleven Rudras of Surabhi

Indra spent his time in *Swargaloka*, the heavenly realm, trying to save the loka from the repeated attacks of terrorists and demons. Once, when a very large group of killers came to his doorstep, he ran away from heaven and went to his father Maharshi Kashyapa. He told his father, "My stepbrothers, the daityas and the danavas, who represent other races, are bothering us a lot. We, the gods, try to live a good life, with good jobs, good houses: everything in swargaloka is good. These wicked people envy our prosperity and harass us. Now these demons have driven me out from my house and established themselves there. What do I do?"

Maharshi Kashyapa said, "Come, let us both worship Shiva. We have to seek his help." When the son is in trouble, he comes and complains to the father; it's normal, isn't it? It is said in the Shaiva agamas that after having a bath in the Ganga at Varanasi, Maharshi Kashyapa and Indra established a Shivalingam and performed their tapasya there.

Rudra was pleased with their tapasya and manifested himself. Maharshi Kashyapa introduced his son and said, "This is the person with whom you were angry sometime ago, as he could not recognize you. Now his brothers have driven him and all the gods out of heaven. He has to be sent back to heaven and we seek your help for that." Shiva replied, "What you want will happen", and disappeared.

Maharshi Kashyapa had a cow called Surabhi. Rudra now invoked the eleven Rudras and told them, "The time has come for you to manifest once again. Now you must manifest in the womb of Surabhi." The eleven Rudras who were established in the body of Brahma, followed Rudra's instructions and manifested in Surabhi's womb. When the eleven Rudras manifested in Surabhi's womb, the whole world became permeated with Shiva. The eleven Rudras are Kapali, Pingala, Bhima, Virupaksha, Vilohita, Shasta, Ajapada, Ahirbudhnya, Shambhu, Chanda and Bhava. These eleven Rudras were known as sons of Surabhi and they were

37

instructed by Shiva to return heaven to the gods. Thus, these Rudras helped the gods to regain their control of heaven, and started living in heaven as its protectors. The reference to the eleven Rudras appears twice. We first come across them when they are born in the body of Brahma and become the eleven pranas, and the second time they are born as Surabhi's sons to become the saviours of heaven.

Shiva as Nilakantha

After regaining control of heaven, the devatas or gods started contemplating how to ensure that they would maintain this control without losing it repeatedly to the *asuras* or demons. "What should be done? Why don't we get the nectar and make ourselves immortal? Once we are immortal, nobody will be able to attack us and displace us from our homes." Thinking thus, they invited the demons, "Come, let us churn the ocean. Brahma has said that there are a lot of jewels and nectar in the ocean. After churning the ocean, we will get all these things and share them half-half." In this way, the gods made peace with the demons, and began the churning.

The churning began with the help of the mountain Mandarachala and the snake Vasukinaga. However, soon the mountain, which was above the water, started drowning. Vishnu came to the rescue by taking the form of a tortoise, and lifted Mandarachala on his back and put him back on top of the water. This was the *Kacchapa avatara*, tortoise incarnation of Vishnu, which is one of his ten incarnations.

The churning continued, and whatever Paramshiva had promised to the gods started coming true. Shivaa manifested as Lakshmi and went to Vishnu, and as Vagdevi or Saraswati she went to Brahma. Jewels and other items like horses and elephants emerged from the churning. These were shared equally by the gods and the demons.

At one stage, poison also came out of the ocean in its undiluted form of *halahala* poison. Halahala poison has the unique feature of being both black and green in colour. It started emitting green and black smoke, which soon engulfed the whole sky. As the gods and the demons inhaled the poisonous fumes, they started writhing in pain. The halahala poison itself cannot be seen or recognized, nor smelt, yet its effect is felt immediately. All of them started praying to God for deliverance.

My guru, Swami Satyananda, used to say that in this world everyone would like to digest the good things of life, but only some exceptional people have the capacity to digest the bad things. For the growth of society, its evolution and balance, it is necessary to have some people who are able to digest the bad things. Shiva manifested himself, drank the halahala poison and held it in his throat. After finishing this work, he returned to Kailash. Upon reaching there, his body started burning because of the poison. His throat started burning, turned blue and he lost his voice. From then on, Shiva became known as *Nilakantha* or the blue-throated one, as he held the poison in his throat.

Meanwhile, the churning of the ocean continued, and the moon emerged from the ocean. As soon as the moon came out, coolness spread everywhere. Vishnu then told the moon, "Shiva has drunk the halahala poison and held it in his throat, and as a consequence his whole body is burning. Go to Shiva's service and help him. Wherever he desires to hold you, stay there and help him cool down." Following Vishnu's instructions, the moon reached Kailash. When he arrived, Shiva held him in his head. The coolness of the moon neutralized the pungent halahala poison and Shiva went back to his meditation.

Kedareshwara

When he resumed his meditation, Shiva felt, 'Someone is calling me.' He saw that in the caves of the Himalayas, in the area of Badrikashrama, two rishis called Nara and Narayana were performing tapasya. When Shiva manifested himself in front of Nara and Narayana, they told him, "We request you to stay in this place and accept our worship." Shiva said, "It

will be as you say," and disappeared. Kedareshwara became
the first Shivalingam on the earthly plane.

Vande devamumaapatim suragurum
vande jagatkaaranam
Vande pannagabhooshanam mrigadharam
vande pashoonaam patim;
Vande sooryashashaanka-vahninayanam
vande mukundapriyam
Vande bhaktajanaashrayam cha varadam
vande shivam shankaram.

Vande sarvajagadvihaaramatulam
vande'ndhakadhvamsinam
Vande devashikhaamanim shashinibham
vande harervallabham;
Vande naagabhujanga-bhooshanadharam
vande shivam chinmayam
Vande bhaktajanaashrayam cha varadam
vande shivam shankaram.

Vande divyamachintyamadvayamaham
vande'rkadarpaapaham
Vande nirmalamaadi-moolamanisham
vande makhadhvamsinam;
Vande satyamanantamaadyamabhayam
vande'tishaantaakritim
Vande bhaktajanaashrayam cha varadam
vande shivam shankaram.

Vande bhoorathamambujaaksha-vishikham
vande shrutitrotakam
Vande shailasharaasanam phanigunam
vande'dhitooneerakam;
Vande padmajasaarathim puraharam
vande mahaabhairavam
Vande bhaktajanaashrayam cha varadam
vande shivam shankaram.

40

Vande panchamukhaambujam trinayanam
vande lalaatekshanam
Vande vyomagatam jataasumukutam
chandraardhagangaadharam;
Vande bhasmakritatripundrajatilam
vandeshtamoortyaatmakam
Vande bhaktajanaashrayam cha varadam
vande shivam shankaram.

Vande kaalaharam haram vishadharam
vande mridam dhoorjatim
Vande sarvagatam dayaamritanidhim
vande nrisimhaapaham;
Vande viprasuraarchitaanghrikamalam
vande bhagaakshaapaham
Vande bhaktajanaashrayam cha varadam
vande shivam shankaram.

Vande mangalaraajataadrinilayam
vande suraadheeshvaram
Vande shankaramaprameyamatulam
vande yamadveshinam;
Vande kundaliraaja-kundaladharam
vande sahasraananam
Vande bhaktajanaashrayam cha varadam
vande shivam shankaram.

Vande hamsamateendriyam smaraharam
vande viroopekshanam
Vande bhootaganeshamavyayamaham
vande'rtharaajyapradam;
Vande sundarasaurabheyagamanam
vande trishoolaayudham
Vande bhaktajanaashrayam cha varadam
vande shivam shankaram.

Vande sookshmamanantamaadyamabhayam
vande'ndhakaaraapaham

41

Vande phoolananandi-bhringivinatam
vande suparnaavritam;
Vande shailasutaardha-bhaagavapusham
vande'bhayam tryambakam
Vande bhaktajanaashrayam cha varadam
vande shivam shankaram.

Vande paavanamambaraatmavibhavam
vande mahendreshvaram
Vande bhaktajanaashrayaamaratarum
vande nataabheeshtadam;
Vande jahnusutaambikeshamanisham
vande ganaadheeshvaram
Vande bhaktajanaashrayam cha varadam
vande shivam shankaram.

Shiva as Someshwara

Chandradeva, the moon, married the twenty-seven daughters of Daksha. In a household where there are twenty-seven wives and one husband, you are asking for trouble. Chandradeva's favourite among the twenty-seven was Rohini and the other twenty-six were very unhappy on account of this. They used to say, "He married us all at the same time, yet he spends all his time with Rohini." One day they went and complained to their father that Chandradeva did not even turn around to look at them. Daksha told Chandradeva, "Look, when you married them, you resolved to give equal attention to all of them. Now it is time to implement that resolve. You desire Rohini more than the others; that is not practising even-mindedness, *samabhavana*. The rest are also your wives and you should give as much attention to them as to Rohini."

Chandradeva agreed to this instruction from his father-in-law; however, when he returned home, he again started spending all his time with Rohini. When Daksha saw that Chandradeva had gone back on his word and did not follow instructions, he became angry and cursed him. He told him that he would be afflicted with leprosy and his body would waste away. He would become weaker and weaker and one day his body would just melt away. The curse took effect and Chandradeva's body slowly started melting away.

Chandradeva knew that Daksha had done the right thing and he became depressed. When the devatas came to know of Chandradeva's disease, they became worried. They said, "We have drunk the nectar of immortality, so how is it possible that we can fall sick? How did Chandradeva fall sick?" Until then, no devata had fallen sick, yet now Chandra's life was in danger and there was consternation everywhere. What could be done?

Brahma came and told Chandradeva to go to Prabhasa Tirtha, a place of pilgrimage, and perform aradhana of Shiva, as he was the only one who could save him. Chandradeva followed his instructions and established a Shivalingam at Prabhasa Tirtha and started doing the sadhana of the Mahamrityunjaya mantra, the healing mantra, as laid down in the tradition. Shiva, as Lord Mahamrityunjaya, was pleased with his tapasya and manifested before him. He treated his disease. The father of all therapeutic sciences is Shiva in the form of Lord Mrityunjaya. He told Chandradeva, "Your body will reduce in size for fifteen days and increase for fifteen days." Chandradeva prayed to him, "Please enter this lingam where I have worshipped you." Shiva said, "It will be as you say," and disappeared. From that time on, Shiva is also known as *Someshwara*, lord of Soma, as the moon god is also called Soma.

Devi's promise

Once, Brahma went to meet his son Daksha. He saw that all the devis and devatas were seated there and he told them, "Paramshiva has said that at this time in creation it is necessary for the male and female elements to unite. Paramshiva has given me Vagdevi and he gave Lakshmi to Vishnu, yet he himself remains a brahmachari as Rudra. In creation only couples exist now, with the sole exception of

Rudra. We have to strive to get him married. Let us go and ask Vishnu how this can be done. He is the only person who can tell us."

Vishnu said, "Brahma, Paramshiva told you to take care of creation and that I would take care of sustenance. He also said that his own self would manifest from you, and would be known as Rudra. Rudra will be able to satisfy all your demands and expectations. He will be the destroyer of creation, the witness of all the gunas and will perform the highest yoga. His better half will be Sati, who will be an incarnation of Shivaa herself. Brahma, you will recall that you asked Shivaa for the boon that she be born as the daughter of your son, and she agreed. Now it is time to remind Shivaa of her promise and ask her to be born in Daksha's house. Therefore, go and tell Daksha to perform aradhana of Devi and pray that she incarnate as his daughter."

Following these instructions of Vishnu, Daksha went to the northern corner of the ocean of milk, the residence of Vishnu, and started performing aradhana of Devi. Devi was pleased and manifested before him, asking, "What do you want?" "I want you to be born in my house as my son's daughter and get married to Rudra. Please become Rudra's shakti." Devi said, "All right, but there is one condition." She then said something mysterious: "Prajapati, if you ever insult me or fail to respect me, then I will leave you. I will abandon this body given by you. This is my condition." Daksha agreed. Devi said, "I will be born in your house at an appropriate time," and disappeared. Daksha went back to his house.

Daksha and Narada

Until this time, Daksha's lineage consisted mainly of daughters, whom he married off to various rishis, *manishis* or thinkers, and devatas. After doing this aradhana, Daksha tried to beget sons. First he got ten thousand sons who were called the Haryashvas. He commanded his sons to get on with the work of increasing the population and sent them out of the house. When they came out of the house, they

44

met Narada, the mind-born son of Brahma. He asked them, "Where are you going?" They replied, "We are going to carry out the commands of our father." Narada said, "Is that so? What are the commands of your father?" They said, "Our father has said that we must try to increase the population of the world and we are going out to do that."

Narada asked them, "Have you ever seen the world?" The Haryashvas said, "No, we are leaving our house for the first time." Narada said, "First, you should know the world which is going to come under your control. Your progeny will populate the whole world, so you should know what the world is." The Haryashvas thought, "Narada is right. Unless we know what our kingdom is like, what can we do about it?" Thinking in this manner, they set out to get to know the world and the universe. To date, they are roaming around in the universe. The universe is infinite, so they are still wandering around and will do so eternally. They are unable to find the beginning or end of creation.

Somebody once asked, "What is the centre of creation?" The answer is, "Wherever you are, that is the centre of creation. No planet, star, constellation or galaxy is the central point of creation. Wherever you are, that is the central point of creation, and creation exists all around you until infinity." The Haryashvas are still searching for this infinity.

Daksha came to know that his ten thousand sons had been misled by Narada and were wandering around in search of the end of the infinite creation. He thought, 'These sons will be of no use to me any more.' If a child comes into the company of a sadhu, he no longer belongs to the household, but to the sadhu. The children of Bal Yoga Mitra Mandal here in Munger are an example. If they were at home, they would be listening to film songs all the time. By coming here, they have learnt to chant stotras, and sing bhajans and kirtans. This is the effect of a sadhu's company! I do not want to turn them into sadhus or sannyasins; I just want them to become winners in life. There are many sadhus who are busy scheming to make disciples. Narada belonged to that category. He sent ten thousand Haryashvas on a tour of the infinite universe!

Daksha then produced one thousand sons through the womb of Askini, the daughter of Panchajanya. These sons were called Shabalashva. They were also asked to carry on with the work of increasing the population. When they came out of the house, they too met Narada, who was standing there, chanting, "Narayana, Narayana." Once again Narada asked, "Where are you going?" "We are going to increase the population" they replied. Narada then advised them, "Before you embark on this work, have a bath in this *Narayana Sarovar*, the lake of Narayana, and then get on with your work."

When these brothers took a dip in the sarovar, they became pure, enlightened and liberated, just like Narayana. Who would like to go back home after that? So they went off to sing the praise of the Lord. In this way, the Shabalashvas also went out of Daksha's hands.

Daksha became aggrieved and angry at the loss of his sons and cursed Narada: "Narada, from today, you will not remain in one place. Nobody will be able to identify your abode. You will forever wander and will never be able to sit quietly in one place." Since that time, Narada has been wandering around like a gypsy. He does not belong to any country. After that, Daksha begat seven daughters through the womb of Virani. After getting them married, Daksha and his wife performed aradhana of Jagadamba, the Cosmic Mother, and prayed to her, "Oh Mother, now please incarnate as our daughter." Shivaa sent a message that she would incarnate in Virani's womb.

Birth of Sati

After a certain time, a part of Devi, the Cosmic Mother, came to reside in the womb of Virani. At the appointed time, the Devi took birth. Brahma came down to see his granddaughter and join in the celebrations. One is always happy to see one's grandchildren, and Brahma was no exception. He was extra happy to know that this girl, who was none other than the Cosmic Mother, was born out of his wish and his son's worship. Brahma gave her the name of Sati and foretold that she would have Rudra as her husband. Daksha and his whole household were overjoyed to hear this news. Sati grew up and soon reached the age of marriage, and Daksha started thinking about how to get her married to Rudra. Sati was also very keen to get married to her *aradhya*, her object of adoration and worship, as soon as possible.

Shiva's acceptance

As per instructions from Brahma, Sati commenced an aradhana at her home to please Shiva. Brahma reached Kailash and told Rudra, "Lord, for the welfare of the world, you now have to accept a wife. You had foretold that Shivaa would manifest later on as the consort of Vishnu in the form of Lakshmi, as my consort in the form of Saraswati, and as Sati, the consort of Rudra. Sati has already taken birth in Daksha's house and has reached a marriageable age, so now please accept her in marriage."

Rudra smiled and said, "Whatever you want will happen." On *navami*, the ninth lunar day, Rudra manifested at Daksha's place, where Sati was performing tapasya, and told her, "You are not different from me, so come with me." Sati said, "It is true beyond debate that you and I are not different from each other, yet now we have to do a lila. According to that lila, you have to ask for my hand in marriage from my father. Only then can I get married according to the prevalent custom." Shiva said, "All right", and went back to Kailash. He then called Brahma and told him, "Send information to Daksha that I will come to get married to his daughter, Sati."

Shiva's marriage

Brahma went to Daksha and told him, "Shiva has agreed to marry to Sati. Start making all the arrangements, send invitations to everyone." The auspicious date and time for the marriage was also decided upon. Brahma invoked all his mind-born sons and they promptly appeared. He told them, "All of you will come with Shiva as the bridegroom's party." He invoked all the devatas and told them the same thing. He then invoked the rishis and munis and told them, "All of you start making the arrangements for the marriage. The arrangements have to be perfect. The invitation card has to be nice; everybody's name must appear on the guest list. Proper arrangements have to be made for everyone's stay: food, gifts, and so on." Thus, all the rishis and munis started their work in right earnest.

Vishnu came to the marriage along with Lakshmi, seated on his eagle, Garuda. On the thirteenth day of the bright fortnight of the month of Chaitra, on Sunday, under the constellation of Poorva Phalguni, Shiva, in the form of Rudra, started his journey from Kailash and reached Daksha's city. He told Daksha, "Please complete the marriage rites, I am ready." Daksha completed the *kanyadana*, the handing over of his daughter to Shiva, in a beautiful and auspicious manner, and Sati was married to Shiva.

Shiva began the journey back to Kailash with Shivaa. Midway, he sent Daksha back to his home saying, "Please go back and do your work. As *Prajapati*, lord of created beings, you have a lot of work to do." Rudra then returned to Kailash with his close assistants and lived happily with Sati.

Evolution of creation

Shiva would spend a lot of time on pleasure trips in Kailash with Sati. During these excursions, Shiva would tell Sati about creation: how first Vishnu was born, and then Brahma; how the different lokas or bhuvanas were created; how creation proceeded from the mind. Shiva then told Sati the story of how Brahma became angry and frustrated at the refusal of his sons to increase the population due to their desire to meditate and seek God, and how Brahma's tears of anger and frustration subsequently gave birth to the ghosts, lower beings, vampires, and so on.

He explained how, before creation arose out of sexual union, it was mental and did not have a material body. The material body manifested with the birth of Swayambhu Manu and Shatarupa. They have been accepted as the first man and woman and were the first to have the material body composed of the five elements. The created beings that came before did not have a material body. The devatas or the gods had divine, light-filled, lustrous bodies. The mind-born sons of Brahma had a body of *sankalpa* or resolve. The ghosts, the lower beings and vampires had bodies similar to air.

When the soul enters a material body, it becomes bound by the fetters of Prakriti or Nature and suffers due to the bondage of karma. A being becomes deluded by *maya*, the veiling power, forgets his own self and runs after momentary pleasures, transient objects and happiness. He wants to fulfil his desires, for which he struggles and generates tensions and suffering.

God resides within

Sati asked, "Is there some means, some karma, some anushthana through which one can be relieved from one's sufferings, conflicts, mental unrest and the bondage of the world, and achieve the ultimate state?" Shiva replied, "Yes. The actions or *karmas* should be such that one is aware that one is Brahman, the ultimate, ever-expanding reality; that God or Ishwara, the non-decaying reality, is in you."

Whoever takes birth in this world, his main karma in life is to experience the God within. He is born to find this out. The *Amarkosha* has defined *samsara*, the world, as *Samsarati iti samsara* – "That which keeps moving like a snake is samsara." The world or the *samsara* is the interaction of the senses and their objects, nothing more than that. The senses and their objects: sound, touch, taste, form and smell, interact in the process of life. We desire our happiness based on this interaction only. We want to listen only to the pleasant and not the unpleasant. We want to see only good things and we get disturbed when we see bad things. Everyone tries to attain the desired object of the particular sense in different forms: as gross matter, as emotions or as thought. However, while doing all this, you should also become aware that God resides within you in the form of the ultimate reality.

Navadha bhakti

Sati then asked, "What are these different anushthanas or methods through which one can realize this infinite God element within oneself?" Shiva replied, "The method is bhakti", and he explained the ninefold bhakti or *navadha bhakti*.

The karma which helps you realize God within you is bhakti. This bhakti should have a connection with *jnana*, wisdom or knowledge. The fulfilment of jnana is bhakti. If this is not so then both jnana and bhakti are incomplete. If bhakti and jnana don't coexist then the form of bhakti is *sakama*, based on fulfilment of desires. However, when jnana is an integral part of bhakti, then the final state reached is *satmaka*, union with the self, a state in which all one's actions are offered to God and one does not desire the fruits of action. Jnana and bhakti are complementary to each other; they are not different from each other. Jnana means "I am That" – *Sah aham* or *So-ham*. When one realizes that the same God is within and without, it becomes a living experience, and that state of jnana is transformed into bhakti. Bhakti is the highest experience of jnana.

Shiva has explained *navadha bhakti*, the nine elements or components of bhakti. They are listed in the *Shiva Purana* as: shravana, kirtana, smarana, sevana, dasya, archana, vandana, sakhya and atmanivedana or atmasamarpan:

> *Shravanam keertanam chaiva smaranam sevanam tathaa;*
> *Daasyam tathaarchanam devi vandanam mama sarvadaa;*
> *Sakhyamaatmaarpanam cheti navaangaani vidurbudhaah.*

If we consider the first step of this ninefold path of bhakti, *shravana* or listening, it is essentially a method of focusing the mind. There is sound all around: people are talking, there is sound of the traffic, yet you are focusing your attention

50

on me, listening to me and trying to understand what I am saying. You are one-pointed and meditative. However, if your mind wanders and becomes attached to the surrounding noise, and there is a break in your concentration then you will not be listening to what I am saying. Therefore, shravana is a type of meditation in which the mind is focused on one thought, one point, or one discourse.

The second step is kirtan. The meaning of *kirtan* is singing the names of God, singing his glories. When the mind sings the names and glories of God, the *bhava* or feeling that manifests at that time connects you to your *aradhya* or object of worship. Otherwise, what is the difference between kirtan and a normal song? People sing film songs, love songs and many other songs. However, when you sing these, your *bhavana* or emotion is not purified, awakened or evolved. It is just entertainment, and entertainment is only a mental experience, not an awakening of bhavana, pure feeling or emotion. Kirtan is a manifestation of pure and awakened bhavana. That bhavana helps you in connecting with your ishta. It is said: *Jaki rahi bhavana jaisi, prabhu murata dekhahi tina taisi* – "Whatever is the nature of your feeling, you will behold God in that form."

In the *Ramacharitamanas*, we come across the episode of Rama reaching Sita's *swayamvara*, the reception where she chooses her husband. All those present there saw Rama in a different form: mothers saw him as their son, young girls saw him as their husband, the kings saw him as an emperor, killers and demons saw him as the lord of death, and saints and the learned saw him as luminosity. The person was one, Rama, but people were seeing him in different forms according to their feelings, their emotions. This is the reason kirtan is given so much importance in our tradition. Not because you are chanting God's name, but because through this practice you are awakening your pure feelings and connecting with your personal deity. Kirtan is a means of positive self-transformation.

Third is *smarana*, remembrance or contemplation. Normally when you remember something, you try to bring that subject in front of you. Does remembrance mean remembering God all the time, twenty-four hours a day? No. It is something that overshadows your mind and remains with you all the time.

A mother keeps her little baby by her and does the housework. The child plays on the floor and the mother does all the work: cutting vegetables, cooking food, making rotis, everything that must be done. She does not forego the household work just to take care of the child; instead, one part of her mind is always focused on the child, no matter what she is doing. When the child picks up a knife or eats dirt, she immediately rushes to him, takes the harmful things away from him, ensures that he is safe, and then gets back to the work. Just as a mother has a constant awareness for her child, similarly, if a bhakta has constant awareness of God then he does not need to meditate, do sadhana or go to satsang. That remembrance, that awareness develops a connection with God and makes him aware of God; it awakens him.

Fourth is *padasevana* or worship of the guru's feet. Once when Swami Satyananda was resting, two of his disciples went to him with the intention of massaging the guru's feet. I was one of them. At that time we were very young and energetic, so I took hold of one leg and my friend the other, and both of us started massaging his legs quite vigorously as if we were kneading flour. Imagine the condition of someone whose legs are being massaged like that! Sri Swamiji never said anything and quietly bore it; however, there was another person who was watching us and he asked us later on what we were up to. We said that we were massaging the guru's feet. He said, "Is that so? It seemed that you were kneading flour in the kitchen." He then showed us how to do it properly. We felt so bad that after that, we did not show our face to Sri Swamiji for a month.

God never asks you to massage his feet. In this context, service to God's feet means to walk in His footsteps and keep control over your pride. For one who follows in the footsteps of God and offers his faith to God, there is no place for ego or vanity. The same sentiment is echoed in the *Bhagavad Gita* when Sri Krishna says to Arjuna, "Offer every action to Me." This means making yourself humble, devoid of pride and vanity. This allows your consciousness to evolve.

Walk the path your guru has shown you without any vanity or ego. With simplicity of heart, believe that you will be benefited by walking the path. Develop a firm connection with your faith and belief. Devoid of ego, walk on the path following the guru's instructions, and keep walking, keep walking. Apply the guru's teachings in your daily life, in your behaviour. This is the meaning of padasevana or service to the guru's feet.

The fifth is *dasya bhava* or the feeling of being a servant of God. Through these different bhavas, you can easily experience your aradhya or worshipped deity. Dasya bhava gives an indication of your relationship with God: that you are only a servant obeying the commands of the master. You are not worried about the result, about what is going to happen, good or bad. This is dasya bhava.

There can be no bhakti without bhava or feeling, and that bhava gives an indication of your relationship with your aradhya or personal deity. Our paramaguru, Swami Sivananda, used to say, "I am a servant of God. I do whatever he says." My guru, Swami Satyananda, said, "I have experimented with different relationships with God. I have thought of him as a friend, as my son, as my lover; however, none of these relationships gave me any satisfaction, any fulfilment, until I became his *dasa* or servant. That is the feeling with which I live today."

A person's relationships are based on his bhavana or feelings. Sri Swamiji has always said, "First decide what your relationship with God should be. The relationship between God and his devotee is very expansive. Until you are able to establish the feeling inside and recognize your relationship with God, you will not be able to become a bhakta in the true sense. The day you are able to recognize your relationship as a result of your bhava, you become a bhakta and your relationship is established."

In the bhakti shastras, the first two bhavas are *shanta*, peaceful, and *dasya*, servitude. As long as the mind is restless, you cannot become focused on God or His symbol. That is why the first instruction is, "Become peaceful, become quiet." Thereafter, hold this thought in your mind: "I am only a servant of God." The bhakti shastras say that these two bhavas are for those who have just started their journey on the path of bhakti.

How do we normally start our practices of yoga, anushthana, mantras, and so on? First we still the body, quieten the senses, and then make the restless mind peaceful. Next, you are asked to focus on a symbol. You start your practices only after that. First is body stillness, then stillness of the mind and then the practice sequence. This is the method of yoga. When you practise bhakti, withdraw your mind from the disturbances of the world and focus on the *shanta bhava* or the feeling of peace. At that point there is nothing else besides you and your deity. There is no other cause to make your mind restless. Then bring to mind the feeling that you are a *sevaka*, a servant. Though this feeling, you start your journey on the path of bhakti.

The sixth part of bhakti is *archana*, offering your karmas to God. How is it possible to offer your karmas? All beings live in this world bound by their karmas and suffer and enjoy the fruits of action. Offering the karmas and not feeling any connection with them is a difficult process. When we are asked to offer our karmas, normally we interpret this as the feeling of *Naham karta, Hari karta, Hari karta hi kevalam* – "Whatever actions I am doing are done by God and I am only his medium." However, this feeling is limited to the mental and intellectual plane and has no relevance to the spiritual plane. If you carry this sentiment, yet are unable to cut your connections with karmas, it is an indication of your hollowness within. If you are able to cut all connections with karmas and their enjoyment, only then can you rightly say, "I am not the doer; God is the doer." Then all your actions, whether internal or external, become only the expressions of the *indriyas,* the senses.

Offering the karmas can also mean that you are offering a pure consciousness, pure intellect and pure mind to God. When the karmas become a tool for the expression of the senses, and do not cause any obstruction to the free flow of the infinite consciousness, at that time the consciousness becomes free of distortions, it becomes polished and pure. That consciousness is then offered to God with the feeling, "This is yours, please take it."

When you renounce karma and doership, then there is no self-interest and bondage. Whatever you are doing is offered to God for the welfare of all. When this feeling is awakened and becomes strong, a person is no longer under the bondage of karma. The individual soul's connection with karma is broken and remembrance of God is spontaneous. This spontaneous remembrance purifies and refines the other karmas.

The seventh step of bhakti is *vandana,* which means bowing down before God, and letting go of your ego. Do not interpret this literally. It does not mean, "Oh God! You are so good, you are so beautiful," and so forth. Vandana means that you live like the person you are worshipping. If you like a person, you try to live that person's behaviour, his philosophy. You try to live his qualities without any hypocrisy. If hypocrisy comes in, then it becomes a show, and a show has no place in bhakti.

If, like a cat wearing a tulsi mala and sitting in an assembly of rats pretending to be a bhakta, you also put up an act, then you are deceiving yourself. However, if you sincerely try to live an ideal, that will surely transform your personality. This is the culmination of sadhana. The gross form of this is praising or performing vandana of God in order to merge oneself with the omnipresence of God, renouncing all pretences, hypocrisy and show.

The eighth step is *sakhya* or friendship: I am a friend of God, His companion, I play with Him, I am His follower. The examples of this bhava are Sudama and Krishna, or Sugriva and Rama. When two people become close to each other then this bhava develops.

Sakhya bhava, dasya bhava and atmasamarpan develop faith or *shraddha*. The relationship which develops with your ishta or personal deity has no negativity in it. The relationship of friendship is a very close one. I notice that children listen more easily to their friends than to their elders. In friendship, things are accepted quicker; where there is no friendship, it is more difficult to accept any idea, and the mind becomes critical and analytical.

The ninth step is *atmasamarpan* or *atmanivedana*, surrendering oneself to the divine. The thinkers of India have visualized life as a boat crossing the ocean of worldly existence with two oars: the mind and the intellect. From life to death, a person lives with the help of these two oars. In spiritual life, when you reach the stage of surrender, you hand these oars over to God so that He then takes the boat forward. The feeling at this time is, "I have surrendered the oars to the ocean. Let the boat to go to whichever shore it wants to go to." For surrender, one requires strength and ability. Just thinking, "I am surrendering to you," or saying, "I am offering you everything I have," is not enough. Until you develop equal vision and perform your karmas accordingly, your mentality is not transformed, and surrender remains limited to the intellectual plane. In order to reach this state, your bhakti and karma must have a solid base. Bhakti and freedom from karma are the two sankalpas or resolves which, when awakened, make you a *siddha*, a perfected being.

Requirements for bhakti
Radha once asked Krishna, "You are very fond of the flute. You always keep your lips close to it. What is the reason?" Krishna replied, "I like the flute because it's empty inside.

As it is empty within, I can fill it with whatever I want, with whichever form and colour." The aim of human life should be to empty oneself of desires, selfishness, and negative actions. Therefore, when describing the nine modes of bhakti to the Cosmic Mother, Sati, Shiva has presented them not only as aradhana or worship, but also as a means of bringing about a positive transformation in life.

This path has a combination of dhyana, jnana and bhakti. Now you are listening, you are in a meditative state, *dhyana*. Your mind is focused on one object, my discourse. This is necessary for the first stage of bhakti. For meditation, it is not necessary that you close your eyes and sit. In meditation, one has to attach the mind to some focus and make sure it does not stray from that. Attaching the mind to the ishta or chosen object of worship is *dhyana*. Attaching the mind to working for the ishta, thinking of the ishta, or visualizing the ishta is meditation. If one-pointedness is there, it does not matter whether the eyes are open or closed.

Sri Swamiji used to say that people go to the Himalayas searching for peace or *shanti*, but remember that peace is not found in the Himalayas. People say that there is a lot of noise and disturbance in the world, but really there is no noise and disturbance in the world; whatever is experienced is within you. Due to your mental state and desires, you come to the conclusion that this place is peaceful and that place is disturbing, the environment here is pleasant and there unpleasant. However, if you are in control of your mind then even in the middle of the market you will not be disturbed; your mind will remain one-pointed. Similarly, if you are not in control of your mind then even if you sit in the caves of the Himalayas, your desires will not leave you, and will make you restless.

The sign of a good sadhaka is that he is able to have control over his mind in all situations. In the *Bhagavad Gita*, Sri Krishna has given this advice (5:11):

Yoginah karma kurvanti sangam tyaktvaa' atmashuddhaye.

57

The yogi does all his actions devoid of attachment, for self-purification alone.

One who is attached must practise *samabhava*, the feeling of equality (2:48):

Yogasthah kuru karmaani sangam tyaktvaa dhananjaya;
Siddhyasiddhyoh samo bhootvaa, samatvam yoga uchyate.

Perform actions, O Arjuna, being steadfast in yoga, abandoning attachment and balanced in success and failure. Evenness of mind is called yoga.

One must maintain equanimity in success and failure. This is *samatvam yoga*, the yoga of equanimity. It is the highest yoga, and it comes when the mind achieves one-pointedness. You cannot have equanimity with a restless mind.

The process of bhakti integrates the three components of dhyana, jnana and aradhana. Right now you are practising shravana, you are listening to me. There is noise in the surroundings, yet you are not listening to that; you are listening only to my speech, you are concentrated on my discourse. This becomes your shravana sadhana, your meditation, your concentration.

While a mother works in the house, her attention is always on her child; there is constant remembrance, constant attention. Can you do that with your ishta or chosen deity? You chant his name for five minutes and your mind wanders around to the shoes left outside the temple, to food, and so on. The mind does not remain still for even five minutes. You keep on struggling with yourself, fighting with yourself; you do not follow a simple approach.

Bhakti is simple, and this is the reason why it is of primary importance. Bhakti has jnana hidden in it. When you have jnana or wisdom, then bhakti manifests. When you have jnana, experience, then your faith enhances, your belief grows. It is only when you have jnana that you come to realize, "Until now I have been stuck in the bondage of karma and maya", and it is only with bhakti that you are able to realize the Self.

Definitions of suffering

After talking about bhakti, Shiva imparted the teachings of Pashupata philosophy to Sati. There is suffering in everyone's life. In the scriptures, three types of sufferings are defined: *adhidaivika*, suffering due to natural causes; *adhibhautika*, suffering due to external causes; and *adhyatmika*, suffering due to one's own internal causes. The mental suffering leads to mental disease. Anger, jealousy and hatred are all mental diseases; they are all distorted states of the mind that make a person suffer. Jealousy and hatred make the mind sick, attachment weakens the mind, and repulsion brings out the negativities of the mind. All these come under the category of mental sickness, just like diabetes, arthritis, asthma, etc., are physical diseases.

Other than these three types of suffering, Shiva talks to Sati about five other sufferings: that of the womb, birth, ignorance, old age and death. The suffering of the womb is experienced when a soul enters the confined space of the womb and his potential becomes restricted. He loses his infinite nature and sees himself only as a limited being.

The suffering of birth is experienced when the soul enters the world and his senses become active. He starts breathing and connects with the outside world. At this moment, he realizes that when a connection is made with the world, he will forget his divine origin and look in the opposite direction.

The suffering of ignorance is experienced when, as a result of ego, you forget your infinite self and identify with the limited self; when you are influenced by the external circumstances and break down due to their overload.

The suffering of old age comes when the senses weaken and the energy levels decrease. Lastly, of course, there is the suffering of death. A person becomes so attached to this world, he thinks that this world is everything. While leaving this world, he fondly remembers his children and remains attached to them. At that time, he forgets that he is now leaving to merge with his ishta. He fails to realize that death is also the grace of God. Death is not a punishment; it is grace from God. Nonetheless, a person lives in constant fear of these five types of suffering.

End of suffering

Mother Sati then asked, "Lord, what needs to be done?" Shiva said, *Sarva dukha poho dukhanta* – "Suffering also has its end." You have to make an effort to end the suffering. Only when the suffering ends can you realize the ultimate reality. The end to suffering is of two kinds: anatmaka and satmaka. *Anatmaka* means the end of all *kleshas* or afflictions. *Satmaka* means that along with the end of all kleshas, there is also attainment of bhakti and jnana.

Everyone tries to get rid of their suffering. At the same time, they go on increasing their desires and trying to satisfy them. Nobody wants an end to their desires; you want an end to your suffering so that you go on performing your karmas for the fulfilment of your desires. This attitude is called anatmaka. In the satmaka end to suffering, along with the end of suffering, there is attainment of *shraddha* or faith, bhakti to God, love and affection. The feeling comes: *Naham karta, Hari karta, Hari karta hi kevalam* – "I am not the doer; Hari or God is the doer and I am only a medium." Once you have this feeling then you can free yourself from the tensions of karma and evolve your bhakti and shraddha.

Bhakti should be the primary *anushthana* or spiritual practice. In this world, it is necessary that you are involved in the transactions of the senses, and so you should never look at this negatively; it is God-given. He has created the system that when you come into this world, you become involved in the transactions of the senses. When you go to a shop, you look at the goodies; you do not meditate. Therefore, continue to transact business with the senses. In the *Ishavasya Upanishad* it is said:

> *Eeshaa vaasyam idam sarvam, yat kincha jagatyaam jagat;*
> *Tena tyaktena bhunjeethaa maa gridhah kasyasvid dhanam.*

60

The world is permeated by Him and everything is His; therefore, enjoy everything without being greedy towards the wealth of others.

Enjoy and experience life, yet at the same time make a place in your life for this anushthana of bhakti, so that you are freed from the afflictions and kleshas and reach God. Liberation or *mukti* is the freedom from kleshas and suffering and the attainment of *aishvarya*, the inner wealth of God. In the *Shiva Purana* it says:

Tathaahi shaastraantare dukha nivrittireva dukhaantah iha tu param aishvarya praaptish cha.

Hence, through this knowledge one obtains the cessation of suffering and the divine qualities of the Supreme.

61

Dāridrya-dahana-stotram

1. Viśveśvarāya narakārṇavatāraṇāya
karṇāmṛtāya śaśiśekharadhāraṇāya.
Karpūrakāntidhavalāya jaṭādharāya
dāridryaduḥkhadahanāya namaḥ śivāya.

2. Gauripriyāya rajanīśakalā-dharāya
kālāntakāya bhujagādhipakaṅkaṇāya.
Gaṅgādharāya gajarāja-vimardanāya
dāridryaduḥkhadahanāya namaḥ śivāya.

3. Bhaktipriyāya bhava-roga-bhayāpahāya
ugrāya durgabhava-sāgaratāraṇāya.
Jyotirmayāya guṇanāmasunṛtyakāya
dāridryaduḥkhadahanāya namaḥ śivāya.

4. Charmāmbarāya śavabhasmavilepanāya
bhālekṣaṇāya maṇikuṇḍalamaṇḍitāya.
Mañjīrapādayugalāya jaṭādharāya
dāridryaduḥkhadahanāya namaḥ śivāya.

5. Pañchānanāya phaṇirājavibhūṣaṇāya
hemāṃśukāya bhuvanatrayamaṇḍitāya.
Ānandabhūmivaradāya tamomayāya
dāridryaduḥkhadahanāya namaḥ śivāya.

6. Bhānupriyāya bhavasāgara-tāraṇāya
kālāntakāya kamalāsanapūjitāya.
Netratrayāya śubhalakṣaṇa-lakṣitāya
dāridryaduḥkhadahanāya namaḥ śivāya.

7. Rāmapriyāya raghunāthavara pradāya
nāgapriyāya narakārṇavatāraṇāya.
Puṇyeṣu puṇyabharitāya surārchitāya
dāridryaduḥkhadahanāya namaḥ śivāya.

8. Mukteśvarāya phaladāya gaṇeśvarāya
gītapriyāya vṛṣabheśvaravāhanāya.
Mātaṅgacharmavasanāya maheśvarāya
dāridryaduḥkhadahanāya namaḥ śivāya.

Om śāntiḥ śāntiḥ śāntiḥ. Hariḥ om

Satsang 3

16 February 2009

Pashupata tantra

While talking about the means of ending suffering, Adideva Mahadeva, Shiva, gave the teachings of Pashupata tantra to Cosmic Mother, Sati. This became the base or foundation of tantra, and thereafter tantra evolved into different branches: in Kashmir it developed as the Pratyabhijna tradition, in the South as Virashaiva, and in the West as Lakulisha tantra. Thus, all the different branches of tantra in our country have originated from Pashupata tantra.

What is the meaning of tantra? People think that it is some kind of magic ritual, yet this is not the real tantra. The lord of the universe, Adideva Mahadeva, gave this teaching to the Cosmic Mother; it is not a magic ritual. The teachings that he gave to Sati are to describe his own nature, to explain how changes take place in this world, and how a human being, immersed in sensory life, can free himself from the bondage of the sensory world and its objects.

Symbolism of Shivalingam

The lingam is placed on its base, which is called an argha. The argha or peeth symbolizes Shakti, and in the centre is the lingam, which symbolizes Shiva. Therefore, the Shivalingam is not only a symbol of Shiva; it is a symbol of the integrated form of Shiva and Shakti.

Shiva is the flame, the light, yet there is a covering over this light. Shiva is hidden; he is not visible, as there is a layer of darkness over him. This sheath is that of Shakti. If you can remove this covering of Shakti, you will automatically see the effulgent nature of Shiva. The Shivalingam is an indication of this truth, this teaching.

The evolution of the Shiva tattwa is always upwards and continuous; consciousness evolves upwards. Shiva is the symbol of the cosmic consciousness, which continuously and sequentially evolves upwards.

Shiva is Brahman

This evolving element is also called Brahman. Shiva is Brahman. The word *Brahman* has come from the root *brinh*, which means continuous evolution, continuous expansion. Thus, the consciousness or Shiva is always evolving and expanding. However, the evolution and expansion of the Shiva element is restricted by Shakti, who involves the human being in *maya*, illusion, and *karma*, action, to such an extent that one forgets the real essence of one's existence. Yet, even this occurs through the *lila* of Shiva, the play of the world as desired by him.

Tantra is the method of evolution of consciousness, Shiva, and awakening of energy, Shakti. The word *tantra* is composed of *tan*, derived from *tanoti*, which means expansion; and *tra*, derived from *trayati*, which means liberating, freeing from a bondage. This refers to freeing the Shakti, which until now has bound itself to the physical body, matter and the elements. When this Shakti is liberated from its material bondage, it then travels upwards to merge with Paramshiva in sahasrara chakra.

Nature of Shakti

The electricity that is generated at the substation is of a very high voltage, of the order of many thousands of volts, yet when it comes to your house, its power is stepped down by the transformer and you get only 220 volts. If the

64

transformer was not there in between to step down the power, your house wiring would simply explode with that high level of power. House wiring can handle 220 volts only, not 220,000 volts. With that 220-volts system, you can run all the household equipment, such as the refrigerator, fan, air conditioner, and so on.

We can use this example of electricity to understand the manifest aspect of Shakti. Shakti was transformed from an unmanifest, infinite form to a manifest and limited form. In the unmanifest, the power of Shakti is high, like 220,000 volts, whereas in the manifest it is 220 volts only. Shakti has limited herself because she has to run this body and interact in this world. Therefore, we now have to expand this limited Shakti. When we break the boundary that has been built around Shakti, then Shakti is freed. This process is called trayati. Tantra is the utilization of Shakti to attain Shiva.

Essence of Pashupata tantra

Commentators have defined tantra in different ways: as a system, as a method or sadhana, as a technique or a tool. However, when we go to the root and see that the teachings are given by Paramshiva to the Cosmic Mother, then clearly it cannot be a hocus-pocus magic ritual. Tantra is the teaching of awakening yourself and attaining your own Self.

Pashupata tantra is the source of all tantric thoughts and philosophies. What does Pashupata tantra literally mean? To explain this, Shiva tells Sati that when a being is born through sexual union, it becomes bound. It becomes deluded, infatuated, and ties itself down to the senses, sensory objects and karmas. The bondage is self-created. This bound creature is called a *pashu*, an animal, whereas a being who is free, liberated, is called a *jivanmukta*. Such a perfected being is the *pati* or master of the animal nature.

Bondage and liberation are both experienced in the world. When the being is bound by the senses, sensory objects and karmas and is completely immersed in the world, like sugar in water, there is bondage. We are all like that.

We are so immersed in the world that we cannot separate ourselves from it.

We are on a leash and that leash is held by our master. Take the example of a dog. If a dog is let loose, it will run around, play and jump and approach everyone, but the moment you tie a leash on it, it will stay with the master and obey his orders. If the master says, "Sit down" or "Stand up" it will do so. As long as a creature is free, it roams about freely, but the moment it is tied to a leash, it comes under the domination of its master, and if it doesn't follow the master's orders, it gets the stick!

Our leash is in the hands of Shakti. In this world she is making us dance to her tune and Shiva is only the witness. Shakti tells us, "Son, since you have this material body, enjoy the material pleasures. When you receive the inspiration and the grace of God, then I will release you from this bondage. When you are freed from my leash and become liberated, you will experience the nature of Shiva. Thus the word 'pashu' means a being who is in bondage, and 'pati' means God or Ishwara. The main subject of tantric philosophy is how to strengthen the bond between Ishwara and the individual.

Pashupata tantra is not a philosophy or a system of thought; rather, it is a sadhana, a spiritual practice. Pashupata tantra evolved as a sect of yogis, not as an organized system. The yogis are wanderers: *Ramata jogi bahata pani* – "Just as water is never still, the yogi never stays in one place; he keeps on moving." Since the establishment of ashrams, yogis do have a responsibility thrust on them; otherwise, they are habitual wanderers.

In the past, Pashupata tantra was the method of sadhana for yogis; it was never an organized system of philosophy. The yogi would go wherever his wanderings would take him and do his sadhana. It might happen that the king of a particular kingdom liked the practices. He would learn those practices and also teach them to his subjects. The teachings would cover karma, sadhana, behaviour, conduct, and the efforts one needs to make in life. In this way, tantra evolved in different parts of the country. After a period of time, different sects and systems formed in those areas. However, the core philosophy of these different systems is the same. It says that when one comes to the world, one encounters suffering, and the aim of life is the elimination of suffering. One has to understand the suffering, bear it and become free from it.

Understanding suffering

Pashupata tantra first explains the nature of suffering. According to commentators, there are three types of suffering: adhibhautika, adhidaivika and adhyatmika.

Adhibhautika suffering comes from the world, creating problems such as fever, asthma, diabetes or cancer. The root cause of these illnesses is the environment in which you live; the way you cope with your environment and with what attitude you live your life.

Adhidaivika means that whatever is happening is God's will. One has no control over this suffering. There might be a famine with no water or food; there will be suffering. If it does not rain, what can you do? That suffering which arises from a situation over which one has no control, and which is happening in accordance to God's will, is called adhidaivika.

The third suffering is adhyatmika, which originates from within the self. You are the cause of your suffering. Your mind is the cause of your suffering. Your association with the world of sense objects is the cause of your suffering, as are your expectations. In this group you can include things like stress, tension, anxiety, fear, phobias, inhibitions, complexes, neurosis, psychosis. You go to a doctor to treat your physical diseases, but how do you treat your mental diseases? Every day you face hatred, jealousy, arrogance, greed, yet you are not able to treat them and you suffer as a result of these mental diseases.

The traditional scriptures talk of these three types of suffering; however, the Shaiva agamas talk of five other types of suffering: that of the womb, birth, old age, death and ignorance. When the jiva enters the mother's womb, suffering arises due to the restrictions of space and action. All the actions of the being are limited to this small area and one suffers.

In the process of birth, the being undergoes extreme pain. When he comes to the world and takes his first breath, he cries in anguish. In the painful process of taking birth, he forgets his previous *samskaras* or impressions. This is the suffering of birth.

The suffering of ignorance occurs when the *jiva* or individual forgets the nature of reality due to his ego and does not consider, 'Who am I? From where have I come? Who do I belong to? What is my bondage? What is the cause, what is not the cause? What is the truth, what is false? What is *jnana* or knowledge and what is *ajnana* or ignorance?' Instead, he thinks, 'I am the doer, I am the enjoyer: I am everything.' He is then immersed in ignorance and thereby suffers.

The suffering of old age occurs when the organs of action and perception become weak, the limbs become weak, one finds oneself helpless and incompetent, one remembers one's earlier health and happiness, becomes depressed and suffers. Ultimately, one's memory also becomes feeble.

Next comes the suffering of death. At the time of death, all the organs and senses become lifeless, the breath stops and one starts thinking about one's possessions. One suffers intensely with the feeling, 'I am dying.' In the beginning when one took birth, one suffered and cried, and now, when dying, one suffers and cries again.

Divine union

These five types of suffering take away the aishvarya of the jiva. The term *aishvarya*, which is discussed in the tantra agamas, is to be understood as a balanced and controlled state of mind; the mind is awakened and intuitive. When the mind is peaceful and discriminative, free from pride and arrogance, when the light of sattwa shines in the mind, then the mind becomes still. When the mind becomes still, it acquires all the divine qualities. Acquiring these divine qualities is the *dharma*, the enjoined duty, of every being who has taken birth.

Explaining the Pashupata philosophy to Mother Sati, Lord Shiva explained that the subject matter comes under five headings: *karana* or cause, *karya* or action, *yoga* or union, *vidhi* or method, and *dukhanta*, the cessation of suffering. The main topic of this philosophy is yoga: *Atmeshvara samyogo yogah* – "The union of *atma* or individual soul with *Paramatma*, Cosmic Soul, is yoga." According to tantra, the requirement of yoga is the union of atma with Paramatma. Pashupata philosophy maintains that this is the correct definition of yoga, as through this path the jiva, who is now bound, attains Paramatma.

In Sage Patanjali's raja yoga, yoga is defined as *Chitta vritti nirodhah* – "The cessation of mental modifications is yoga." In the Pashupata philosophy it is said that stopping the *vrittis*, the mental modifications, and diverting them fully towards the Divine is yoga.

Shiva yoga

The yoga that is described in Pashupata tantra is neither hatha yoga nor raja yoga; rather, it is a yoga which I have named *Shiva yoga*. *Shivena saha yogah: Shiva yogah* – "The teachings of yoga as associated with Shiva will be called Shiva yoga."

If you are asked which yoga is the most important, it is Shiva yoga. Shiva yoga has four parts: hatha yoga, raja yoga, bhakti yoga and karma yoga. These four yogas are for the individual soul.

When the individual soul comes to the world, it comes under the bondage of karma maya and to get out of this bondage it needs karma yoga. *Karma maya* means becoming attached to karmas, and through *karma yoga* one eliminates the karmas. Eliminating the karmas means renouncing the fruit of actions. You have to eliminate the expectations of the results of actions and focus only on the actions. What may happen, what may not happen, and your expectations about the result should not be in your mind. In the *Bhagavad Gita* (2:47) it is said: *Karmanye vadhikaraste ma phaleshu kadachana* – "You have the right perform actions but no right to the results." This means that the expectations with which you always perform actions should be removed. When you remove the expectations from the karmas, they become complete and creative, and the results will be good, auspicious and beneficial.

The Pashupata philosophy views bhakti yoga as an *anushthana* or systematic spiritual sadhana. While giving the teachings of raja yoga, Shiva says that this practice can focus the mind, and thereafter one can turn away from the objects of the world and focus on God. Hatha yoga and raja yoga are practices through which one can awaken the pranas. In this way, Shiva yoga combines the four yogas and this is how the path of Pashupata has defined the means of sadhana.

Two categories of yogas are also discussed: kriyatmaka and kriyoparama. *Kriyatmaka yoga* includes the practices of hatha yoga, raja yoga, karma yoga and bhakti yoga. Japa, mantra, pratyahara, dharana, dhyana: all the systematic and organized forms of yoga, are part of the kriyatmaka category. When one perfects these yogas and becomes established in the state of yoga, that is called *kriyoparama yoga*. At this point, all the actions or practices end; there is no need to do these practices as one is now established in yoga.

Mantra

The main mantra of the Shaiva agamas is *Om Namah Shivaya*. In the Shaiva agamas it is said that the sannyasin, the sadhu, the dispassionate and the non-attached, all those who are not drawn towards the attractions of the world, should worship the symbol of the formless: *Om*. Those who are involved and immersed in the world should do japa of the mantra *Namah Shivaya*; and those who live in the world, yet aspire for both

70

nivritti, renunciation of the world, and *pravritti*, involvement with the world, should do japa of *Om Namah Shivaya*.

Those who are following the path of pravritti should practise with the *panchakshara* or the five-lettered mantra, *Namah Shivaya*; those who are following the path of nivritti should practise the *ekakshara* or one-lettered *Om*; and those who are following both pravritti and nivritti should use *Aum Namah Shivaya*. These are the instructions Paramshiva himself gave to Mother Sati.

The main mantra is *Om Namah Shivaya*. This mantra has been given various names, such as the panchakshari, shadakshari or Shaiva sutra. It is called the Shaiva sutra as the complete knowledge of Shiva is inherent in these five letters.

Mantra has been described in different ways. The main point is that through mantra the jiva experiences oneness with the transcendental reality. *Mananat trayate iti mantrah* – "Mantra is that power which liberates the mind from its bondages." In this sutra, *manana* means focusing your mind on one thought, contemplation of one idea. Mantra is the power through which the mind is freed from its whirlpool of thoughts and becomes one-pointed and centred. That power which frees us from the worldly objects and attaches us to God is mantra. Through mantra, the jiva and Shiva attain oneness and there is an awakening of pure knowledge. Mantra is a very important sadhana in itself.

In the Shaiva agamas it is said that the Cosmic Father, Paramshiva, imparted the teachings of yoga, tantra, astrology, medicine and every other discipline and science that is known today, to the Cosmic Mother, Sati. He even propounded politics, statecraft, and similar subjects. If one thinks deeply then one will realize that Sati took birth only for this purpose. The story goes that Sati took birth and later immolated herself at her father's place, so what was the purpose of Sati's birth? Adi Shakti herself said that she would take birth to do Shiva's work. What was that work? It was the establishment of vidya after creation was complete.

Vidya

Vidya is that teaching, that sadhana, through which you can reach the summit of self-development. Vidya always takes the human being towards light. Its opposite, *avidya,* is that which plunges you to the depths of darkness.

In the journey of life, at birth we are in a stupefied, dull state called *mudha*, and as we evolve through the teachings we gain vidya. In the scriptures it is said: *Janmana jayate shudrah samskaro dvija uchyate* – "At birth one is in a state of ignorance; positive samskaras raise one to the twice-born state." Through positive samskaras you can get rid of your dullness and ignorance, the state of mudha, and become a dwija. *A dwija* is that person who has been reborn through knowledge or jnana.

First, you are created and then you obtain vidya. Likewise, first the universe is created and then vidya is established. Sati was born to establish this vidya, as Sati was one who could be given the teachings that could make one attain perfection of this *loka,* or plane of existence, and also of *paraloka,* the existence beyond this loka. The perfection of this life or loka lies in *purushartha,* individual effort, and karma for self-development. The perfection of paraloka means removing the impurities through sadhana and experiencing the light within.

After creation was set in motion and the beings began increasing in number, in order to give the individual an aim or direction in life, Shiva placed his thoughts clearly before Sati. She then divided the main thoughts of these teachings into different points, and spread them in the form of Shakti tantra, especially through the ten Mahavidyas.

In *Satya Yuga*, the age of purity and truth, Shiva and Shivaa took the form of Rudra and Sati to carry out their lila. Shiva, as guru, first gave the teachings to Sati, and then Sati, as guru, gave the teachings of the sixty-four traditions of tantra.

Ten forms of Devi

After the long discussion between Shiva and Sati about pashu and pati, Sati said, "We will continue this discussion later."

Quite some time passed, yet Sati did not show any further interest in the matter. Shiva thought, "Perhaps Sati's mind is full with this teaching. Let me now go and do some tapasya." As he departed from Kailash with this thought in mind, he found Sati standing on the road blocking his way. He tried a different road, yet again he found Sati standing there, in another form. He tried a third road, but again Sati was there in yet another form. He tried ten different directions, yet everywhere he went he found Sati standing there in a different form.

Shiva wondered, "Why is Sati blocking my path?" Sati smiled and said, "Lord, it seems that you are also in the grip of maya." Shiva said, "Sati, if you wish to delude someone, not even I can escape. Now, tell me why you have blocked my path with these ten different forms." Sati replied, "You have told me about the Pashupata philosophy, which essentially relates to the Shiva tattwa. I want to tell you about some other secret teachings: the ten Mahavidyas of Shakta tantra, which essentially relate to the Shakti tattwa. These ten forms of mine, which you have seen, are the ten forms of the mysterious teachings of Shakti tantra." These ten forms of Sati are known as the *Dasha Mahavidya*, or ten great repositories of knowledge.

Ten incarnations of Shiva
When Shiva saw Sati standing in front of him in these ten different forms, he also assumed ten different forms and said, "Sati, your first form is that of Kali. I will remain with her as Mahakaala." Kali and Mahakaala have been accepted as the first of the ten Mahavidyas; to deserving people, this form gives enjoyment, *bhoga,* and liberation, *moksha.* The second incarnation of Sati was Taraa and that of Shiva was Tara; these two have the ability to give enjoyment and liberation, and also happiness. The third form of Shakti was Bhuvaneshi and that of Shiva was Bala Bhuvanesha; these two also give happiness to deserving people. The fourth form of Devi was Shodashi Sri Vidya and the corresponding

form of Shiva was Shodasha Sri Vidyesha; they give enjoyment and liberation.

The fifth incarnation of Devi was Bhairavi who grants the desired fruits to worshippers. The fifth form of Shiva was Bhairava, who always grants the desires of his devotees. The sixth incarnations were Chinnamastaa and Chhinnamastaka. The seventh was famous as Dhumavati and Dhumavan, who fulfil the desires of evolved worshippers. The eighth was Bagalamukhi and Bagalamukha. The ninth was Matangi and Matanga, who fulfil all the desires of the worshippers. The tenth was Kamalaa and Kamala, who give enjoyment and liberation and nourish the devotee in all ways.

In tantra, these ten incarnations have been said to have the capacity to fulfil all wishes. They destroy the negative forces and illumine the higher consciousness. Shiva and Shivaa complement each other in their lila and present the teachings of Shakti tantra, in which Shakti is predominant and Shiva is her assistant. The predominant figures are devis such as Kali and Taraa, and their helpers are Mahakaala, Tara, and so on. In this way, Shakti tantra also evolved along with Shaiva tantra.

Incarnation of Durvasa in Satya Yuga

In Satya Yuga, when Rudra and Sati were having their dialogue and were engaged in their lila and other pastimes, a rishi couple named Atri and Anasuya were performing tapasya in a different area with the aim of begetting a son. Brahma, Vishnu and Shiva were all pleased with their tapasya and gave them the boon that aspects of each of their divine beings would be born as the couple's three sons. Chandrama was born from Brahma's aspect; Dattatreya, who spread the sannyasa system, was born from Vishnu's element; and Durvasa, from Shiva's aspect.

The nature of Shiva is perceptible in Sage Durvasa. The task of Rudra is to destroy, and to bring about that destruction he has to become angry. We see this nature in Sage Durvasa. He was a very aggressive person, yet underlying this aggressiveness was Shiva's grace and blessings. Everyone used to be mortally afraid of Sage Durvasa, apprehensive of receiving his thunderbolts. At the same time, they would feel blessed by his anger, for they knew that underlying his wrath there was a blessing.

There are some prevalent stories about Sage Durvasa and one of them is about Ambarisha, who was tested by Sage Durvasa. He had instigated a lila with Ambarisha regarding food, which resulted in the sudarshan chakra, Vishnu's discus, pursuing Durvasa, and only when he prayed and Shiva intervened did the chakra withdraw.

During the Pandavas' exile in the forest, a similar lila took place. Sage Durvasa reached the forest with his ten thousand disciples and asked for food. They had no food, so Draupadi, the wife of the Pandavas, prayed to Sri Krishna, who immediately reached her and gave one grain of rice which satiated Durvasa's hunger.

If Durvasa had not had this interaction with Ambarisha or the Pandavas, we would not know how God cares for a true devotee. Whenever a person wanted to receive grace, Durvasa would reach there beforehand and create a situation wherein God would manifest. Durvasa would arrive before God and God would follow him with his blessings.

Durvasa's third test was on Sri Rama. *Kaala*, Time, had taken the form of a mendicant, and made Rama take a vow that when they were talking with each other, nobody would interrupt them. If someone came, that person would be exiled. Durvasa prevailed upon Lakshmana to go to Rama and Rama was forced to exile him from the kingdom.

Daksha's anger
Shiva had been spending his time in Kailash, creating lilas with Mother Sati. It was a joyous time. The whole world knew that Rudra and Sati were Shiva and Shivaa. They were being worshipped everywhere. At this time, Daksha arranged an elaborate yajna in Prayag and invited all the sages and gods. Sati also arrived at the yajna along with her husband Rudra.

75

The organizers of the yajna escorted the guests to their allotted places. Rishis, munis, saints, *kinnaras* and *yakshas*, celestial beings, had all reached the yajna and were seated in their respective places. The yajna was about to begin, and everyone was waiting for the arrival of Prajapati Daksha, the host of the yajna. An announcement was made, "Behold, Prajapati Daksha is arriving." On hearing this, all those present including Brahma, Vishnu, the devatas, rishis, munis, kinnaras and gandharvas stood up respectfully. The only exception was Rudra, who remained seated quietly in his place. On entering the program hall, Daksha was very pleased to see everyone stand up, as he was proud of the fact that creation was populated with his progeny. He thought, "I have given my daughters in marriage to the rishis and devatas, and I am worshipped in all the realms."

When Daksha entered the hall, he saw that everyone had stood up except Rudra. He started trembling with rage. He shouted, "He is not of the four *varnas*, the castes. Throw him out of the yajna! He has not stood up and offered me respect. Who does he think he is? Brahma has stood up, Vishnu has stood up, all the devatas and rishis have stood up, yet he doesn't bother!"

When Nandi and other assistants of Shiva heard this, they were incensed at the temerity of someone abusing the father of the universe and asking for his expulsion, and they got involved in a brawl with Daksha. Rudra sat quietly through all this. Daksha exclaimed, "This chap lives in graveyards and burning ghats. His lineage is abominable. Why is he here? He is of lowly birth and different from all the castes."

Shiva is neither brahmin, nor kshatriya, nor vaishya, nor shudra: he is separate from all the castes. Some of the devatas and rishis are brahmins, some are kshatriyas. Brihaspati was a brahmin. Indra was both a brahmin and a kshatriya; being Kashyapa's son he was a brahmin, and being the king of gods he was a kshatriya. Similarly, all the devatas, rishis and others are connected to one caste or another.

When Daksha abused Shiva, Nandi became angry and cursed Daksha. The master was sitting quietly, but his servant could not bear the insult meted out to the master. A sevaka is not dispassionate; the master can be non-attached but not a sevaka, because he is faithful to the master. How can a faithful sevaka be non-attached? Therefore, Nandi cursed Daksha saying, "You will lose all your prosperity and deviate from the path of karma! One day you will get a goat's head in place of your own head, as all the time you are bleating 'me, me, me' which is the sound a goat makes!"

After saying this, Nandi turned towards Shiva and found him smiling. Shiva said, "Nandi, relax. Whatever is destined to happen, will happen. Nobody can stop that, not even me. Certainly I am formless, attributeless, but as Rudra I have a job to do; I am bound. Everything will happen at the appropriate time."

Saying this, Adideva Rudra and Sati left the yajna, along with their retinue, and returned to Kailash, where Rudra became busy with his pooja, sadhana and tapasya, and remained in samadhi for extended periods. Meanwhile, Daksha completed his yajna and everyone went back home.

Tryambakeshwar in Treta Yuga

Time passed, and after the end of Satya Yuga, began the Treta Yuga. In Treta Yuga, Rishi Gautama lived with his wife Ahalya in the Brahmagiri mountains, which are in Tryambakeshwar, near Nasik in western India. At one time there was a disastrous famine in that area, which lasted for many years. There was not a wisp of cloud in the sky, the earth was scorched, and people left the place in search of food and water. Eventually, Maharshi Gautama peformed worship of the rain god, Varuna. Pleased with his efforts, Varuna appeared before him, and asked him the reason for the worship. Rishi Gautama said, "For years now there has not been a drop of rain in this area. Please give your blessings and let there be rain." Varuna said, "I cannot go against the laws of Nature; I cannot give you rain. However, there is one thing I can do. Dig a hole and I will give you the blessing of perennial water there. The water from that hole will never run dry."

Gautama dug a hole of about an arm's length and Varuna filled it with divine water, which would never be depleted. He said, "This water will be like the water of a *tirtha*, place of pilgrimage, and its fame will spread far and wide." In this way, Gautama established his ashram in Brahmagiri with the blessings of Varuna. He utilized the water to make the entire area lush and green.

When this news spread, people who had left in search of water slowly started coming back. The animals and birds that had left also returned, and slowly the place again became populated with birds, animals, sages, and other people who lived in peace and happiness. Everybody used the water given by Varuna to satisfy their needs.

One day, some brahmin wives came to the well to collect water. At that moment, some lower caste women were drawing water from the well. The brahmin wives told them, "Vacate the place, we will take water first." Ahalya heard this exchange and told them, "Everyone has equal right to this water. Let them take some first and then you take your turn."

The brahmin wives became angry on hearing this. They did not say anything at the time and left quietly after collecting the water, but when they reached home they complained to their husbands, "Today Ahalya has insulted us in front of the lower caste people. You have to avenge this insult. Please do something so that we are able to teach a lesson to both Ahalya and Gautama. Unless you do something, we will not eat any food or drink water."

The brahmins realized that in order to avoid domestic discord, it would be better to do something, so they started performing tapasya and invoked a god. When the god appeared, the brahmins asked him, "Could you please manifest as a dying cow and graze in Gautama's fields. When Gautama comes to shoo you off, you die. When you die, we will raise hell with Gautama and insult him." The god said,

"Remember one thing: whenever someone harbours ill-will towards someone else, it rebounds on him. I am now helpless and am bound to do your bidding, as I have committed myself before hearing your request. However, do remember that the result of this action will not be favourable." Saying this, the god took the form of a dying cow and went to Gautama's fields.

When the cow ventured into the fields and started eating the crop, Gautama came out and touched her with a blade of grass, saying, "Come mother, please move from here." As soon as the blade of grass touched the cow, she fell down and died. The brahmins, who were waiting for this opportunity, jumped forward and exclaimed, "Gautama Rishi, what have you done? You have killed a cow! This was not expected from you. You will have to suffer the consequences. Please leave this ashram. Go two miles away from this ashram, where there is no water, and make your dwelling there. Go around the world three times and maintain a *vrata* or vow for one month. Do a circumambulation of Brahmagiri mountain and perform its worship after constructing one thousand lingams. Only then will you be free of this sin of killing a cow."

Rishi Gautama said, "All right, I will do as you say." He established a small ashram two miles away from Brahmagiri and began the worship of Shiva. Shiva was pleased with his worship and manifested before him. Gautama folded his hands in prayer and addressed him, "Lord, please make me free of sin. Take away the burden of the sin upon my shoulders." Shiva said, "Gautama, you have always been sinless and pure. These wicked people have played a trick on you. In truth, they are the sinners. You have always been sinless and will remain so."

Gautama said, "Lord, I thank those priests, for if they had not punished me thus, I would not have done this aradhana or received your darshan. They have done me a great favour and I thank them from the bottom of my heart. Please do not be angry with them and let them also receive your blessings."

Shiva was extremely pleased to hear this and said, "Excellent! Only a person like you could have said this. In fact, now you have proved that you bear negativity towards no one, you are verily sinless. Now, tell me what you want. I am willing to give you whatever you desire." Gautama said, "If you are pleased with me then give me the river Ganga." Shiva said, "So be it." As soon as he said this, Mother Ganga appeared next to him. Upon seeing her, Rishi Gautama praised her thus with the *Ganga Stotram*:

Jaya jaya gange jaya hara gange
jaya jaya gange jaya hara gange;

Devi suredhvari bhagavati gange
tribhuvanataarini taralatarange;
Shakaramauli-vihaarini vimale
mama matiraastaam tava padakamale.
Bhaageerathi sukhadaayini maatastava
jala mahimaa nigame khyaatah;
Naaham jaane tava mahimaanam
paahi kripaamayi maamajnaanam.
Haripada paadya tarangini gange
himavidhu muktaa dhavala tarange;
Dooree kuru mama dushkriti bhaaram
kuru kripayaa bhavasaagara paaram.
Tava jalamamalam yena nipeetam
paramapadam khalu tena griheetam;
Maatargange tvayi yo bhaktah kila
tam drashtum na yamah shaktah.
Patitoddhaarini jaahnavi gange
khanditagirivaramandita bhange;
Bheeshma janani he munivara kanye
patita-nivaarini tribhuvana dhanye.
Kalpalataamiva phaladaam loke
pranamati yastvaam na patati shoke;
Paaraavaara vihaarini gange vimukha
yuvati krita taralaapaange.
Tava chenmaatah srotah snaatah

punarapi jathare so'pi na jaatah;
Naraka-nivaarini jaahnavi gange
kalusha-vinaashini mahimottunge.
Punarasadange punyatarange
jaya jaya jaahnavi karunaapaange;
Indramukutamani-raajita charane
sukhade shubhade bhritya sharanye.
Rogam shokam taapam paapam
hara me bhagavati kumati kalaapam;
Tribhuvana saare vasudhaa haare
tvamasi gatirmama khalu samsaare.
Alakaanande paramaanande kuru
karunaamayi kaatara vandye;
Tava tata nikate yasya nivaasah
khalu vaikunthe tasya nivaasah.
Varamiha neere kamatho meenah
kim vaa teere sharatah ksheenah;
Athavaa shvapacho malino
deenastava na hi doore nripatikuleenah.
Bho bhuvaneshvari punye dhanye
devi dravamayi munivara kanye;

Jaya jaya gange jaya hara gange
jaya jaya gange jaya hara gange.

Pleased with this praise, Mother Ganga asked her, "Son, what do you want?" Gautama said, "Mother, I want you to stay here forever." Ganga said, "It will be as you say." She immediately appealed to Shiva to reside there with Mother Sati and his close followers, stating that only then would she reside on this earthly plane. Shiva said, "All right, as you wish." In this manner, at the place where Gautama performed tapasya, Shiva manifested as the Shivalingam at Tryambakeshwar, and Mother Ganga became the Godavari river.

Descent of Bhagirathi Ganga
In India, a king named Sagar was hosting the ashwamedha yajna. As per the tradition of this particular yajna, a horse

is set free to roam the lands, and wherever it goes the land comes to belong to its owner unless the horse is challenged and captured. Thus, King Sagar released the horse. It reached Maharshi Kapila's ashram, at which point Indra tied the horse up, as he was worried that if King Sagar completed the yajna he might acquire the title of *Indra*, king of heaven. Therefore, he created an obstacle to the completion of the yajna and went off to his realm. Maharshi Kapila was in samadhi at the time and did not come to know of this.

When the horse did not return, King Sagar asked his sons to find out where in the earthly plane the horse was hiding. They went out in all directions in search of the horse and eventually found the horse tied up in Maharshi Kapila's ashram. They assumed that Maharshi Kapila had tied the horse up and started abusing him. On hearing the commotion, Maharshi Kapila came out of his samadhi. He opened his eyes, only to see that eight thousand sons of King Sagar were abusing him. He became furious and that anger took the form of fire and sound, and burned the sons to ashes in a flash.

When his sons did not return, the king became worried. He told his youngest son, Anshuman, "Please see what has happened to your brothers and also find out why the horse has not come back." Anshuman went around the entire world and eventually reached Maharshi Kapila's ashram. He found the horse tied there and small mounds of ashes all around. He waited patiently for the Maharshi to come out of samadhi.

When Maharshi Kapila came out of samadhi, Anshuman bent down to do his pranam and said, "Sir, the horse from the yajna is tied here in your ashram. With your kind permission, I would like to take this horse." Maharshi Kapila said, "Yes, you can take the horse. You are humble and well-behaved. Your brothers came here, but as they were ill-mannered and abusive, I burnt them to ashes. The ashes you see here belong to them." Anshuman inspected the ashes and asked, "How is it possible to revive them?"

Maharshi Kapila said, "That will be possible only when the Ganga comes down and washes away their sins." Anshuman asked, "But where does Ganga exist on this earthly plane?" Maharshi Kapila instructed him, "Try to get the flow of Ganga from the Himalayas to this ashram. When the water of the Ganga touches the ashes, your brothers will be freed of their sins and attain heaven."

Anshuman came back with the horse, told his father what had happened and asked, "Please give me permission to make an attempt to bring the Ganga down." Generation after generation they made this effort. King Dilip tried, and then King Bhagiratha. During King Bhagiratha's tapasya, Brahma manifested and asked him the reason for this arduous penance. Bhagiratha said, "I am trying to bring the Ganga to this earthly plane so that my ancestors are liberated." Brahma advised him to worship Shiva and Mother Ganga and please them. "Ask Ganga to descend on earth and ask Shiva to hold Ganga in his head. If he does not do this, she will come down from space with such tremendous force that she will pierce the earth and reach the nether worlds."

Accordingly, Bhagiratha started the worship of Ganga. She manifested and said, "I will surely fulfil your desire, but you must first please Shiva." Bhagiratha then worshipped Shiva, who agreed to help in this momentous task. At the appointed time, Shiva opened his locks and stood on a mountain. The descent of Ganga began. Ganga flowed down and Shiva absorbed her flow on his head. Ganga flowed here and there within the locks of Shiva, yet there was no way for her to flow out from there. Then Bhagiratha again prayed to Shiva, "Lord, please let one stream come out." Shiva was pleased with his praise and took one stream from his head and let it flow to earth. This river, which came from the Himalayas, followed Bhagiratha and reached Bihar.

In ancient times, Maharshi Jahnu had his ashram near Sultanganj. Ganga was flowing with such force that Maharshi Jahnu stopped her there and did not let her proceed. Bhagiratha had gone ahead and suddenly realized that he could not hear the sound of Ganga behind him. In the *Amarkosha* it is said that Ganga has a specific sound: *Gam Gam gamayate, iti Ganga.* When he realized that Ganga was not following him, he turned around and retraced his tracks. He saw that Maharshi Jahnu had stopped Ganga, and he prayed to him to release her. Maharshi Jahnu released Ganga from his right thigh and from that time on she is known as Jahnavi.

Bhagiratha then went ahead with Ganga and reached Maharshi Kapila's ashram, where Ganga washed the ashes of the sons of Sagar and liberated them. They were freed from the bondage of the world and Ganga merged with Gangasagar. From that time on, Ganga has been flowing continuously from the Himalayas to Gangasagar. She is the symbol of purity and ceaseless activity.

Incarnation of Shiva as Pippalada in Treta Yuga

Maharshi Dadhichi used to live in his ashram with his wife Suvarcha and would impart spiritual teachings and sadhana on a regular basis. The maharshi and his wife were both devotees of Shiva. He refused to go to the yajna in Prayag, at which Shiva was insulted by Daksha. He said, "Where God in the form of Shiva has no place of honour, what will we do there?" All the devatas, rishis and munis went, yet he refused to go. His devotion to Shiva was strong and unbroken. He had received a very special blessing and the bones of his body were as hard as diamond. He knew that he had received this boon for a purpose and his body would someday be of use to the gods.

One day, when Dadhichi was sitting in the ashram with his pregnant wife, the gods came to meet him. They said, "Maharshi, you are aware that the demons are harassing us and we need weapons to defend ourselves. We all know that your bones are as strong as diamond. We can make spears out of them.

At that time, one demon named Vrittasura was terrorizing the whole world, and he could not be conquered by any divine weapon. In a way, he was invincible, as he had received the boon that he could not be killed by any weapon.

Vrittasura had made a list and given it to the Cosmic Father, Brahma. His wish was that he should not be killed: neither inside nor outside, neither by human nor animal, neither in the morning nor in the evening, neither through liquid nor any hard material, and Brahma had agreed to it. After receiving the boon, Vrittasura attacked the empire of the gods. He drove the gods out and started ruling there.

That was when the gods came to Dadhichi and said that they needed weapons, as their divine weapons were useless against Vrittasura. Dadhichi spontaneously agreed to give his bones. He entered into samadhi and the divine cow Surabhi came and started licking his body. As soon as her tongue touched his body, Dadhichi's body dissolved into energy and merged into space. Only the bones remained and Vishwakarma made weapons out of them.

The plan was to fashion many different types of weapons out of the various bones that had been made as hard as diamond through Shiva's grace. Weapons were made out of different bones and distributed to various gods. Vrittasura was finally killed by these weapons and the gods regained control of their kingdom.

When Maharshi Dadhichi left his body, his wife also wanted to enter the funeral pyre. However, there was a voice from heaven which said, "Suvarcha, you cannot leave your body now as you are carrying a baby. If you leave your body now, you will be guilty of infanticide. Therefore, do not enter the funeral pyre; you must stay alive."

Suvarcha was the wife of a rishi, and she had her own powers. She sat down in samadhi and instructed the baby in her womb to come out. The heavenly voice had said that a pregnant woman should not leave her body and she was honouring those instructions. This is how Pippalada, an aspect of Shiva, took birth. After his birth, Suvarcha entered the funeral pyre along with the remains of Maharshi Dadhichi and left for the heavens.

When the child was born, all the gods and goddesses arrived and named him Pippalada. This name was given because it was under a peepal tree that Suvarcha had commanded the baby to come out of the womb. Therefore, the child was born under the peepal tree.

Pippalada was an aspect of Shiva, and had the brilliance and vitality of Dadhichi. The gods nourished the boy, and for a long time Pippalada remained under the peepal tree and did his sadhana and tapasya there. After being engaged in tapasya for a long time, and authoring many scriptures, he married King Anaranya's daughter, Padma, and ruled over the kingdom. In this incarnation, Shiva fulfilled the roles of a sadhu, a rishi and a powerful king.

Shiva's incarnation as Dwijeshwara in Treta Yuga

Once a king named Bhadrayu and his wife Kirtimalini entered a dense forest on an adventure trip. Both of them were staunch devotees of Shiva. In order to test the king's devotion, Shiva and Sati manifested as an old brahmin couple and, through the power of maya, created an old tiger. The tiger chased the old brahmin couple and when they met the king they begged him to save them. The king assured them of protection and started shooting various arrows, throwing spears and attacking the tiger with a sword, but all to no avail. Nothing happened, as the tiger was made out of maya.

The tiger leapt on the brahmin wife, grabbed her in his jaws and dragged her into the jungle. When he saw his wife being dragged away like this by the tiger, the brahmin, who was none other than Shiva, appeared very upset and cried to the king, "You have not kept your word. My wife has been taken by the tiger. Now what will I do here all alone? Who will look after me?" The king said, "Sir, I am ready to give you whatever you want. I am sorry that I could not keep my word. I am ashamed. Please give me an order and I will do whatever you say." Shiva in the form of the old brahmin said, "Please give me your wife. She will stay with me and look after me." King Bhadrayu took water in his hands and took

a sankalpa, "From today I give you my wife, Kirtimalini."
After this, the king thought, "I have not been able to keep
my word, I have not been able to protect my subjects; what
right do I have to live?"

He arranged wood for his funeral pyre, lit the fire
and got ready to enter it. He circumambulated the fire,
meditated on Shiva and was on the point of entering the fire,
when Shiva manifested and said, "Bhadrayu, this was a test of
your devotion. The brahmin wife was none other than Shivaa
and the brahmin was me. The tiger was made of maya. This
entire lila was created to test you."

Dwija means a brahmin, therefore this manifestation of
Shiva is known as Dwijeshwara. After testing Bhadrayu, Shiva
returned to Kailash with Sati.

Shiva's incarnation as Hanuman in Treta Yuga

One day in Kailash, Shiva was narrating to Sati the story of
the churning of the ocean and the distribution of nectar.
After hearing the story, Sati said, "The story is incredible;
particularly Vishnu taking the form of Mohini, the most
beautiful woman. Have you seen that form?" Shiva said, "No,
I have not seen that form because after drinking the poison,
my throat was burning and I came straight to Kailash to cool
down." Sati said, "Then how can I believe that this actually
happened, since you were not really there and you are telling
me of something that you have just heard about?" Shiva said,
"Yes, what you are saying is correct."

Shiva invoked Vishnu, who immediately manifested and
asked, "Did you call me?" Shiva said, "Yes, I want to see your
Mohini form." Vishnu smiled and said, "That was an event
of a bygone era. Are you serious that you want me to show
that form now?" Shiva said, "Yes, because I have only heard
of this form and have not actually seen it." Following Shiva's
instruction, Vishnu manifested as the beautiful woman called
Mohini. The moment she appeared, Shiva's mind became
restless and he started chasing her. Mohini ran in front and
Shiva was behind her. Shiva got excited and frustrated at

not getting her, and in this way, his seed fell. The *saptarishis*, the seven rishis who were watching this lila of their ishta, collected Shiva's seed on a leaf and placed it in the womb of Gautama's daughter Anjani, via the ear passage.

Anjani was the daughter of Gautama and Ahalya, and she was married to the king of the monkeys, named Keshari. Gautama's ashram was in Tryambakeshwar, near Nasik; therefore, Hanuman was born on one of the mountains in the Brahmagiri range. There are different variations of this story. In some, it is mentioned that Shiva's seed was put in Anjani's womb by the saptarishis, and in some it is said that the god of the wind, Vayu, put it there. In any case, the valiant and strong Hanuman was born from that seed of Shiva. We all know him as a great devotee of Rama, the killer of the demons or *rakshasas*, and as the most famous proponent of Rama bhakti; however, Hanuman was also a partial incarnation of Shiva.

Hanuman started his lila right from his birth; he ate up the morning sun, mistaking it for an apple, and as a consequence, darkness descended everywhere. However, later, at the request of the gods, he vomited it out. Knowing him to be an incarnation of Shiva, the gods gave him all their powers. Thereafter, Hanuman went to Surya, the sun god, and imbibed all the teachings and vidyas. Surya became Hanuman's guru, and on Surya's instructions assumed the responsibility of being minister to Sugriva, who was an incarnation of the sun. Surya told him, "Go to Sugriva, serve him and stay with him in Kishkindha. There you will meet your aradhya, Sri Rama." Hanuman imbibed this instruction and spent his time with Sugriva; he then met Sri Rama and devoted himself to doing all his work. We praise Hanuman with the *Sri Hanuman Chalisa*:

Shreeguru charana saroja raja, nija manu mukuru sudhaari;
Baranaum raghubara bimala jasu jo daayaku phala chaari.
Buddhiheena tanu jaanike, sumirau pavana-kumaara;
Bala budhi bidyaa dehu mohi, harahu kalesa bikaara.

Siyaavaraa Raamachandra Shankara Hari Aum.

88

Jaya hanumaana jnaana guna saagara;
Jaya kapeesa tihum loka ujaagara.
Raama doota atulita bala dhaamaa;
Anjani-putra pavanasuta naamaa.

Mahaabeera bikrama bajarangee;
Kumati nivaara sumati ke sangee.
Kanchana barana biraaja subesaa;
Kaanana kundala kunchita kesaa.

Haatha bajra au dhvajaa biraajai;
Kaamdhe moomja janeoo saajai.
Sankara suvana kesareenandana;
Teja prataapa mahaa jaga bandana.
Bidyaavaana gunee ati chaatura;
Raama kaaja karibe ko aatura.
Prabhu charitra sunibe ko rasiyaa;
Raama lashana seetaa mana basiyaa.

Sookshma roopa dhari siyahi dikhaavaa;
Bikata roopa dhari lanka jaraavaa.
Bheema roopa dhari asura samhaare;
Raamachandra ke kaaja samvaare.
Laaya sajeevana lakhana jiyaaye;
Shreeraghubeera harashi ura laaye.
Raghupati keenhee bahuta baraaee;
Tuma mama priya bharatahi sama bhaaee.

Sahasa badana tumharo jasa gaavaim;
Asa kahi shreepati kantha lagaavai.
Sanakaadika brahmaadi muneesaa;
Naarada saarada sahita aheesaa.
Jama kubera digapaala jahaam te;
Kabi kobida kahi sake kahaam te.
Tuma upakaara sugreevahim keenhaa;
Raama milaaya raaja pada deenhaa.

Tumharo mantra bibheeshana maanaa;
Lankesvara bhae saba jaga jaanaa.
Juga sahasra jojana para bhaanoo;

89

Leelyo taahi madhura phala jaanoo.
Prabhu mudrikaa meli mukha maaheem;
Jaladhi laanghi gaye acharaja naaheen.
Durgama kaaja jagata ke jete;
Sugama anugraha tumhare tete.

Raama duaare tuma rakhavaare;
Hota na aajnaa binu paisaare.
Saba sukha lahai tumhaaree saranaa;
Tuma rachchhaka kaahoo ko dara naa.
Aapana teja samhaaro aapai;
Teenom loka haamka tem kampai.
Bhoota pisaacha nikata nahim aavai;
Mahaabeera jaba naama sunaavai.

Naasai roga harai saba peeraa;
Japata nirantara hanumata beeraa.
Sankata te hanumaana chhuraavai;
Mana krama bachana dhyaana jo laavai.
Saba para raama tapasvee raajaa;
Tina ke kaaja sakala tuma saajaa.
Aura manoratha jo koee laavai;
Soi amita jeevana phala paavai.

Chaaron juga parataapa tumhaaraa;
Hai parasiddha jagata ujïyaaraa.
Saadhu santa ke tuma rakhavaare;
Asura nikandana raama dulaare.
Ashta siddhi nau nidhi ke daataa;
Asa bara deena jaanakee maataa.
Raama rasaayana tumhare paasaa;
Sadaa raho raghupati ke daasaa.

Tumhare bhajana raama ko paavai;
Janama janama ke dukha bisaraavai.
Anta kaala raghubara pura jaaee;
Jahaan janma hari-bhakta kahaaee.
Aura devataa chitta na dharaee;
Hanumata sei sarba sukha karaee.

Sankata katai mitai saba peeraa;
Jo sumirai hanumata balabeeraa.

Jai jai jai hanumaana gosaaeen;
Kripaa karahu guru deva kee naaeen.
Jo sata baara paatha kara koee;
Chootahi bandi mahaa sukha hoee.
Jo yaha parihai hanumaana chaaleesaa;
Hoya siddhi saakhee gaureesaa.
Tulaseedaasa sadaa hari cheraa;
Keejai naatha hridaya mamha deraa.

Pavanatanaya sankata harana, mangala moorati roopa;
Raama lakhana seetaa sahita, hridaya basahu sura bhoopa.

Shiva's incarnation as Krishnadarshan in Treta Yuga

In every age, there will be a *Manu*, the original man. To date there have been twenty-seven Manus. The first Manu was Swayambhu Manu. The current Manu is Vaivasvat Manu. The story that is being narrated is not related to the current *chaturyuga*, the cycle of the four yugas. There was a chaturyuga in the past and there will be a chaturyuga in the future. We are able to see only the current chaturyuga and do not have any idea about the past chaturyuga nor the future chaturyuga. However, in the scriptures, indications have been given about the future chaturyuga and also the bygone chaturyuga. The past chaturyuga becomes history or mythology, and the future remains unknown.

In Treta Yuga, the Manu named Shraaddhadeva had nine sons. His ninth son was called Nabhaga. Nabhaga was very fond of studying. The others brothers liked to rule the kingdom and indulge in pleasures and pastimes, but Nabhaga stayed for a long time in the ashram of his guru in pursuit of knowledge. In the meantime, Shraaddhadeva Manu divided his kingdom between his eight sons and left for the forest with the sankalpa of *vanaprastha*, the third stage of life in which one retires from worldly life to practise sadhana in relative seclusion. Shraaddhadeva built a small hut and remained in the forest.

After many years, when Nabhaga returned after finishing his studies, the brothers received him with respect and gave him all the news. After hearing them, Nabhaga asked, "Where is my share? The kingdom has been divided into eight parts; has any share been kept for me?" "No. That was not our decision. Father made the division and he should have thought about it. You were engaged in your studies, and he might have thought that you did not need a kingdom. Your name is not there in the partition deed." Nabhaga said, "How is this possible? I will ask my father how he forgot me."

With this thought in mind, he went to his father in the forest. His father was happy to see him. Nabhaga told him, "Dear father, it seems that you have forgotten that I am also your son. You have distributed the kingdom to all my brothers without giving me any share." His father said, "Nabhaga, you also had a share, but your brothers have cheated you; they have taken your share and are casting the blame on me. How could I possibly not keep your share? Anyway, it does not matter now. There are other means of livelihood.

"Near this ashram, the brahmins of Angirasa lineage are performing a yajna. In this yajna, on every sixth day, they are unable to complete a prescribed ritual. They do not know two necessary *richas* or compilation of mantras. Go there and tell them these two richas, which are connected to Vaishvadeva. After the yajna is complete and they go to heaven, they will be so pleased that they will give you their entire wealth."

As advised by his father, Nabhaga went to the Angirasa rishis and chanted the two suktas of Vaishvadeva. On completion of this chanting, the Angirasa rishis achieved their desired goal and left for heaven. While leaving, they told Nabhaga, "Whatever is lying here is now yours." As Nabhaga was collecting the goods, Shiva decided to test his devotion and appeared there as a brahmin *tapasvi* or ascetic, and asked him, "Who are you to take all this wealth? This is not yours." Nabhaga said, "My father told me that whatever share was given to me by the rishis would be mine. The Angirasa rishis also told me that whatever is left over from the yajna is my share. Therefore, all this wealth is given to me by the rishis and is mine."

During this darshan, the form of Shiva was pitch black, yet extremely beautiful; whoever looked at him was so mesmerized that they could not remove their eyes from him. *Krishna* means black, and so this incarnation is known as 'Krishnadarshan'. Shiva as Krishnadarshan then told Nabhaga, "The rishis may have told you all this, but that is not relevant now. Go and ask your father what to do with the goods lying in the yajna. Make your father the arbitrator, and whatever decision he makes, I will accept it."

Shraaddhadeva Manu told his son, "The person who is stopping you from taking the wealth is none other than Lord Shiva. He has full right over all the items received from a yajna. Whatever items are leftover in a yajna go to Lord Rudra; he has the first right. If you want it, take his permission first. Whatever the brahmin has said is correct. You go to the brahmin, apologize to him and then pray to him."

As advised by his father, Nabhaga went back to the site of yajna, where Shiva was waiting in his form of Krishnadarshan. He joined his hands in prayer and said, "Lord, please forgive me. I was making a grave blunder." Shiva as Krishnadarshan said to him, "Your father is right, and due to your good nature you accepted it unquestioningly. If you had some ulterior motive, you would not have accepted his instructions. You would have taken away everything like your brothers and would not have listened to him. I am pleased with your behaviour and am bestowing *brahmajnana*, supreme knowledge, upon you." In this way, Paramshiva as Krishnadarshan gave Nabhaga the highest knowledge and also all the wealth of the yajna.

Shiva's incarnations as Yatinatha and Hamsa in Treta Yuga
In Treta Yuga, near the Arbudachala mountain, there lived a Bhil (a tribal community) couple who were great devotees of

Shiva. They used to worship him regularly. One day, Shiva in the form of a sannyasin arrived at their house to test them. They lived in a small hut in the forest. They slept, ate and worshipped in that small hut. Shiva, as a mendicant knocked at their hut late in the evening and said, "I need to stay here for the night and will leave in the morning." The man started wondering how to extend hospitality to his guest. He told his wife, "We have an honoured guest with us. The guest will stay inside the hut, and since you are a woman, you will also have to stay within. I will stay outside on guard and will ensure that the wild beasts of the jungle do not disturb our honoured guest during his sleep."

With this thought in mind, the man sat down outside with his bow and arrow and commenced his guard duty. However, the lila was such that the Bhil was killed that night by wild beasts. In the morning, when his wife opened the door, she saw her husband lying dead. She went to the sannyasin and told him, "My husband is fortunate to have given up his body while doing seva. I will follow him." Saying this, she collected the wood for her husband's funeral pyre and, after lighting it, climbed on to it herself. Shiva now appeared in his original form and said, "I have created this lila in order to test your devotion. Please ask for whatever boon you want."

The woman was overwhelmed at this turn of events and did not know what to say. Shiva understood this and said, "You have seen me now as an ascetic, and in your next birth you will see me as a *hamsa*, a swan. Your husband will be born in a royal family in his next birth and you will also be born in a royal family. I will come as a hamsa to make the two of you meet. Thereafter, you will rule over your kingdom for a long time."

In his next birth, the Bhil was born as Nala, the son of King Virsena in the city of Naishadha, and his wife was born as Damayanti, the daughter of King Bhima in the city of Vidarbha. Shiva came as a hamsa to bring Nala and Damayanti together and bestowed on them the happiness a royal couple can enjoy. The tapasya and sadhana of the Bhil and his wife was rewarded by Lord Shiva as kingly happiness in the next birth.

Sati's testing of Rama

One day Lord Shiva told Sati, "Come, let us go to Dandakaranya." As Shiva and Sati were roaming in the Dandakaranya forest, Vishnu, in the form of Rama, was searching for Sita there. Ravana, who had worshipped Shiva to become the almighty conqueror of the world, had kidnapped the Cosmic Mother Lakshmi, in the form of Sita, and taken her to Lanka. Rama, who was *maryada purushottama*, a person with the highest ideals, was also enacting his lila and searching for Sita in the forest, loudly lamenting, "Oh Sita, Oh Sita, where are you?" He was asking the plants, the flowers, the trees, the birds and the animals, "Have you seen my Sita?"

Astride his bull, Shiva saw Rama and Lakshmana searching for Sita. There were tears in Rama's eyes. There was the pain of separation from Sita in his being. The words, "Sita, Sita" were spontaneously coming from his lips. Shiva saw Rama and Lakshmana from a distance, did his pranams, and praising them with the words, "Jaya Satchidananda, jaya Sri Rama", went off in a different direction.

Sati was extremely surprised to witness this lila of Shiva and said, "Why are you bowing down to this ascetic who is shedding tears? Why are you giving him your respectful salutations as 'Jaya Satchidananda'? You are the *aradhya*, the chosen deity, of Rama, so why are you saluting him?" Shiva replied, "The person whom you are seeing as Rama is none other than Vishnu, who in the human form of Rama is performing this lila." The various lilas of Rama are praised with the *Nama Ramayanam*:

Baalakaandam
Shuddha brahma paraatpara raama;
Kaalaatmaka parameshvara raama.

Sheshatalpa-sukhanidrita raama;
Brahmaadyamara-praarthita raama.

Chandakirana-kulamandana raama;
Shreemaddasharatha-nandana raama.

Kaushalyaa-sukhavarddhana raama;
Vishvaamitra-priyadhana raama.

Ghora-taatakaa-ghaataka raama;
Maareechaadi nipaataka raama.

Kaushika-makha-samrakshaka raama;
Shreemadahalyoddhaaraka raama.

Gautama-muni-sampoojita raama;
Suramunivaragana-samstuta raama.

Naavika-dhaavita mridu-pada raama;
Mithilaapura-janamohaka raama.

Videha-maanasa-ranjaka raama;
Tryambaka-kaarmuka-bhanjaka raama.

Seetaarpita-vara-maalika raama;
Kritavaivaahika-kautuka raama.

Bhaargava-darpa vinaashaka raama;
Shreemadayodhyaa-paalaka raama.

Ayodhyaakaandam
Aganita-gunagana-bhooshita raama;
Avanee-tanayaa-kaamita raama.

Raakaa-chandra-samaanana raama;
Pitri-vaakyaashrita-kaanana raama.

Priya-guha-vinivedita pada raama;
Tatkshaalita-nija mridupada raama.

Bharadvaaja-mukhaanandaka raama;
Chitrakootaadri-niketana raama.

Dasharatha-santata-chintita raama;
Kaikeyee-tanayaarthita raama.

Virachita-nija-pitrikarmaka raama;
Bharataarpita-nija-paaduka raama.

Aranyakaandam
Dandaka-vana-jana-paavana raama;
Dushta-viraaha-vinaashana raama.

Sharabhanga-suteekshna-archita raama;
Agastyaanugraha-vardhita raama.

Gridhraadhipa-samsevita raama;
Panchavatee-tata-susthita raama.

Shoorpanakhaartti-vidhaayaka raama;
Khara-dooshana-mukha-soodaka raama.

Seetaapriya-harinaanuga raama;
Maareechaarti-kridaashuga raama.

Apahrita-seetaanveshaka raama;
Gridhraadhipa-gatidaayaka raama.

Shabaree-datta-phalaashana raama;
Kabandhabaahuchchhedana raama.

Kishkindhaakaandam
Hanumat-sevita-nijapada raama;
Natasugreevaabheeshtada raama.

Garvita-baali samhaaraka raama;
Vaanara-doota-preshaka raama.

Hitakara-lakshmana-samyuta raama;
Kapivara-santata-samsmrita raama.

Sundarakaandam
Tadgati-vighna-dhvamsaka raama;
Seetaapraanaadhaaraka raama.

Dushtadashaanana-dooshita raama;
Shishta-hanumad-bhooshita raama.

Seetaaveditakaakaavana raama;
Krita-choodaamani-darshana raama.

Kapivara-vachanaashvaasita raama;
Raavana-nidhana-prasthita raama.

Yuddhakaandam
Vaanara-sainya-samaavrita raama;
Shoshita sarideeshaarthita raama.

Vibheeshanaabhayadaayaka raama;
Parvata-setu-nibandhaka raama.

Kumbhakarna-shirashchhedaka raama;
Raakshasa-sangha-vimardaka raama.

Ahimahiraavana-chaarana raama;
Samhrita-dashamukha-raavana raama.

Vidhibhavamukha-surasamstuta raama;
Khasthita-dasharatha-veekshita raama.

Seetaadarshana-modita raama;
Abhishikta-vibheeshananata raama.

Pushpakayaanaarohana raama;
Bharadvaajaabhi-nishevana raama.

Bharata-praanapriyakara raama;
Saaketapuree vibhooshana raama.

Sakala-sveeyasamaanata raama;
Ratnalasat-peethaasthita raama.

Pattaabhishekaalankrita raama;
Paarthivakula sammaanita raama.

Vibheeshanaarpita-ranjaka raama;
Keeshakulaanugrahakara raama.

Sakalajeeva-samrakshaka raama;
Samasta lokoddhaaraka raama.

Uttarakaandam

Aagata-munigana-samstuta raama;
Vishruta-dashakanthodbhava raama.

Seetaalingana-nirvrita raama;
Neeti-surakshita-janapada raama.

Vipina-tyaajita-janakajaa raama;
Kaarita-lavanaasura-vadha raama.

Svargata-shambuka-samstuta raama;
Svatanaya-kushalava-nandita raama.

Ashvamedha-kratu-deekshita raama;
Kaalaavedita-surapada raama.

Aayodhyakajana-muktida raama;
Vidhimukha-vibudhaanandaka raama.

Tejomaya-nija-roopaka raama;
Samsritibandha-vimochaka raama.

Dharmasthaapana-tatpara raama;
Bhaktiparaayana-muktida raama.

Sarvacharaachara-paalaka raama;
Sarva-bhavaamayavaaraka raama.

Vaikunthaalaya-samsthita raama;
Nityaananda-padasthita raama.

Raama raama jaya raajaa raama;
Raama raama jaya seetaa raama.

Shiva talked to Sati about Rama's divinity, his completeness as a person and his lila. He said, "Rama is not a partial incarnation of Vishnu, but a full incarnation. Vishnu has manifested himself on the earth in order to establish *dharma* or righteousness and *maryada*, the highest ideal. He is also my chosen deity of worship, my aradhya. If I did not offer him my pranams, it would be a great offence on my part."

If God, guru or your chosen deity is in front of you, and you do not bow down to him, there can be no greater offence. You can steal, or even murder, and still be forgiven by God; however, if you do not offer your pranams to your aradhya or your ishta, and do not show them due respect then that is unpardonable, because that bowing down expresses your feeling of surrender to God and guru. When Arjuna was suffering from the delusion of guilt and remorse on the Mahabharata battlefield, he assailed Lord Krishna with question after question. However, until Arjuna surrendered to him with the words: *Shishyaste'ham shadhi mam tvam prapannam* – "I am your disciple, please instruct me", Krishna did not solve his problems. The advice of the *Bhagavad Gita* began only after Arjuna surrendered.

When you are in front of your guru or ishta, you should restrain your ego and surrender it to him. Only then can you awaken true *shraddha* or faith, bhakti and surrender, which then connects you with God. Otherwise, your bhakti becomes *vyabhicharini*, flirtatious like a bee. A bee sits on a flower for only a moment, draws some nectar from it and then goes on to the next flower, and the next, and the next. It does not suck the nectar from one flower only, but goes on collecting it from many different flowers. If the bee collected the honey from one flower then it would not have to wander so much. Likewise, when a person worships various deities or people and keeps on wandering around without focusing his faith on one ishta, then that bhakti is called vyabhicharini. Concentrate your faith on one ishta; only then is there a possibility of attainment.

It is very simple. If you need to dig for water, you should dig one hole fifty feet deep, and not fifty holes one foot deep. In the first case you will definitely get water, but in the latter case it will be failed labour.

Shiva's ishta is Vishnu, and Vishnu's ishta is Shiva. They worship each other and are devotees of each other. Before creation, Shiva and Vishnu met and agreed that they would be on the same level and there would be no difference between them.

Adishakti, who was present as an embodied being in the form of Sati, was deluded by this lila of Shiva. She asked Shiva, "Who is this person to whom you are offering your pranams?" Shiva said, "He is verily pure Brahman, who lives in Vaikuntha. He is my chosen deity, my ishta, the form of Mahavishnu." Yet, the lila of the lord had to take place and Sati's mind did not accept these words.

Sati is *Parashakti*, the transcendental energy, and saying that the Parashakti accepted or did not accept is meaningless. However, in the physical body of Sati there was a mind that was worldly in nature, and that mind did not accept it. She thought, "There is some other mystery behind this and Shiva is misleading me; he is confusing me." Shiva was a bit annoyed that Sati did not believe him and said, "If you want to test Rama, you can go ahead; satisfy yourself that Narayana has taken the form of Rama." Sati was ready, as this lila was about to culminate.

Sati transformed herself into a likeness of Sita thinking, 'If Rama addresses me as Sita and fails to see through this disguise, that will prove he is not *Parabrahman*, the transcendental reality, and if he recognizes my real self then I will of course accept him as the supreme reality, as Vishnu.'

When Sati approached Rama as Sita, Rama offered his pranams to her and said, "Oh Mother, why are you wandering around alone in this dense forest? Where is Baba Bholenath, Lord Shiva? Why have you renounced your original form and taken this new form?" Sati was shocked to hear this. She thought, "O Lord, what have I done? I have done something utterly wrong!"

Following the proper etiquette, Sati folded her hands in prayer and said, "Rama, Lord Bholenath was touring the earthly plane, accompanied by me and his close assistants. Here he saw you and Lakshmana searching for Sita in the

101

forest. He did his namaskara to you and went his way; he is standing over there under the banyan tree. He was overjoyed to have your darshan and was suffused with bliss. There was a doubt in my mind regarding your true identity and that is why I took his permission to test you. Please forgive me for this unpardonable act. You are verily Lord Narayana." Rama smiled and said, "Oh Mother, it is not befitting for you to talk like this. After all, this is your lila, so where is the question of forgiving you?"

Rama uttered these sweet words in order to assuage the pain, the guilt that Sati was feeling. Sati then asked, "My Lord, please tell me how you and Bholenath became equal and complementary to each other. How did you become mutual worshippers?" Rama told Sati, "At the beginning of time, Shiva called me to Kailash and made me sit on a throne bedecked with jewels and precious stones, and worshipped me at an auspicious time. He told the assembled gods, 'From now on, Vishnu is my chosen deity, my aradhya. He is in me and I am in him. From today, I instruct that Vishnu's worship be accorded the highest status and be the primary ritual. Let the Vedas give this same teaching.' Lord Shiva's grace and blessings have put me in the same position as him."

These words of Rama made Sati more ashamed and embarrassed. She joined her hands, offered her pranams to him and said, "Lord, please keep on showering your blessings and grace on me." She then went back to Shiva. While the omniscient Shiva knew what had happened, still he asked her, "Did you test him?" "Yes," Sati said. "What were your findings?" Sati replied, "Rama is Narayana himself. There is no difference between you and Rama. This means that when I tested Rama, I was also testing you. This has been my greatest offence."

Shiva said, "It is now time to go back. We have done enough sightseeing and holidaying." They went back to Kailash and Shiva entered straight into samadhi.

The story of Ravana

At this time, in the south, the king of demons, Ravana, was expanding his empire. He would move around in his aircraft to see which kingdom he could gobble up. One day, when he was flying over the Himalayas in his Pushpaka plane, he found that his plane was stuck in a certain place and was not moving forward. When all his efforts to move the plane proved futile, Ravana started wondering, 'What is this miracle, this power, which can stop the Pushpaka plane from moving?'

He looked down and saw some sadhus chanting. He went down and asked, "What is this area, in which my plane is not able to move forward?" The chief of those ascetics, Nandi, got up and said, "This is Kailash, where Paramshiva resides. All around Kailash there is a protective wall of energy, which does not allow even birds to fly. Planes cannot fly over here, and if someone makes an effort to, he is stilled midair. This is the domain of Lord Shiva, Mahadeva, the greatest and highest god.

When Ravana heard that there was a person who was mightier than him, due to whom his plane could not go forward, he became curious and asked, "Is it possible for me to meet this Paramshiva who lives in Kailash?" Nandi said, "If you perform aradhana to worship him then he will certainly manifest and give you darshan."

The king of Lanka performed aradhana with the following *Tandava Stotra*.

Jataatavee-galajjala-pravaaha-paavitasthale;
Gale'valambya-lambitaam bhujanga-tunga-maalikaam.
Damad-damad damad damad-ninaada-vaddamarvayam;
Chakaara-chanda taandavam tanotu nah shivah shivam.
Jataakataahasambhrama-bhramannilimpa nirjharee;
Vilola-veechi-vallaree viraajamaana-moorddhani.
Dhagad-dhagad-dhagad-jvalallalaata-patta paavake;
Kishora-chandra-shekhare ratih pratikshanam mama.
Dharaa-dharendra nandinee vilaasa bandhu bandhura-

Sphurat diganta santati pramodamaana maanase.
Kripaa-kataaksha-dhoranee niruddha durdharaapadi;
Kvachid-digambare mano vinodametu vastuni.
Jataa-bhujanga-pingala-sphurat-phanaa-mani-prabhaa-
Kadamba-kunkuma-drava-pralipta-digvadhoomukhe.
Madaandha-sindhura-sphurat-tvaguttareeyamedure;
Mano-vinodamadbhutam bibhartu bhootabhartari.
Sahasra-lochana-prabhritya shesha lekha shekhara-
Prasoona-dhooli-dhoranee vidhoosaraanghripeethabhooh.
Bhujangaraajamaalayaa nibaddha-jaata-jootakah;
Shriyai chiraaya jaayataam chakora-bandhu shekharah.
Lalaata-chatvarajvalad dhananjaya-sphulingabhaa;
Nipeeta-pancha-saayakam namannilimpa-naayakam.
Sudhaa-mayookha-lekhayaa-viraajamaana-shekharam;
Mahaakapaali-sampade shiro jataalamastu nah.
Karaala-bhaala pattikaa dhagad-dhagad-dhagad-jvalad-
Dhananjayaahutee-krita prachanda pancha-saayake.
Dharaa-dharendra-nandinee kuchaagrachitra patraka-
Prakalpanaika-shilpinee trilochane ratirmama.
Naveena-megha-mandalee-niruddha-durdharasphurat-
Kuhoo-nisheethineetamah-prabandha-baddha-kandharah.
Nilimpa-nirjhareedharastanotu kritti-sindhurah;
Kalaa-nidhaana-bandhurah shriyam jagaddhurandharah.
Praphulla-neela-pankaja-prapancha-kaalima-prabhaa-
Valambi-kantha kandalee-ruchi-prabaddha-kandharam.
Smarachchhidam purachchhidam Bhavachchhidam
makhachchhidam;
Gajachchhidaandhakachchhidam tamantakachchhidam bhaje.
Akharva-sarva-mangalaa kalaa-kadamba-manjaree-
Rasa-pravaaha-maadhuree-vijrimbhanaa madhuvratam.
Smaraantakam puraantakam bhavaantakam
makhaantakam;
Gajaantakaandhakaantakam tamantakaantakam bhaje.
Jayatvadabhra-vibhrama-bhramad-bhujangamashvasad-
Vinirgamat-kramasphurat-karaala-bhaala-havyavaat.
Dhimid-dhimid-dhimid-dhvanan-mridangatunga-mangala;
Dhvani-krama pravartita-prachanda taandavah shivah.

Drishad vichitratalpayorbhujanga-mauktika-srajoh-
Garishtharatnaloshthayoh-suhrid-vipaksha-pakshayoh.
Trinaaravinda-chakshushoh prajaa-mahee-mahendrayoh;
Samapravrittikah kadaa sadaashivam bhajaamyaham.
Kadaa nilimpa-nirjharee-nikunja-kotare vasan;
Vimuktadurmatih-sadaa shirahsthamanjalim vahan.
Vilola-lola-lochano lalaama-bhaala-lagnakah;
Shiveti mantramuchcharan kadaa sukhee bhavaamyaham.

Lord Shiva was pleased with Ravana's worship and manifested before him, asking, "What do you want? Why have you performed this worship? Ask for a boon." Ravana said, "Firstly, accept me as your disciple. Secondly, give me a symbol that I can keep in my native city and thirdly, please grant me true bhakti." Lord Shiva said, "As you wish" and gave him the three boons. He gave his own Chandrahasa sword and said, "Take this to Lanka and worship it daily. The day this sword disappears from your court, realize that your end is near."

Ravana took the sword, installed it in Lanka and worshipped it daily. Ravana lived for a very long time, conquered the whole world and established the rakshasa culture. The rakshasa culture is a degeneration of *rakshya* culture which comes from the phrase *Vayam raksham* – "We protect our own society, clan, sect and lineage." In time, this culture became distorted and degenerated to *rakshasa*, demonic thinking. Today's society is also guided by this philosophy of rakshya. In this system, all the arrangements are for made for the progress of society, but when it is distorted it becomes a rakshasa or demonic culture.

Initially, Ravana was a high-class brahmin, bhakta and scholar. The *Krishna Yajurveda* emanated from Ravana's mouth. He was a great scholar, yet his inclinations were different. He began to expand his empire further after receiving the boons from Shiva. He abducted Mother Sita and threatened, coaxed and cajoled her, as well as tried other means to make her submit to him. He even took the Chandrahasa sword to her. Before Hanuman's entry into

Lanka, Shiva had placed a condition on Ravana that if he ever lifted this sword against any innocent person then the sword would disappear and the whole kingdom would become insecure. However, Ravana's good sense was blinded by his passion and he had forgotten this warning of Shiva. The moment he lifted the Chandrahasa sword against Sita, it disappeared, as it was being used against an innocent woman, to frighten and hurt her.

The moment the Chandrahasa sword vanished, Ravana came back to his senses and realized that he had committed a great offence and his kingdom was no longer protected. He had a foreboding at that time that Sita would be the cause of his death and the destruction of his empire. Even so, he thought, 'Let me make one more attempt. Let me go to Lord Shiva and ask him to come himself now that his sword has gone. I will ask him to accept this earnest plea from his bhakta. If the Lord himself comes then I will become invincible and nobody would be able to defeat me.' Thinking thus, Ravana started out for Kailash.

Baidyanatheswar in Treta Yuga

Ravana had become a friend of Shiva and so this time his plane was not stopped over Kailash. He landed and Shiva's attendants brought him inside with respect. When the Lord received the news of his arrival, he came out and asked the reason for his arrival. Ravana said, "Lord, I have misused your Chandrahasa sword and it has vanished." Shiva said, "That was the dictate of the Almighty. Now your death is certain." Ravana said, "Lord, I know that Rama is the incarnation of Narayana, but I also know that I am your staunch devotee, your servant. Please listen to the prayer of a bhakta and come with me to Lanka." Shiva said, "That is not possible, I am going to sit for samadhi now." Ravana said, "If you cannot come with me then at least give me your symbol."

Shiva gave him a Shivalingam and said, "This is my symbol. Take this with you, but remember one thing. Put this lingam down only when you reach Lanka. If you put it down at any place before reaching there, the lingam is not going to move; you will have to go to Lanka without it, and do not come to me requesting for another lingam." Ravana accepted these words of Shiva and said, "I will follow these instructions. I will hold the lingam in my hands and will not put it down anywhere on the way." Saying this, Ravana took the lingam in his hands, boarded his plane and started for Lanka.

The gods, however, had other plans for him. Varuna, the water god, obeying the wishes of Shiva, placed himself in Ravana's stomach. He created a strong urge in Ravana for urination. Ravana could not hold himself and was in great distress when he looked down to see a small Bhil boy grazing cows.

Ravana was a learned man and knew a lot, but Varuna had created such distress in him that he failed to see that the boy was none other than Narayana himself, who had assumed this form as per Shiva's wishes. Ravana landed his Pushpaka plane and told the boy, "I have to relieve myself urgently, but this Shivalingam is in my hands. Please hold it for a few minutes until I relieve myself." Vishnu, in the form of the boy, agreed and said, "Return quickly, otherwise my cows will wander away." Ravana said, "Yes, I'll be back in two minutes." However, Varuna had other designs, as he was following the wishes of Shiva. Ravana's urination just would not stop. It became a small river, which exists even today. Vishnu in the form of the boy called out to Ravana, "Come back immediately! The lingam is becoming heavy and I can't hold it any longer. Unless you return immediately, I'll have to put it down on the ground." However, Ravana did not hear him, as he was relieving himself with great bliss.

Vishnu in the form of the boy waited for some time, and when he saw that Ravana was not coming back, he yelled at him, "My cows are disappearing out of sight and I have to go. I am putting the lingam on the ground." Saying this he disappeared along with the cows.

When Ravana eventually came back after relieving himself, he saw the lingam on the ground. He tried to lift it from the ground, but to no avail. As Shiva's will was for it to remain there, no power could move it. Ravana tried again with all his strength but it proved futile. When repeated efforts failed, he became angry and gave a hard punch to the lingam, pushing it down into the ground. Ravana boarded his plane realizing that his defeat was now certain, as he had lost his protection and also the blessings of the Lord.

When Ravana asked the name of the boy, Vishnu had said, "My name is Baiju." Since the boy had placed the lingam on the ground and established it there, that lingam became known as Baijnath. Some people see Shiva's healing power in this lingam and this is another reason for calling it *Vaidyanath,* as a *vaidya* is a therapist or a doctor.

Daksha's yajna

One day, while Shiva was in samadhi, Sati was wandering around in the Gandhamardana mountain range along with her companions when she saw several aircrafts following each other in the sky. Gods and goddesses were seated inside. She told her companions, "It seems that all the devis and devatas are going to the same place, as they are all travelling at the same time and in the same direction. Find out where they are going."

Sati's assistant named Jaya stopped one plane and asked, "Sir, where are you going?" Seated in that plane with his twenty-seven wives was Chandradeva, the moon god, who was going to attend Daksha's yajna in Kankhal, Haridwar. He said, "I am going to the Daksha's yajna. He has invited all of us."

Jaya reported back to Sati that her father was conducting a massive yajna and they were all going to attend it. Sati was surprised to hear this. She exclaimed, "My father is doing a yajna and he has not invited us! We are his favourite daughter and son-in-law and we have a rightful share from every yajna. How is this possible? It is very likely a mistake." These types of thoughts went around in Sati's head. Then one other thought came to her mind: 'A daughter does not need an invitation to visit her father's place. She can go any time. The door of the father's house will always be open for his daughter.'

When she saw all the devis and devatas going for the yajna, she had a strong urge to accompany them. She went to Shiva and humbly asked, "Lord, I have come to know that my father has arranged a big yajna near Kankhal and all the devis and devatas are going there. Should we not also go?" Shiva said, "Mahadevi, we have not received an invitation, so how can we go? If we go anywhere without an invitation we will not receive due respect, and that is greater than death. My opinion is that we should not go." Sati said, "After all, he is my father and I can go at any time to my own father's house." Shiva repeated, "Sati, if you go without an invitation, the consequences will not be favourable."

Sati then had a premonition that the purpose of her incarnation was finishing. Since *vidya*, spiritual knowledge, was now established in creation, this part of the lila was to end, the next part was to begin and the yuga was on the verge of changing. She said, "Lord, please allow me to go." Shiva said, "As you remember, the last time your father conducted the yajna he banished me, so as long as an invitation is not there, I am not going. However, if you are so keen to go, then of course you go. My *ganas*, close attendants, will go with you, and you will ride on Nandi, my bull."

Shiva spoke these soothing words to Sati and sent her off to the yajna with Nandi and his ganas. When Sati reached Kankhal, she saw that all the arrangements for the yajna had been made. Her sisters were of course happy to see her, but from the expression on their faces it was evident they were apprehensive about Daksha's reaction when he saw that Sati had come uninvited.

After wandering around the yajna, Sati reached the main *mandapa* or ceremonial tent. The seats for all the devis and devatas were placed around the main yajna *vedi*, platform, and the rishis and munis were making the final arrangements for the ceremony. All the devatas were arriving and proceeding to their appointed seats. Sati reached her father's seat and offered her pranams to him.

Daksha took a long hard look at her and said, "Why have you come here? Your husband lives in graveyards and smears himself with ashes. He is not a civilized person; in fact, he is mad, and you stay with him. I threw him out of my previous yajna, as he did not offer me the due respect which should have been accorded to me as *Prajapati*, the creator of beings. He will not get any share from this yajna. Since you have come, you can partake of a small portion of the wealth which is being distributed; however, after that you must leave."

When Daksha had prayed to the Cosmic Mother to be born as his daughter, she had said one thing very clearly, "The day you show me disrespect, I will discard this body given by you." However, Daksha had forgotten the Cosmic Mother whose worship he had performed and was seeing Sati as his daughter.

Sati knew that this lila had to end and she said, "Where Shiva is not present, I am not there either. This body is cursed because it has come from your seed and you are enemy of Shiva. I am going to abandon this body." Taking this decision, the Cosmic Mother walked up to the yajna vedi and, with her yogic power, burnt herself to ashes. She burnt up the body given by Daksha, freeing herself from the physical bondage and, as Shivaa, merged back with Shiva. Thus ended this chapter of Sati, who was the incarnation of vidya.

The ganas, the assistants of Shiva who had come with Sati, lost their heads at Sati's immolation. Some were frightened, some were angry, some started yelling and running around the place, dragging people around the mandapa, hitting them, throwing them about and generally destroying everything. It seemed that the ganas would destroy the whole yajna. However, the chief brahmin named Bhrigu, who was to conduct the yajna, manifested several warriors through his mantra chanting. These warriors then started fighting with the ganas. It was a devastating battle,

110

which neither side could win. Ultimately, the ganas returned to Kailash, as they had lost heart on account of having to convey to their master that Sati had immolated herself. However, the information had to be delivered, so they went back to Kailash and gave a detailed report to Shiva.

Hearing everything, Rudra went into a terrible rage and became ready to destroy the entire world. He tore apart his locks of hair, and tearing out one part, he dashed it down the mountain. From the two parts of his matted locks, were born Mahabali Virbhadra and Mahakali. Mahadeva instructed them to go and destroy the yajna.

Virbhadra and Mahakali reached Kankhal and a war began between Bhrigu's warriors and Shiva's ganas. However, this time the ganas of Shiva were implementing Shiva's orders and so they went all out and destroyed the mandapa, beat up all the rishis and munis, pulled their long beards until blood started flowing, beat up the devatas and threw them all out of the mandapa. Even Brahma and Vishnu had to go back to their lokas. The yajna was finished, totally destroyed. Virbhadra caught hold of Daksha, cut off his head with his sword and put his head in the fire where Sati had burnt herself. Thereafter, Virbhadra and his followers went back to Shivaloka, to Kailash.

When Brahma saw the yajna completely destroyed, he thought this was wrong. A yajna should be completed, as it is conducted for the welfare of the world. He thought, 'We should pray to Lord Shiva that he revive Daksha in some way and let the yajna be completed.' Brahma, along with other devatas, went to Shiva and prayed to him to revive Daksha. "We accept that he made a big mistake, but you are almighty and can change his mind. In order to complete your lila you had the yajna destroyed, but with your grace you can surely revive him and see that the yajna is completed."

When the devatas appeased Shiva in this way, he cooled down and acquisced to fulfil their desire. He came to the yajna mandapa with the devatas and saw the destruction carried out there. When Brahma requested him to revive

Daksha, Shiva asked him to bring his body before him. When the body was brought, Shiva exclaimed, "Where is the head?" Virbhadra said, "How can the head, the mouth which hurled abuses at you, be joined to the body? That head is burned to ashes." Shiva said, "All right then, bring the head of the sacrificial animal." The head of a goat was brought to him and he joined that to Daksha's body. Thus, Nandi's curse on Daksha came to be true. Nandi had told Daksha, "That head which is abusing Shiva and continuously saying, 'Me, me, me' will one day become a goat's head and will keep on bleating 'Meh, meh, meh'."

The moment Nandi's curse was fulfilled, Daksha received new life. He stood up in front of Shiva and started singing his praise; unfortunately, however, only the bleating of 'Meh, meh, meh' came out of his mouth. He started praying to the Lord fervently with full surrender and apologies. Shiva put his hand on his head and showered his grace on him. The moment Shiva's hand touched Daksha's head, he received all spiritual knowledge. He became fully aware of his mistake and once again begged Shiva for forgiveness. Lord Shiva was appeased and forgave him.

Satsang 4

17 February 2009

Shaktipeeths

After giving life to Daksha, Shiva lifted Sati's charred body on his shoulders and left the yajna mandapa. The story says that Shiva seemed like a madman. He went around the entire world with Sati's corpse on his shoulders, like a man possessed. He became so totally oblivious of himself that the *devatas*, the gods, became worried. They wondered, "When will Shiva get rid of the corpse and become his normal unaffected self?" Yet, Shiva showed no signs of regaining normalcy. Vishnu thought of a way out: "If we get rid of this corpse from Shiva's shoulder so he does not see it any longer, then it is possible that he will go back his normal serene state." With this plan in mind, Vishnu threw his sudarshan chakra, his discus, which had been given to him by Paramshiva, at the corpse and started cutting it up.

The story says that each place where a part of Sati's corpse fell, became transformed to a *Shaktipeeth*, a centre of divine power and a place of pilgrimage. We should remember that Shiva, as Paramshiva, the ultimate transcendental Self, knew that Sati's birth was needed for the establishment of *vidya*, spiritual knowledge; *jnana*, wisdom and knowledge; *siddhanta*, spiritual principles; *darshan*, philosophy; and *sadhana*, spiritual practice. His behaviour as a person lamenting Sati's demise was a passing lila.

113

Vishnu also knew about this lila since he is another form of Shiva. There is no difference between them. They are two beings, but they have the same *prana* or energy; they have one mind, one aim, one destiny. Whether you surrender to Shiva or to Vishnu, it does not matter, because ultimately you will attain liberation. The difference between them is seen only during the lila, as according to the requirement of their *krityas* or duties, they have to perform various lilas. Paramshiva has given the kritya of *sthiti* or sustenance to Vishnu, and accordingly he has to perform lilas with that aim. Paramshiva as Rudra must also perform different lilas. They support each other.

Vishnu knew that Sati's incarnation was for a specific purpose, and that aim would be fulfilled when the teachings and systems of sadhana which Shiva taught Sati were revealed as vidya, through the different forms of Shakti that Sati had manifested. The teachings were meant for the evolution of humankind and they had to be established in the world.

It is said in the Puranas that in Satya Yuga, it was possible to fulfil one's desires merely by thinking about them. The trees, the plants, the herbs and the vegetable kingdom would always produce the right item at the right time. Everything was available easily and people did not have to try hard for anything. Whatever a person would think and say during Satya Yuga would come true.

The souls of the people who were born in that age were stainless. The people of Satya Yuga were always connected with the Divine, with the devatas and higher souls. They were able to travel around the entire world by just wishing it. However, with the advent of Treta Yuga, as suffering and evildoers started increasing, minds became polluted, the emotions and karmas became polluted, and this led to a decrease in the amount of energy in creation. It then became necessary for a person to earn a living. As the mind becomes polluted, the emotions gather impurities, and one moves away from God; with purification of the mind and emotions one comes closer to God.

114

It was necessary to establish the vidyas and the schools so that, through the process of sadhana and self-education, the minds would become pure. This episode of Narayana cutting Sati's corpse into pieces and Rudra moving around like a lunatic is symbolic. Paramshiva would never move around like a madman with the corpse of Shakti on his shoulder. After all, it is only through his will that Shakti manifests, and it is only through his will that she merges back into him. There was an arrangement between Paramshiva and Vishnu that all the teachings, given in the form of dialogue between Shiva and Sati, be established in the world as sadhana for the awakening of discrimination and intelligence. Therefore, with the help of Vishnu, Shiva established the Shaktipeeths, the centres of Shakti, where one could imbibe the teachings of spiritual life and sadhana, free oneself from the clutches of maya and reconnect with the Self.

Purushartha

What is the need of schools, colleges and universities? What is the need of education? When you study and learn something, the aim is to improve your life. You acquire different skills and qualifications required for living in society. Today, everyone is interested in earning wealth and becoming prosperous. Therefore, the aim of these schools is to provide you with sufficient knowledge to earn a living, earn wealth, fulfil your desires, raise a family and provide for your old age. This arrangement has essentially been made for Kali Yuga as, in this age, a person's mind is running after the material world. This was not the case in Satya Yuga or Treta Yuga; in those ages people would perform their karmas as duty. They would work towards all the *purusharthas*, the four aims or efforts of life as given in the scriptures: *artha*, material fulfilment; *kama*, emotional fulfilment; *dharma*, appropriate living; and *moksha*, liberation.

Artha purushartha means material wealth and prosperity. Only when you are materially affluent and do not lack the basic material needs are you in a position to easily perform the other purusharthas. It is said: *Bhukhe bhajana na hoi Gopala, le lo apni kanthi mala* – "A hungry man is not in a position to chant Gopala's name." Affluence and prosperity are needed for sadhana, as it is only then that you can sit peacefully and make your mind one-pointed. If you lack wealth then you will not be able to do sadhana because you will be worrying about arranging your food all the time. How long will you meditate for? Ten hours? At the eleventh hour, you will feel hungry. You will have to get up, light the fire and bake your bread. Even if you meditate for twenty-four hours, at the twenty-fifth hour you will have to eat because that is the inherent nature of the body. This is one reason why the scriptures have given directions for the four purusharthas.

The scriptures have prescribed four purusharthas; however, in Kali Yuga, only two purusharthas are performed: artha and kama. Dharma and moksha purusharthas are not attended to. The mental involvement and dedication to artha and kama is matched by a total negligence of dharma and moksha. It is when all the purusharthas are performed properly that a person attains peace.

A car has four wheels and if even one tyre is punctured, can you drive the car? No, you should stop the car, change the tyre, and only then can you drive the car. Yet, have you done that with your life? There are four wheels of your life: artha, kama, dharma and moksha, yet you have punctured the wheels of dharma and moksha and pumped in more than the needed pressure into the wheels of artha and kama. Often, so much air is pumped in that these two tyres burst!

You are running your car on two tyres; how long will it last? This is the reason that although all of you desire material happiness, it remains elusive, and spiritual happiness is, of course, out of reach for the average person. The material happiness which you experience is fleeting, as the purusharthas are not balanced and harmonious in your life.

In Satya Yuga and Treta Yuga, a human being would perform all the four purusharthas and then leave the body.

However, the creator, the sustainer and the destroyer of the universe knows what is in store in the four yugas. He knows what is going to happen because he is performing the lila. Therefore, with Vishnu's help, Shiva established the Shaktipeeths all over the country in memory of Sati. In these Shaktipeeths, a person can go and practise sadhana and tapasya, perform worship of *Adishakti*, the primeval energy, and become a fit receptacle for her blessings and grace.

In the *Shiva Purana*, it is said that Sati's corpse was cut into sixty-four pieces by the sudarshan chakra, and the place where each piece fell became a Shaktipeeth. In Kamakhya, Devi's *yoni*, womb, fell. Deoghar has Devi's heart and Munger her eyes. Munger is a Shaktipeeth; it is called Netrapeeth. In Chandisthan, the temple of Chandi, Devi's left eye fell. The power of the eye is vision, the ability to see. Understanding, knowledge and jnana become clearer with the eyes; form, colour and a scene are all perceived by the eyes, not by the nose, ear or other organs.

There is a unique book called *Netratantra*, 'tantra of the eyes'. Possibly the home of this tantra was Munger, because this is the *Netrapeeth*, the Shaktipeeth where Devi's eye fell. *Netratantra* has two parts: the first explains how to cure diseases of the eyes and the second part deals with awakening of inner vision, the eye of wisdom. It describes the means, the techniques and the sadhana for this inner awakening. This tantra is not only a physical science but an integration of the physical and spiritual sciences.

Every Shaktipeeth has an associated text that explains the sadhana and the method of that peeth. Nowadays, people know them simply as tantric texts; however, if you study them in depth, you will find what its specific teachings are and what its application is.

Paramshiva and Mahavishnu propagated the teachings of the sixty-four tantras. Sixty-four centres of Shakti were founded, which were called Shaktipeeths, and in each of these peeths, a particular tantra from the sixty-four tantras and one form of Shakti, a yogini, were established. These

117

days, school principals run schools and in ashrams, acharyas head the institutions. Similarly, the yoginis were made the controlling authority of these peeths. Thereafter, the material and spiritual sciences were established all over the world. This work was done by Lord Shiva, assisted by Vishnu, in the memory of Sati. After establishing these Shaktipeeths, Shiva went back to Kailash and Vishnu returned to Vaikuntha.

Sixty-four Shaktipeeths

	Place	Body Part	Name of Shakti	Name of Shiva
1	Puri	Crown (kirita)	Vimala/Bhuvaneshi	Samvarta
2	Vrindavan	Hair	Uma	Bhutesha
3	Karveer	Third eye (trinetra)	Mahishamardini	Krodhisha
4	Sri Parvat	Right temple	Srisundari	Sundarananda
5	Varanasi	Ear ornament (karnamani)	Vishalakshi	Kaala Bhairava
6	Godavari Tata	Left cheek	Vishweshi/Rukmini/ Vishwa Matrika	Dandapani/ Vatsapani
7	Shuchi	Upper teeth	Narayani	Sanhara/Sankura
8	Panchasagar	Lower teeth	Varahi	Maharudra
9	Jwalamukhi	Tongue	Siddhida Ambika	Unmatta
10	Bhairav Parvat	Upper lip	Avanti	Lambakarna
11	Attahasa	Lower lip	Fullara Devi	Vishwesha
12	Janasthana	Chin	Bhramari	Vikritaksha
13	Kashmir	Throat	Mahamaya	Trisandhyeshwara
14	Nandipur	Necklace	Nandini	Nandikeshwara
15	Srisaila	Neck	Sri Bhramaramba Devi/Mahalakshma	Mallikarjuna/ Sanvarananda/ Ishvarananda
16	Nalhati	Intestine	Kalika	Yogisha
17	Mithila	Left shoulder	Uma/Mahadevi	Mahodara
18	Ratnavali	Right shoulder	Kumari	Shiva
19	Prabhas	Stomach	Chandrabhaga	Vakratunda
20	Jalandhar	Left breast	Tripuramalini	Bhishana
21	Ramgiri	Right breast	Shivani	Chanda
22	Baidyanath	Heart	Jayadurga	Baidyanath
23	Vaktreshwara	Mind	Mahishamardini	Vaktranath

118

24	Kanyakashrama	Back	Sharvani	Nimisha
25	Bahula	Left hand	Bahula	Bhiruka
26	Ujjaini	Elbow	Mangala Chandika	Mangalyaka-Pilambara
27	Manivedik	Both wrists	Gayatri	Sharvananda
28	Prayag	Fingers of hand	Lalita Devi	Bhava
29	Utkala	Navel	Vimala	Jagannatha
30	Kanchi	Skeleton	Devagarbha	Ruru
31	Kaala Madhava	Left buttock	Kali	Asitanga
32	Shona	Right buttock	Narmada/Shonakshi	Bhadrasena
33	Kamgiri	Yoni	Kamakhya	Umananda
34	Hastinapur	Left thigh	Jayanti	Kramadishwara
35	Magadh	Right thigh	Sarvanandakari	Vyomakesha
36	Trisrota	Left foot	Bhramari	Ishwara
37	Tripura	Right foot	Tripura Sundari	Tripuresha
38	Vibhasha	Left ankle	Kapalini/Bhimaroopa	Sarvananda Kapali
39	Kurukshetra	Right ankle	Savitri	Sthanu
40	Yugadya	Right foot – big toe	Bhootadhatri	Kshirkantaka
41	Virat	Right foot – toes	Ambika	Amrita
42	Kalipeeth	Rest of the fingers	Kalika	Nakulesha
43	Manasa (Tibet)	Right palm	Dakshayani	Amara
44	Sri Lanka	Ankle	Indrakshi	Rakshaseshwara
45	Gandaki (Nepal)	Right cheek	Gandaki	Chakrapani
46	Nepal	Both knees	Mahamaya	Kapala
47	Hingula (Karachi)	Top of the head (brahmarandhra)	Bhairavi	Bhimalochana
48	Sugandha (Bangladesh)	Nose	Sunanda	Tryambaka
49	Kartoyatata	Left temple	Aparna	Vamana
50	Chattal (Bangladesh)	Right hand	Bhavani	Chandrashekhara
51	Yashora (Bangladesh)	Left palm	Yashoreshwari	Chandra
52	Karnataka	Both ears	Jaya Durga	Abhiru
53	Sarvashaila	Left temple	Shakini	Vatsanabha
54	Munger	Eyes	Chandi	Kaala Bhairava
55	Himadri Hill	Not Available	Bhima	NA
56	Kishkinda Hills	NA	Tara	NA
57	Amarkantak	NA	Chandika	NA

58	Vindhyachal	NA	Vindhyavasini	NA
59	Chitrakut	NA	Sita	NA
60	Mathura	NA	Devaki	NA
61	Dwarika	NA	Rukmini	NA
62	Gaya	NA	Mangala	NA
63	Pushkar	NA	Puruhuta	NA
64	Kanyakubja	NA	Gauri	NA

Shiva as Rameshwara in Treta Yuga

In Vishnu's incarnation as Rama, he reached the shore of the ocean, along with Sugriva and eighteen battalions of the monkey infantry, in pursuit of Ravana, who had abducted Sita. The army was wondering on how to cross the sea to Lanka. There were various suggestions. Some suggested crossing with a boat, but then others said this would be dangerous as the demons might sink their boats before they reached the shore. That idea was discarded and the suggestion was made to construct a bridge, which would enable the army to cross over safely.

When the arrangements were being made for the construction of the bridge, Rama said, "Before we start on this undertaking, I would like to worship my aradhya, Lord Shiva, and receive his blessings." Rama built a Shivalingam on the beach out of sand and performed his aradhana with a stuti:

*Namaami shambhum purusham puraanam
namaami sarvajnamapaarabhaavam;
Namaami rudram prabhumakshayam tam
namaami sharvam shirasaa namaami.*

*Namaami devam paramavyayam
tamumaapatim lokagurum namaami;
Namaami daaridryavidaaranam tam
namaami rogaapaharam namaami.*

*Namaami kalyaanamachintyaroopam
namaami vishvodbhava-beejaroopam;*

Namaami vishvasthitikaaranam tam
namaami samhaarakaram namaami.

Namaami gaureepriyamavyayam tam
namaami nityam ksharamaksharam tam;
Namaami chidroopamameyabhaavam
trilochanam tam shirasaa namaami.

Namaami kaarunyakaram bhavasya
bhayankaram vaa'pi sadaa namaami;
Namaami daataaramabheepsitaanaam
namaami someshamumeshamaadau.

Namaami vedatrayalochanam tam
namaami moortitrayavarjitam tam;
Namaami punyam sadasadvyateetam
namaami tam paapaharam namaami.

Namaami vishvasya hite ratam tam
namaami roopaani bahooni dhatte;
Yo vishvagoptaa sadasatpranetaa
namaami tam vishvapatim namaami.

Yajneshvaram samprati havyakavyam
tathaagatim lokasadaashivo yah;
Aaraadhito yashcha dadaati sarvam
namaami daanapriyamishtadevam.

Namaami someshvaramasvatantramumaapatim
tam vijayam namaami;
Namaami vighneshvara-nandinaatham
putrapriyam tam shirasaa namaami.

Namaami devam bhavaduhkhashokavinaashanam
chandradharam namaami;
Namaami gangaadharameeshameedyamumaadhavam
devavaram namaami.

Namaamyajaadeesha-purandaraadi-suraasurairarchita-
paadapadmam;

121

*Namaami deveemukha-vaadanaanaameekshaarthamakshit
ritayam ya echchhat.*

*Panchaamritairgandha-sudhoopadeepairvichitra-
pushpairvividhaishcha mantraih;
Annaprakaaraih sakalopachaaraih sampoojitam
somamaham namaami.*

When Rama repeatedly invoked his aradhya with this stuti,
Shiva could not remain unmoved in Kailash. He broke his
samadhi and manifested in the Shivalingam. When Rama
had darshan of his aradhya in the lingam, the following stuti
came out of his mouth spontaneously:

*Damrupaani Shoolapaani
He nataraajana namo namo.*

*Tuma aadi deva anaadi ho tuma antaheena ananta ho
Shreemanta ho, bhagavanta ho he naatha karunaakanta ho*

*Shashilalaata tana viraata
He trilochana namo namo.*

*Nihsaara isa samsara men shiva naama kevalam saara hai
Shiva shakti hai, shiva bhakti hai, shiva mukti kaa aadhaara hai*

*Roma roma Om Om
He aghanaashana namo namo.*

Praising his aradhya thus, Rama also prayed to him for
victory in the ensuing battle with Ravana. Hearing this, Shiva
did not offer his blessings or a boon, but said with palms
joined in pranam mudra, "Victory to you, Rama!"

When Rama heard this call of victory, he realized that
his victory over Ravana was now certain. Thereafter, Rama
took permission from Shiva for the war and said, "You have
blessed me by giving me darshan in this earthly lingam. I
wish that at this place where I have performed your worship,
you would come and stay permanently." Shiva agreed and
entered the lingam. From that time on, this Shivalingam
became known as Rameshwaram.

Thereafter, Rama crossed the sea, entered Lanka, fought with the demons and killed them. Eventually Ravana was also killed and Rama came back to Ayodhya with Sita. Rama's reign began in Ayodhya. During this *Ramarajya*, Rama's reign, no one anywhere, in any house, lacked anything. There is suffering when there is a lack of something. When there is no want, there is happiness. In Rama's time, nobody lacked anything, in any house or in any family. Each person was content and happy in whatever work he was engaged in. All his needs and desires were fulfilled through his work. This is called Ramarajya. If a beggar is happy and content then it is Ramarajya for him. Contentment, happiness, fulfilment, absence of any want is the true meaning of Ramarajya.

Shiva as Bhimashankar in Treta Yuga

After Ravana's death, when Rama was ruling over his kingdom, some of the remaining demons escaped to various places. One of those surviving demons was called Bhima. Bhima was the son of Karkati, who was married to Viradha and they lived in the forest. When Rama was going to Vishwamitra's ashram, accompanied by Vishwamitra, he killed the demons Maricha and Subahu, along with many others. Among these was Viradha, so Karkati became a widow. After some time, Kumbhakarna had come to the forest, met Karkati and had an affair with her.

Bhima was born from the seed of Kumbhakarna. Like Kumbhakarna, he was immensely strong. One day he asked his mother, "Who is my father? Where is he? I want to meet him." Karkati replied, "Son, Ravana's younger brother Kumbhakarna is your father. That pillar of strength was killed by Vishnu, in his form of Rama." Upon hearing this, Bhima became furious and said, "Vishnu has caused the destruction of our lineage. If I am my father's son then I will make sure that Vishnu does not go unpunished. I will also harass the other devatas and take revenge for my father's death."

With this oath, he went off to perform tapasya and started the worship of Lord Brahma. Brahma was pleased with his worship and as a boon he gave him infinite strength. Bhima conquered the world with this boon and eventually reached Kamarupa, the present state of Assam. Bhima fought a terrible war with the king of Kamarupa, called Sudakshina. He imprisoned the king, who was a devotee of Shiva, and started ruling like a tyrant. Inside the prison, King Sudakshina made a lingam out of clay and started worshipping Shiva. Lord Shiva came to save his devotee and stayed there in disguise. Meanwhile, Bhima came to know from his spies that the king was worshipping inside the prison, with the express aim of killing him. Bhima became incensed, took out his sword and rushed off to the prison with the aim of killing the king. He saw that the king was worshipping the lingam inside his prison cell and, in a tearing rage, he struck the lingam with his sword. However, the moment it struck the lingam, the sword was shattered into pieces, and the lingam remained unaffected. Shiva manifested from the lingam and with just one roar of *Hum*, burnt Bhima and all his followers into ashes. After Bhima's death, King Sudakshina worshipped Shiva with the following stuti:

Akaaranaayaakhila-kaaranaaya
namo mahaakaarana-kaaranaaya;
Namo'stu kaalaanala-lochanaaya
kritaagasam maamava vishvamoorte.

Namo'stvaheenaa-bharanaaya nityam
namah pashoonaam pataye mridaaya;
Vedaanta-vedyaaya namo namaste
kritaagasam maamava vishvamoorte.

Namo'stu bhakterhita-daanadaatre
sarvaushadheenaam pataye namo'stu;
Brahmanya-devaaya namo namaste
kritaagasam maamava vishvamoorte.

Kaalaaya kaalaanala-sannibhaaya
hiranyagarbhaaya namo namaste;
Haalaahalaadaaya sadaa namaste
kritaagasam maamava vishvamoorte.

Virinchi-naaraayana-shakramukhyairajnaata-
veeryaaya namo namaste;
Sookshmaa'tisookshmaaya namo'ghahantre
kritaagasam maamava vishvamoorte.

Anekakoteendunibhaaya te'stu namo
gireenaaÆ pataye'ghahantre;
Namo'stu te bhakta-vipaddharaaya
kritaagasam maamava vishvamoorte.

Sarvaantara-sthaaya vishuddha-dhaamne
namo'stu te dushta-kulaantakaaya;
Samasta-tejonidhaye namaste
kritaagasam maamava vishvamoorte.

Yajnaaya yajnaadiphala-pradaatre
yajnasvaroopaaya namo namaste;
Namo mahaanandamayaaya nityam
kritaagasam maamava vishvamoorte.

Shiva was pleased with this worship and once again he manifested, and asked, "What do you want?" The king said, "Oh Lord! Please stay here in this lingam in your essential form." Shiva entered the lingam made by the king and his presence has remained there ever since as Bhimashankar.

After Shiva's effulgence was completely absorbed by the lingam, he returned to Kailash and, in the form of Rudra, remained absorbed in samadhi for a very long time. His eyes remained closed; he had no opportunity to open them as he was totally absorbed in his own Self, in meditation on his aradhya. This is Shiva's essential sadhana: meditation on his aradhya and repetition of his name. While meditating on his aradhya, he would see his own Self, effulgent and formless.

King Himavana in Dwapara Yuga

Time is fleeting by on the earthly plane. Treta Yuga ended and the Dwapara Yuga began. At the beginning of the Dwapara age, there was a king named Himavana, and his kingdom spanned the entire Himalayas. Himavana was a very intelligent, dynamic and well-reputed king. He was known all over the world for his good deeds and people respected him as a noble person. When Himavana reached a marriageable age, the devatas themselves went to the divine ancestor, Divya Pitara, and requested him to give his eldest daughter in marriage to Himavana. He agreed and his daughter Mena was married to Himavana. They spent their time in great joy and happiness, yet there was a deeper reason behind this marriage, and the devatas and Vishnu himself were behind this.

One day, the devatas came to Himavana along with Vishnu and said, "Himavana, you are aware that the Cosmic Mother earlier incarnated as Sati and became the wife of Rudra. She was born as the daughter of Daksha, and later immolated herself in Daksha's yajna and merged back to her immutable form. As Sati did not receive love and affection from her father, she left her body and reached her spiritual abode, in accordance with her earlier promise. Now, if the Cosmic Mother incarnates in your house as your daughter then all our troubles will be resolved and the world will be blessed. Therefore, Himavana, please start your tapasya to please Mahadevi, the Cosmic Mother. Gain her blessings and grace, and request her to incarnate in your house as your daughter."

Himavana liked this idea: 'What could be better than the Cosmic Mother manifesting as my daughter, if she is pleased with my worship? People go through so much penance and hardship in order to have a glimpse of her and I am going to get it so easily! She will be in my house as my daughter; she will play here, she will sit on my lap, she will grow up and then I will get her married! This is such a welcome, auspicious and delightful opportunity!' Himavana and Mena were very happy to hear Vishnu's words.

126

After instructing Himavana to conduct the worship of Mahadevi, the devatas themselves started doing an aradhana of her. They sat on a mountain peak and started their worship. The primal power, Jagadamba, manifested in her eight-armed form and asked, "What do you all want?" They said, "Oh Mother, the last time you showered your grace on us by incarnating as the daughter of Daksha. That lila is now over and this has left the work of the devatas unfinished. We earnestly wish that you again take birth and become Rudra's wife."

Devi asked, "Where do you want me to be born?" The devatas said, "We are just coming from Himavana's place and we want you to take birth there as his daughter." Devi said, "So be it", and disappeared. Receiving this assurance from her, the devatas went back to their homes and Himavana and Mena started their worship. They worshipped Shiva and Shivaa for a number of years. Devi was pleased with their aradhana and, manifesting before them, said, "I am pleased with your worship. I know the intention with which you have done this aradhana and I will fulfil it."

Himavana said, "Oh mother, we have done this aradhana with the intention of having you as our daughter. Yet, we know that your maya is all-powerful and when you incarnate in our house as our daughter, it is possible that we will forget that you are the Mahadevi, the Cosmic Mother, and will see you only as our daughter. Therefore, before you do your lila as our daughter, please give us such jnana of your real self that it remains enshrined in our hearts, and even when we see you as our daughter, we do not lose sight of this glorious, effulgent and divine form." Devi said, "So be it" and then she turned around and said, "You want to know my real form? Listen:"

Param brahma param jyotih pranavadvandvaroopinee;
Ahamevaasmi sakalam madanyo naasti kashchana.
Niraakaaraapi saakaaraa sarvatattvasvaroopinee;
Apratarkyagunaa nityaa kaaryakaaranaroopinee.

Kadaachiddayitaakaaraa kadaachitpurushaakritih;
Kadaachidubhayaakaaraa sarvaakaaraahameeshvaree.
Viranchih srishtikartaaham jaganmaataahamachyutah;
Rudrah sanhaarakartaaham sarvavishvavimohinee.

Kaalikaakamalaavaaneemukhaah sarvaa hi shaktayah;
Mandashaadeva samjaataastathemaah sakalaah kalaah.
Matprabhaavaajjitaah sarve yushmaabhirditinandanaah;
Taamavijnaaya maam yooyam vrithaa sarveshamaaninah.

Yathaa daarumayeem yoshaam nartayatyaindrajaalikah;
Tathaiva sarvabhootaani nartayaamyahameeshvaree.
Madbhayaad vaati pavanah sarvam dahati havyabhuk;
Lokapaalaah prakurvanti svasvakarmaanyanaaratam.

Kadaachiddevavargaanaam kadaachidditijanmanaam;
Karomi vijayam samyak svatantraa nijaleelayaa.
Avinaashiparam dhaama maayaateetam paraatparam;
Shrutayo varnayante yattadroopam tu mamaiva hi.

Sagunam nirgunam cheti madroopam dvividham matam;
Maayaashavalitam chaikam dviteeyam tadanaashritam.
Evam vijnaaya maa devaah svam svam garvam vihaaya cha;
Bhajata pranayopetaah prakritim maam sanaataneem.

This was how the Cosmic Mother described her form to Himavana and Mena. She said, "I am the *Param Jyoti,* the transcendental flame. I am *Param Brahman,* the transcendental reality. After giving them knowledge of her form, she said, "I will incarnate in your house as your daughter and will complete the designated work of Rudra." Giving them this assurance, Devi disappeared and Himavana and Mena went back to their palace.

Parvati takes birth in Dwapara Yuga
Time passed and Mena became pregnant. After some time, the Devi established herself in the womb and was born as Parvati. All over the world there was happiness, peace and joy. When the almighty Shakti had taken birth in Himavana's

house, how could there be absence of anything? Himavana and the entire province were endowed with wealth and prosperity, and in this atmosphere of bliss, peace and fulfilment, Parvati grew up. When she was old enough, she went to a guru for her studies. One day, when Parvati's studies were complete, Devarshi Narada came to Himavana's house. Himavana and Mena welcomed him and requested him to take a seat. Himavana then called his daughter and told her, "A great sage has come. Touch his feet." When Parvati offered her pranams to Narada, he looked at her and said, "Himavana, please hand over this daughter of yours to Shiva, who is in samadhi in Kailash." Himavana said, "Please read her palm and tell us what is in store for her." Narada said, "Who am I to see her palm and what can I say about her future? The Cosmic Mother has incarnated in your house as your daughter; how do I foretell her future? She is the one who determines my future and that of the entire world. Himavana, my earnest request to you is that you hand over your daughter to Lord Shiva, because she is verily Jagadamba, Cosmic Mother, and she will be Shiva's wife and nobody else's."

Shiva's tapasya in Dwapara Yuga
In the meantime, Shiva was contemplating a change in his routine. He thought, "I have been alone in Kailash, in samadhi, for a long time. I need a change. Let me go to some place which is fresh and soothing." With this thought in mind, he came to Gangavatara along with his ganas. The *tirtha* or pilgrimage place known as Gangavatara is very close to Gangotri, in Himavana's kingdom. When the king received the news of Shiva's arrival in Gangavatara, he came to meet him, along with his family and his retinue.

When Shiva saw him, he said, "Himavana, I have come here to remain in solitude. I want to do tapasya." Himavana said, "Lord, the entire creation is yours. What was the disturbance in Kailash that prompted you to come here and

129

stay aloof from everyone? This is your will, your lila. You can sit for samadhi anywhere you like. It is our great fortune that you have come to our kingdom to do tapasya here. I have only one desire: let my daughter look after you while you are here. Parvati will ensure that you do not face any trouble or lack anything during your tapasya. She will try her best to see that you are content and happy."

Shiva said, "Himavana, the learned have said that woman is the manifest form of maya. I am a tapasvi, a yogi, and a person who is never attached to maya, and now you are suggesting that a young girl will look after me? Why do I need a young girl? The company of a woman will soon awaken desire for various objects: this is the opinion of the learned and wise. In fact, this is not only the opinion of the wise, but also the experience of the householder. When one sees a woman, the mind becomes restless and one loses *vairagya*, non-attachment. I have come here to strengthen my vairagya, not weaken it."

When Shiva uttered these words, Himavana could not say anything in response; however, the Cosmic Mother, in her form of Parvati, could not hold herself back. She said, "My Lord, you perform your tapasya through the *shakti* or power of tapasya. If you do not have this shakti within then how can you do tapasya? Only endowed with the shakti of tapas are you able to do tapasya. In fact, this is how you even got the idea of doing tapasya! That force which propels all karmas is known as *Prakriti*. Shambhu, you are under the control of Prakriti. You have come to Gangavatara to do tapasya because Prakriti wants you to. Who has brought you here? Shakti has brought you here. Creation, sustenance and destruction are made possible by association with Prakriti. Who are you? You are forgetting the subtle Prakriti. Is it possible for the lingam form of Maheshwara, Shiva, to exist without Prakriti? No. You are eulogized, worshipped and respected by all creatures only because of the Shakti tattwa."

Hearing these words of Parvati, Shiva smiled and said, "I try to destroy Prakriti through my tapasya and become

130

established as the formless Shiva bereft of Prakriti. The saints should never involve themselves with Prakriti. They should stay aloof and non-attached."

Parvati responded, "Lord, please forgive me, but these words that you are speaking now, your very speech is also Prakriti. Why are you accepting the help of Prakriti to speak? In order to sit, to walk, indeed, for every action, you are taking the help of Prakriti. If you are using Prakriti in these ways, how can you say that you are free from Prakriti? Why have you not transcended it? All these activities are connected with Prakriti. If you say that you have transcended Prakriti then there is no need to speak or do anything, and if you admit that your speech and action is propelled by Prakriti then you are not removed from Prakriti. All these are actions of Prakriti only. If you were beyond Prakriti, why would you come to the Himalaya mountains to do tapasya? Whatever is an object of the senses for all beings is Prakriti, and whatever a wise man thinks, that is also the realm of Prakriti. For, the intellect, *buddhi*, is also part of Prakriti. I am Prakriti and you are Purusha. It is through my grace that you become *saguna*, with attributes, or *nirguna*, without attributes."

Parvati is telling Shiva in very direct and clear words that it is with her blessings that he becomes saguna or *sakara*, with form. Without her, he has no existence, he is nobody. "You cannot do anything without me. You may have conquered the senses, but you perform all your lilas in the domain of Prakriti. Therefore, how do you become non-attached? How are you not involved with me?"

She is throwing a challenge to Shiva: "If you have transcended Prakriti, if you are without any attachments and mutations, why are you afraid that the company of a woman will make your mind restless? If you have gone beyond Prakriti then you should not be afraid; you should remain unperturbed. You should not even be saying that you want to keep a distance from women as they are an obstacle to vairagya. These words suit someone who is under the

131

domination of Prakriti. Therefore, I feel that what you have said is not correct, not justified and not appropriate.

Mahadeva Shiva was testing Parvati when he spoke those words, so he smiled and said, "All right, as you wish. You stay here and look after me." He knew that she was Jagadamba herself, who had incarnated as Parvati, and that in this life of hers he would wed her. He then thought, "There is ample time. She has to do tapasya first; until she does tapasya, how will she win me?" Thinking thus, Mahadeva went into samadhi and Parvati busied herself in the service of Lord Shiva.

Burning of Kama in Dwapara Yuga

When Shiva came to Gangavatara for his sadhana and tapasya, a demon called Tarakasura attacked *swargaloka*, heaven, defeated the devatas and drove them out. Tarakasura was a very powerful asura and he wanted lordship over the three lokas. The devatas, now driven out from the heavens, came to the Cosmic Father Brahma and complained to him, "Oh Lord, we are being badly harassed by Tarakasura. He has captured heaven and driven us out. He is now creating trouble for the entire creation, terrorizing people and making them suffer."

Brahma said, "Oh devatas, it is destined that Shiva's son will kill Tarakasura and no one else. He has attained a boon that if he has to die, it will be by the hands of Shiva's son. He purposely asked for this boon because he knows that Sati has left her body and Shiva is in a completely unattached and withdrawn state of samadhi. The thought of marriage is not in his mind. Tarakasura knows that as long as Shiva remains in samadhi, he will have no son, and as long as Shiva's son is not born, he will not die. This is the reason why Tarakasura considers himself invincible."

Lord Brahma then said, "I gave the boon to Tarakasura that only the son of Shiva could kill him, so now you should all try to see that Shiva gets married. This is the correct time, as the Cosmic Mother has taken birth in Himavana's house as Parvati. This is what you all wanted. At present,

Parvati is engaged in doing seva of Shiva in the Gangotri area. If you can attract Shiva's attention to Parvati by some means then your work will be done. Please make all efforts to see Shiva starts desiring Parvati, and developing love and affection for her."

When Brahma spoke these words, the devatas invoked the god of desire, *Kamadeva*, known in the West as Cupid. He appeared immediately and the devatas entreated, "Please do something to attract Shiva to Parvati and make him become enraptured with her." Kamadeva said, "If this is what you all want then I will surely do it." He came to Gangavatara, where Shiva was doing tapasya and Parvati was serving him, and with the help of his assistants, he created a very enchanting environment there: flowers bloomed all around, the wind was scented with their fragrance, a soft cool breeze started, and it seemed like spring. The whole scenery was truly enchanting and captivating. Everything became beautiful: the scenery, the mountains and the creatures. Beauty spread throughout creation, and at this opportune moment Kamadeva shot his arrow of *kama*, passion, at Shiva.

When the first arrow was shot at the Lord's body, it did not affect him, as he had conquered all the senses. With the second arrow, Kamadeva sought to influence Shiva's mind. However Shambhu had conquered the mind, so this also did not disturb him in any way. A person who has controlled his mind is not affected by any mental unrest; he is never worried and mental restlessness is not present in his life. The third arrow was shot at Shiva to influence his pranas. When the pranas were stirred, Rudra's samadhi was broken. He wondered, "What is happening? My mind is not disturbed, neither are my senses. How were my pranas disturbed?" When he opened his eyes, his gaze fell on Kamadeva. The moment he saw Kamadeva, he became so enraged that both his external eyes closed and his third eye opened.

Lord Shiva has three eyes. Normally, he uses only two eyes and the third eye remains closed. When the Lord appears in a human form, the two eyes function, which is an expression of duality, *dvaita*: me and you, the worshipper and the worshipped, the seen and the seer. This world is seen through our vision of duality. When these twin eyes of duality close, then the third eye of non-duality, *advaita*, opens. When this advaitic eye opens then dvaita is burned to ashes. When the third eye opens, what need is there for the world of duality? The world gives rise to the experience of duality and *samhara* or destruction, which is one of the duties of Shiva; this experience of 'me' and 'you' has to be destroyed.

During this episode, Parvati saw Shiva's dual eyes open for a moment and give her a loving glance, but the next moment those eyes closed and the third eye opened and burnt Kamadeva to ashes. Parvati was also perturbed: "What is the cause of this havoc? Why is he so angry?"

The moment Shiva saw Kamadeva, he realized, "This is the work of the devatas and Kamadeva is just the front." However, since he was very angry due to the disturbance in his pranas, the moment he opened his third eye, fire emanated from it and burnt Kamadeva to ashes. When the eye of non-duality or advaita opens, duality or dvaita does not remain; rather, it dissolves into that advaita.

When huge flames of fire started coming out of Shiva's third eye, there was great panic in the world. The devatas, the siddhas and the rishis became very frightened. They thought that Shiva would now destroy the entire world. Everyone started fervently praying, "Oh Lord, please forgive us, please forgive us!"

Rati, the wife of Kamadeva, started lamenting, "Oh Lord, what has happened to my husband!" The devatas, along with Brahma and Vishnu, started praying, "Oh Lord Rudradeva, please calm down, withdraw your anger. Whatever has happened is in accordance with the dictates of the divine plan, according to your own wishes. Please douse your anger and become calm." Rati also prayed to him, "Oh Lord, this was not Kamadeva's fault. He was only following the instructions of the devatas. They ordered him to come to you and awaken instinctive desire within you. He is an assistant of Indra and was following his instructions. Please forgive him and revive him." Shiva said, "All right, but for now, Kamadeva will remain without a body. In that bodiless form, he will overpower all creatures. He will be all-pervading and all creatures will come under his spell, but he will not be visible. Rati, since you are praying for him, I assure you that in future Kamadeva will incarnate as Krishna's son Pradyumna. Lord Krishna will be the incarnation of Narayana, and when Kamadeva is born as his son and is embodied again then you will again be united with him."

This is such a beautiful lila. Mahadeva, as Shiva, burnt up Kamadeva, and in his other form of Mahavishnu, he gives life back to Kamadeva. Shiva further said, "When Pradyumna is born, the demon Shambarasura will throw the child into the ocean, but the child will survive and will grow up to kill the demon. He will be brought up in Shambarasura's kingdom. Therefore, Rati, please go to Shambarasura's kingdom and spend your time waiting for your husband." After saying this, Shiva went back to Kailash, along with his ganas.

Parvati's tapasya

Parvati, who was engaged in Shiva's seva, was standing to one side in great fear, and she remained standing there. Shiva did not so much as glance at her. Parvati was in great distress at this separation from Shiva and returned home with her companions asking herself if Shiva would ever forgive them: "The Lord went back angry with us; will he ever be pleased with us again?" As soon as she started worrying like this, she lost her peace of mind, and in the back of her mind was the thought: "The lord went back angry and the reason for his anger is me. Will he ever look at me again?"

During this time, Narada visited Himavana's house. When he saw Parvati so depressed and worried, he asked her the reason for it. She said, "Mahadeva has become angry. A tragic event occurred in the Gangotri area. Mahadeva's samadhi was broken at the instigation of the devatas.

Mahadeva became so angry that he burnt Kamadeva to ashes. He went off in great anger to Kailash. Will I ever again have darshan of my aradhya?" Narada said, "Of course. Perform worship of Mahadeva for a long time. When you become the right receptacle through that aradhana, Rudradeva himself will come to marry you. Remember that Shiva can never forsake you; you are his other half. You are the primordial power, Adishakti. At present, you are engaged in doing lila in the human world. That is why sometimes you remember your own self and sometimes you do not. You have now given yourself a body composed of blood, flesh and bones. You will have to perform worship to purify this body and mind. Appease Lord Shiva. He will surely take you as his partner in the accomplishment of his role." Advising her thus, Narada then initiated her into the *panchakshara mantra*, the five-syllabled mantra, *Namah Shivaya*, and also its sadhana.

Parvati accepted that Mahadeva could be approached only through tapasya. She offered her pranams to her parents and went off to a mountain, along with two of her friends. To please her lord, she started performing austerities without a break. The region of the Himalayas which she chose for her tapasya was called Shringitirtha. The particular mountain where she did her tapasya became known as Gauri Shikhara. On this mountain, she made a *parthiva lingam*, a lingam made of earth, and worshipped Shiva by offering bael leaves. While chanting the thousand names of Shiva, she would offer one thousand bael leaves to the lingam. Let us chant the *Bilva Patra Stotram*:

Tridala trigunaakaaraam trinetram cha triyaayudham;
Trijanma papa samhaaram eka bilvam shivaarpanam.

Trishaakherabilvapatraishch achchhidreh komalaistathaa;
Shivapoojaam karishyaami eka bilvam shivaarpanam.

Akhanda bilvapatrena poojitam nandikeshvaram;
Shuddhayate sarvapaapebhyo eka bilvam shivaarpanam.

Shaaligraam shilaamokaam vipraanaam jaatu arpayet;
Somayajna mahaadaanam eka bilvam shivaarpanam.

Danti koti sahasraani ashvamedha shataanicha;
Koti kanyaa mahaadaanam eka bilvam shivaarpanam.

Lakshmyaashchastanautpannam mahaadeva sadaapriyam;
Bilvavriksham prachchhaami eka bilvam shivaarpanam.

Darshanam bilvavrikshasya sparshanm papa naashanam;
Aghora papa samhaaram eka bilvam shivaarpanam.

Moolato brahmaroopaaya madhyato Vishnu roopine;
Agratah shivaroopaaya eka bilvam shivaarpanam.

Parvati performed many difficult sadhanas, such as *panchagni*, sitting amongst the five fires, in order to win Shiva's favour. At the beginning, she would take food, but later on renounced it and started living on leaves. Slowly, she gave up the leaves and subsisted on air alone. As her tapasya became severe, its *tejas*, fire, spread across the whole universe. Tormented by this fire, all the devatas and other beings went to Vishnu and pleaded, "Oh Vishnu, we are being roasted by the fire of tapas generated by Parvati's austerities. You are our only refuge. Please save us!"

Vishnu said, "The reason for Parvati's tapasya is well known; we all know it. We should all go to Lord Shiva. He can solve our problem. He can relieve us of our suffering, afflictions and sorrows in life."

The devatas went to Shiva and said, "Lord, Parvati is doing intense tapasya to attain you. Please give your blessings to her." Shiva said, "I know that Parvati is doing intense tapasya. In fact, the time has now come for the *saptarishis*, the seven rishis, to go and test her. Devatas, please return home. I know what needs to be done and I will fulfil my role."

After the departure of the devatas, Shiva invoked the saptarishis. When they appeared before him, he said, "Parvati is doing tapasya in Gauri Shikhara in Shringitirtha. Please go there and check the strength of her sankalpa and determination. Once her sankalpa becomes firm and she has no other desire in life other than attaining me, please come and inform me."

The saptarishis went to Gauri Shikhara, and witnessed a unique sight. The Cosmic Mother, Adishakti herself, was seated atop a mountain and offering bael leaves to a Shivalingam she had made, completely absorbed in her worship. They waited patiently for her to finish. When Parvati finished her aradhana, she noticed the sapatarishis. She bowed down to them and offered them to sit. They asked her, "Devi, why are doing this difficult sadhana?" Parvati said, "Difficult? No, not at all. This is an anushthana for attaining my dearest Shiva. I do not find this difficult at all. This is an expression of love. Where is the difficulty in this?"

From these words, the saptarishis understood that Parvati was deeply in love with Shiva. If she had said that the tapasya was difficult, it would have meant that she was different from Shiva and she was making a great deal of effort to get close to him. She would have experienced difficulty and strain on account of the difference. However, Devi said frankly, "This is an aradhana of love. There is total affection in it. How can there be strain in it?"

Karma or purushartha feels strenuous and difficult when you have the feeling, 'I am doing this' or, 'I am going to attain this.' The effort of karma or anushthana is based on a desire, and that desire is selfish. Yet, what was the selfish desire of Parvati? She was doing the sadhana with the hope of winning the Lord's grace and attaining him. She had no desire other than this, and this is why she could easily say, "Whatever I am doing is a reflection of my *bhakti*, my devotion, my love, my affection. I want to become one with my Lord. This is not a tapasya for me!"

The saptarishis were very pleased with Parvati's sentiments, and after giving her their blessings they returned to Kailash. They reported to Shiva that the tapasya Parvati was performing to attain him was really extraordinary. Shiva was pleased to hear this, and donning the guise of an ascetic, he came to Parvati and asked, "You are a strikingly beautiful woman; what are you doing here all alone in this dense forest where there are a lot of wild and ferocious animals? There are no facilities here, no comforts. Why are you subjecting your soft body to this stress and strain?" Parvati replied, "I am doing tapasya to attain my aradhya."

Shiva, disguised as the ascetic, asked, "Who is your aradhya, whom you want to attain?" Mother Parvati replied, "I want to attain *Sarveshwara*, the ruler of all, Mahadeva." Mahadeva smiled and remarked, "That Mahadeva? That person who has no house of his own, who wears snakes instead of garlands, who wears a tiger skin instead of fine clothes, who has no father or mother, who has no beginning and no end? You are doing this sadhana to attain that man! You must be crazy!"

Parvati was enraged to hear the ascetic's comments and said, "Stranger, be careful how you speak about my ishta. You don't know anything about Lord Shiva, the transcendental one! You are a creature of this world. You wander here and there, trying to get some divine blessing through your tapasya, but you do not have *shraddha* or faith within you, therefore your tapasya has never been fulfilled. If you make any more derogatory remarks about my aradhya, I will immediately leave this place!"

The disguised Shiva was not going to give up easily. He said, "My girl, you are simply wasting your time, as the person you are trying to please is so engrossed in his samadhi that this time, even if ten Kamadevas come and shoot arrows at him, he is not going to move. He has now regained total composure and is sitting there with total equanimity, indifference and non-attachment. I suggest that you forget him. In the world, there are a good number of emperors and princes who can give you all manner of happiness and wealth. Get married to them and forget this madman, Shiva."

When the ascetic talked like this, Parvati became very angry, but then she said to herself, 'If I get carried away by anger, my tapasya will be affected, so let me remain calm.'

The rules of tapasya say, "Do not be angry." There are disciplines for every anushthana, both physical and mental. Normally, people follow only the physical disciplines and not the spiritual and mental disciplines: this food is to be eaten and not that, this drink is to be taken and not that, this is forbidden and that is accepted, this is taboo and that is okay, and so on and so forth. People impose such rules on themselves, and the focus of these rules essentially relates to the external environment. However, the rules of anushthana say that whatever rules and disciplines you follow in relation to your body, the same rules should be applied to your mind; only then will the anushthana bear fruit.

It is said in the scriptures that when you take a sankalpa and perform an anushthana, the mind should be free from anger, fear, worry or depressing thoughts. The mind should not be agitated, but remain serene and quiet, as the deeper results of the anushthana will be felt in the mind, the pranas and the spirit, not in the body. Are you able to control your body without coming to terms with the mind? People undertake vows and fasts; for example, it is said that during an anushthana one should forsake cereals and live on fruit. This becomes an excuse to eat more of the permitted foods, with the excuse that it is not healthy to remain hungry!

Once a lady was preparing for an anushthana. She had three sons, and when they came to know that their mother was going on a day's fast, each one sent some food items to the mother. The first son sent ten kilos of different types of fruit. The second son sent a litre of good, thick cow's milk. The third son sent permitted vegetables such as pumpkin and water chestnut. This is how the mother fasted! The next day the sons asked their mother, "Mum, how was your fast?" She said, "Son, I feel a little weak." The sons asked, "Why mother? We sent all the fruit, milk and vegetables." She said, "Yes, yes, I had all that, but in spite of that I was still hungry." If a person can eat a plate piled with edibles and drink litres of milk, how can it be called a fast? Whenever there is a vow or *vrata*, an anushthana, then people pay more attention to

140

the food. Nobody bothers about purification of the mind. The mind keeps on playing games throughout the day. The mind is manipulative and hypocritical, and remains so.

Lila of marriage

Parvati knew that if her mind became disturbed by her anger during the anushthana, and she strayed from her aim, her anushthana would not be fruitful and become meaningless. Therefore, she decided not to get into an argument with the ascetic. After taking this decision, she turned her back on him and began walking in the other direction. Shiva, in the guise of the ascetic, caught hold of Parvati's hands and said, "I am Shiva. Come with me to Kailash."

Parvati freed her hands and said, "Why do you hold my hands now? This is not the right decorum, as I am the *upasaka*, the worshipper, and you are the *upasya*, the worshipped. If you want my hand, you should go and speak with my father. You cannot hold my hands in this forest. You should follow the established decorum of marriage: you should ask for my hand from my father." Shiva was pleased with these words of Shivaa and said, "It will be as you say." Saying this, he disappeared. Parvati was now happy that the Lord's graceful glance had at last descended upon her and he would soon come to her father with a proposal. With this thought in her mind, she returned to her father's house in an elated mood. Some time passed, during which Lord Shiva considered going to Himavana's house to ask for Parvati's hands. Shiva is a *liladhara*, a master of divine play, and he appeared in the guise of a *nata*, a performing artist in Himavana's palace and declared, "I will now display my art." He began his lila by displaying various skills in Himavana's court. He walked the tightrope, sang songs, played the drums; he displayed the entire repertoire of an artist. None of those seated in the audience saw through this guise except Parvati, who mentally offered her pranams and said, "Oh Lord! You have come." Shiva also mentally reciprocated, gave his blessings and said, "Yes, Parvati, I have come to ask for your hand."

141

When the performance was over, Himavana and Mena, who were very pleased, said, "That was beautiful. What can we give you? Wealth, property, a palace, elephants, horses, cows, cattle; whatever you desire, you can have." Shiva said, "If you are pleased with my performance then give me your daughter's hand in marriage." Influenced by Shiva's maya, Mena and her husband, the king of the Himalayas, failed to recognize Lord Shiva and assumed that this was an ordinary actor, displaying his art with the expectation of a reward. They said, "You must be crazy. How dare you, an ordinary beggar, ask for the princess' hand?" Himavana called his guards and said, "Throw this man out of here." The moment the guard tried to catch the nata, he disappeared.

The moment the nata disappeared, Himavana put his hands to his head and moaned, "Oh heavens, I failed to recognize the Lord. He himself had come to ask for the hand of my daughter in the guise of this actor; he performed his lila and deluded us through his maya. What do I do now? How do I please him?"

The Lord's lila continued. Himavana was still sitting in his court with Parvati. Shiva discarded his form of the actor, donned the guise of a brahmin and entered the palace again. With a stick in hand, umbrella over his head, crystal mala around his neck, wearing geru clothes, Shiva entered the palace as a mendicant. On one side, Himavana was grieving over how he failed to recognize Lord Shiva, and on the other side, Parvati mentally offered her pranams on seeing her Lord enter a second time. She said to him mentally, "Lord, please finish this lila. My parents are going through a lot of anguish. How much more are you going to test them?" Shiva replied to her in his mental code, "Just wait a bit."

The mendicant asked Himavana, "What happened? It seems that there was some fun and drama going on here. I see flowers lying on the floor; it appears that someone was dancing here, but I see lines of worry on your forehead. Why are you so crestfallen?" Himavana said, "Sir, my daughter is destined to be married to Lord Shiva as per divine mandate.

142

Some moments ago, Lord Shiva himself came in the guise of a performer. He exhibited his skills and when I told him to ask for a reward, he asked for the hand of my daughter. I did not recognize him and after making some derogatory remarks, I asked him to leave. He deluded all of us with his maya and left. I have committed a grave offence. I am thoroughly confused. I do not know what to do in this situation."

Hearing this, Shiva in the guise of the sadhu said, "Why do you want to atone for this? You want your daughter to marry this inauspicious fellow?" Shiva further said, "The groom you have selected for your daughter is not a befitting one. Please do not marry her to Shiva." This was enough for Mena. She blurted out, "Until today, I have not seen Shiva, but whatever I have heard about him is defamatory. It is said that he is a beggar, that he does not wear clothes, has no parents, no family, no lineage, and dwells in the burial grounds. Instead of clothes, he wears a tiger skin, or any animal skin, his whole body is smeared with ashes, his hair dishevelled. How can I give my gentle daughter to such an uncouth fellow? All those who come here to the court have tried to dissuade us from giving our daughter to him. There is something wrong here. If he was a good match, people would have unhesitatingly recommended him. It seems that he is not a suitable match for Parvati. And since the time he lost his first wife, Sati, he has been disconsolate, wandering around aimlessly like a madman. I will not let my daughter get married to him." Making this decision, she left the court and went off to her chambers.

When Mena went off to the *kopa bhavan*, the quarters reserved for the lady of the house when she is annoyed, Himavana dissolved the court assembly saying, "Regarding Parvati's marriage, I have heard both sides. Some are saying, 'Do' and others 'Do not.' Now I will go into seclusion and think deeply on the matter." Saying this, he stayed the proceedings of the court, and went to his chambers.

Shiva went back to Kailash, called the sapatarishis again and said, "Parvati's parents are in a dilemma about her marriage. Please go and talk to them, drive some sense into them and make them ready for the marriage. Let them be rid of the negativity which is in their mind." Accordingly, the saptarshis came and told Himavana and Mena, "Whatever has happened is the lila of the Lord; he has been testing you. He came in the guise of the performer and also the mendicant. He has been testing you to see if you have enough bhakti and shraddha, devotion and faith, or if your mind forsakes Shiva after listening to others. Now, forget all this useless speculation and hand your daughter over to Mahadeva."

Himavana and Mena heeded the advice of the saptarishis and got ready to wed Parvati to Shiva. The saptarishis made the astrological chart, and Himavana sent out invitations to everyone. The rivers and the mountains came in their divine forms to help Himavana with the arrangements, and the decorating of the *mandapa*, the ceremonial tent, began. Invitation letters were sent to all the mountains, rivers and trees of every plane of existence, and they all came in their divine and lustrous bodies.

Brahma instructed Narada to gather all the devatas and prepare them to be part of the bridegroom's party, so Narada went to all the lokas and announced the news. All the gods, goddesses and celestial beings started gathering in Kailash. Brahma and Vishnu also came. Shiva was sitting there, totally non-attached and serene. He said, "All of you go ahead, I will follow on my bull."

In this decision, Shiva displays his cleverness. If the devatas went in front, everyone would be enchanted by their beauty. Shiva is a beggar; he wears no dazzling clothes or ornaments, but he knew that if there are a thousand beautiful people and there is one ugly person in their midst, no one will notice him. Therefore, Shiva thought, 'Let the devatas go ahead. They will brighten up the place with the glamour of their clothes and ornaments. Their aura will light up the place and then I will come astride my bull, accompanied by my close attendants.'

Shiva's companions are a strange lot. Some are ghosts, some are spirits, some are blood-sucking vampires, some have a huge belly, some don't have a head, some have only one eye, some have only one nostril, one ear, one eye, one leg, and so on. The model that was accepted in creation remained in the world and those that did not conform to the accepted specifications were retained by Shiva as his *ganas*, his attendants. Creation accepted the model that had two legs, two hands, one head, two eyes, two ears, one nose, two nostrils, one mouth and thirty-two teeth. All the rest went to Shiva.

Making a lot of noise, playing many different musical instruments, Shiva's party reached Himavana's kingdom. Himavana brought them to his place with due respect and commenced the worship of Shiva with the following stuti:

Tvam brahmaa srshtikartaa cha tvam vishnuh paripaalakah;
Tvam shivah shivado'nantah sarvasamhaarakaarakah.

Tvameeshvaro gunaateeto jyoteeroopah sanaatanah;
Prakritih prakriteeshashcha praakritah prakriteh parah.

Naanaaroopavidhaataa tvam bhaktaanaam dhyaanahetave;
Yeshu roopeshu yatpreetistattadroopam bibharshi cha.

Sooryastvam srishtijanaka aadhaarah sarvatejasaam;
Somastvam shasya paataa cha satatam sheetarashminaa.

Vaayustvam varunastvam cha tvamagnih sarvadaahakah;
Indrastvam devaraajashcha kaalo mrityuryamastathaa.

Mrityunjayo mrityumrityuh kaalakaalo yamaantakah;
Vedastvam vedakartaa cha vedavedaangapaaragah.

Vidushaam janakastvam cha vidvaamshcha vidushaam guruh;
Mantrastvam hi japastvam hi tapastvam tatphalaprada.

Vaak tvam vaagadhidevee tvam tatkartaa tadguruh svayam;
Aho sarasvateebeejam kastvaam stotumiheshvarah.

Ityevamuktvaa shailendrastasthau dhritvaa padaambujam;
Tatrovaasa tamaabodhya chaavaruhya vrishaachchhiva.

This is how Shiva was married, this time to Parvati, and a fresh chapter of lila then began.

Śrīpaśupatyaṣṭaka

1. Paśupatiṃ dyupatiṃ dharaṇīpatiṃ
bhujagalokapatiṃ cha satīpatim.
Praṇatabhaktajanārtiharaṃ paraṃ
bhajata re manujā girijāpatim.

2. Na janako jananī na cha sodaro na
tanayo na cha bhūribalaṃ kulam.
Avati ko'pi na kālavaśaṃ gataṃ
bhajata re manujā girijāpatim.

3. Murajaḍiṇḍima-vādyavilakṣaṇaṃ
madhurapañchama-nādaviśāradam.
Pramathabhūtagaṇairapi sevitaṃ
bhajata re manujā girijāpatim.

4. Śaraṇadaṃ sukhadaṃ śaraṇānvitaṃ
śiva śiveti śiveti nataṃ nṛṇām.
Abhayadaṃ karuṇāvaruṇālayaṃ
bhajata re manujā girijāpatim.

5. Naraśirorachitaṃ maṇikuṇḍalaṃ
bhujagahāramudaṃ vṛṣabhadhvajam.
Chitirajodhavalī-kṛtavigrahaṃ
bhajata re manujā girijāpatim.

6. Makhavināśakaraṃ śaśiśekharaṃ
satatamadhvarabhāji phalapradam.
Pralayadagdha-surāsuramānavaṃ
bhajata re manujā girijāpatim.

7. Madamapāsya chiraṃ hṛdi saṃsthitaṃ
maraṇa-janma-jarā-bhaya-pīḍitam.
Jagadudīkṣya samīpabhayākulaṃ
bhajata re manujā girijāpatim.

8. Harivirañchi-surādhipapūjitaṃ
yamajaneśadhaneśa-namaskṛtam.
Trinayanaṃ bhuvanatrintayādhipaṃ
bhajata re manujā girijāpatim.

Om śāntiḥ śāntiḥ śāntiḥ. Hariḥ om

Satsang 5

18 February 2009

After the wedding ceremony, Shiva returned to Kailash along with Parvati. All the gods, goddesses, celestial beings and sages who had come to take part in this great wedding now departed for their respective lokas. Shiva and Parvati spent their time happily, walking around Kailash and conversing with each other. In the course of their conversations, Shiva told Parvati about her previous birth. This topic came about as one day Parvati had asked Shiva, "Lord, why are you wearing this garland of heads? And whose heads are they?"

Lord Shiva replied, "All these heads are actually yours, Parvati; they represent the number of times you have taken birth in this world to conduct your lila and then merged back into your essential, original form as Adishakti, the primordial power. Your original form is that of Adishakti or Shivaa, and as such, you are not different from me. However, you have incarnated in the world in different ages to accomplish specific tasks, and each time you have discarded your material body. I have kept the heads as tokens, and this is the garland I wear."

Mother Parvati asked Shiva, "What was my previous birth?" Shiva said, "You are my Shakti. Nothing is unknown to you. Yet, since you have asked me, I will tell you what your earlier form was." Shiva then described her previous incarnation as Sati. In the process, he also told her about yoga, tantra, Pashupata philosophy, Samkhya, and other vidyas, the teachings of which he had already given to her, in her form of Sati.

Conquering time

While listening to all this, Parvati asked, "It is evident that any being who inhabits a body made of the *pancha bhootas*, the five elements, is destined to die. Lord, is it possible to conquer time, to attain immortality? If so, what is the method?"

Lord Shiva said, "Parvati, whoever comes to the world is subject to *kaala,* time, and lives his cycle of life here on earth according to the dictates of time. Kaala is quite frightening and it cannot be destroyed by any god, demon, celestial being, or human. Only one who is a yogi, a sadhu, a tapasvi and is untouched by the maya of the transient world, one who has renounced the objects of the world and has focused his mind on God, one who has *bhakti* and *shraddha*, devotion and faith, can win over kaala and, reaching the supreme abode, attain the ultimate wealth of Shivaloka."

Mother Parvati then asked Shiva, "Lord, how do the yogis and tapasvis win over kaala?" Shiva said, "This is a very secret and mysterious vidya, which I cannot disclose before everyone. Come with me to some secluded place. There I will tell you about the means of conquering kaala, and listen carefully to this." Saying this, Shiva took Parvati to a place in the mountains where no god, demon or attendant could reach them, not even a bird. There he propounded the teachings and said, "The first requirement for winning over kaala is to withdraw the mind from enjoyment of worldly objects and focus it on God. This is the first step, for as long as one is influenced by the world and desires the objects of the world, one will be bound by the fetters of karma. Once one is stuck in this bondage of karma, one can only free oneself through *guru kripa,* the grace of guru, or the blessing of God."

This was said to Mother Parvati by Shiva a long time ago, yet it is still applicable today. You cannot ignore the importance of bhakti. Bhakti is such a powerful tool and method, yet people have not understood it properly. They think it is simply worship of God, but in reality bhakti is the means for self-transformation.

Earlier, when Shiva talked about bhakti to Mother Sati, he said that bhakti is an expression of *jnana*: knowledge, knowing and wisdom. Jnana, *dhyana* or meditation, and bhakti are not opposed to each other; they complement each other. The main aspects of bhakti appear in the *Ramacharitamanas*, when Rama gives the teachings of *navadha bhakti*, the ninefold path of bhakti.

Satsang

In Tulsidas' *Ramacharitamanas*, Sri Rama tells Shabari, *Prathama bhagati santana kara sanga* – "The first aspect of bhakti is company of saints." The normal interpretation of this is to be in the presence of saints, sadhus, sannyasins or elevated souls. Whatever is spoken in their company is considered to be *satsang* or spiritual truth. However, people have limited this idea to mere talk. We need to go to the root of the subject.

Who is a saint? In the *Ramacharitamanas* itself, Sri Rama says, *Santa hridaya navaneeta samana* – "The heart of a saint is as soft as butter." Take the example of a potato. When the potato is uncooked, it is not tasty, as it is hard. When the same potato is boiled, it becomes soft, edible and tasty. Likewise, when the heart becomes soft, the sentiments and emotions become soft and pure, and a person becomes saintly. Our guru, Swami Satyananda, would explain the same idea in many ways: how by purifying one's sentiments one can experience the divinity within.

Essentially, the *sanga* or company of saints conveys the idea of a relationship. The modern individual is motivated by relationships. One establishes relationships with one's family, friends, and so on. These relationships then influence one's attitudes, thoughts and behaviour. If there is negativity in there, it becomes so strong that it pollutes even the good. If one fruit becomes rotten in a basket of fruit, it spoils the others also. However, several good fruits cannot purify the

149

rotten one. Likewise, the tamasic forces in one's life are so strong that they destroy and negate the virtues.

If we are surrounded by people whose behaviour, thoughts and life are not saintly or sattwic then our behaviour, attitude and actions and are also influenced by their nature. Thus, one should be in the company of sattwic persons, not tamasic persons. Good company is the beginning of bhakti, as this exposes one to fresh, positive, creative and inspiring thoughts, which give you a new direction in your life.

Shravana

Sri Rama then says, *Duji rati mama katha prasanga* – "One should enjoy listening to kathas." You receive happiness, inspiration and joy from listening to the *kathas* or stories of the lilas of God. When you read a novel or a story, it is essentially entertainment, whereas when you study the qualities of God, or hear about them, it is not just entertainment to give momentary pleasure; it creates a positive transformation and inspires you to live differently. As a result, you become more evolved.

Once a *pandit*, priest, was narrating a story. He used to tell uplifting stories and many people would come to listen to him. Among the listeners was a man who wished that his sons would also come to these sessions, but the sons were not interested. One day, the father prevailed upon one of his sons to come. The son heard the spiritual story with great attention. The katha finished and everybody got up, dusted their clothes and prepared to depart. The father did likewise and asked his son, "How did you like the katha?" The son said, "The katha was very inspiring, but I cannot appreciate one thing. People listen to the kathas and try to imbibe the good points, yet the moment the katha ends they dust themselves off; they shake off everything and leave."

Nobody takes home the jnana, the wisdom, of the katha. However, if the essence, the underlying teaching of the katha is imbibed, one's life becomes divine, and the mind becomes inspired and connected with positive thoughts, which takes

150

one away from suffering. Psychologists have written about the power of positive thoughts, as this is what gives you mental strength. Thus, when your thoughts become positive through *shravana*, listening, then the shakti of the mind is awakened and the path of bhakti becomes easier.

Absence of vanity

Tisari bhagati aman – "The third is being without vanity." When the thoughts, ideas and attitudes become positive, where is the room for pride or vanity? Pride or vanity is narrowness of the mind, in which you do not see anything beyond yourself; you think of yourself as the greatest. The mind that is always engrossed with oneself is deluded. This fattens the ego and vanity. The mind that is not engrossed with oneself is simple and straightforward. That mind becomes filled with devotion for the guru or God. This is the culmination of spiritual life and the true form of bhakti.

In this way, Lord Shiva explained to Mother Parvati that to conquer time or death, one has to connect one's mind and emotions with God and awaken love for Him. The person who is in love with the world is called a bhogi and a person who is in love with God is called a yogi.

Mother Parvati then asked, "Lord, you have described bhakti. What are the other means?"

Shabdabrahman

The Shaiva agamas state that after explaining bhakti to Mother Parvati, Shiva talked about the *navadha* or ninefold *shabdabrahman*. This is a form of mantra sadhana as *shabda* means mantra or sound, and sound is *Brahman*, the ever-expanding reality. That reality or Brahman, which is neither seen by the senses nor cognized by the mind, is glimpsed through mantras. There are very few people who have seen God, and those who have seen Him are not able to describe Him.

Our guru, Swami Satyananda, used to tell us the story of a doll made out of salt who wanted to discover the depth of

151

the ocean. In this pursuit, the doll dived into the depths of the ocean, became fully dissolved in the water and lost its identity. Similarly, the mantra gives you a push from within and takes you from a gross state to a subtle state. When the mantras, *Sri Rama Jaya Rama, Om Namah Shivaya, Om Namo Bhagavate Vasudevaya*, and so on, are chanted, initially it is a physical effort. You take a mala in your hands and rotate the beads with each mantra. While chanting the mantra, you focus your awareness on your ishta, or the different forms of your ishta. This is how it is in the beginning. However, as you enter into the deeper levels of the mantra, it awakens in the mind and starts moving spontaneously. Kabirdas says:

Aisaa jaapa japo mana laaee, soham soham surataa gaaee;
Chhah sau sahasra ikeesau jaapa, anahad upajai aapai aap.

"When you become totally immersed in your *So-Ham* japa, then *anahad*, the source of all sound, awakens spontaneously, and the nada is heard effortlessly with every breath, 21,600 times every day."

The awareness of the mantra should be there the whole twenty-four hours. If the mantra is remembered with each breath, then the mantra sadhana becomes subtle, and *nada*, the subtle sound vibration, manifests within.

In this teaching, Lord Shiva explains how mantra japa takes one to a subtle state of consciousness where the sadhaka hears nine types of nada within. Each nada is associated with a specific state of inner awareness experienced in states of meditation. At one time bells are heard, at another time the flute, sometimes a roll of thunder. After going through and analyzing these nadas, the sadhaka stabilizes himself in the ultimate nada of the *Pranava* mantra: *Om*. He then becomes liberated and a conqueror of time.

Hatha yoga

In this sequence of teachings, Lord Shiva also described hatha yoga. Mother Parvati asked, "Is it possible to achieve immortality through this body?" Shiva answered, "Yes, it is.

In this body there is both poison and nectar. The source of nectar within the body is the bindu chakra. The nectar drops from bindu, but it is burned up by *jatharagni*, digestive fire. If you can stop the nectar from being burned up by jatharagni, and absorb it, then you can overcome old age and also death. You will never grow old and will live forever; you will become a *chiranjeevi*, an immortal being." Shiva described the sadhana of *khechari mudra*: "Fold the tongue back so it touches the palate. The nectar will drop on the tongue and then you can easily drink it." He then went on to describe asana, pranayama, dhyana, mantra, and so on.

The dialogue between Shiva and Parvati went on for a very long time and, while listening, Mother Parvati began to feel very sleepy. Shiva had told her, "I am talking with my eyes closed, therefore every now and then say, 'Yes, yes' so I know you are awake and attentive." This dialogue was taking place by a river and a fish was quietly listening to all these teachings. When the fish noticed that Parvati was sleepy and not responding any more, it started saying, "Yes, yes", as it did not want Shiva to stop. Such is the nature of Shiva that although he knew very well what was happening, he went on describing different vidyas with his eyes closed and the fish went on responding, "Yes, yes."

When Mother Parvati woke up, Shiva asked her, "Have you understood all the secret teachings I have just told you?" Parvati said, "Oh lord, while you were speaking I felt sleepy and dozed off." Shiva said, "Then who was responding, 'Yes, yes'?" He looked around and saw the fish. Mother Parvati said, "This fish has acquired the knowledge of the entire teachings of yoga." Shiva said, "Yes. Now I will change this fish to a human being and send him into the world to spread these teachings for the welfare of all." He gave his blessings to the fish and the fish incarnated as Matsyendranath to propagate the teachings of hatha yoga.

The Nath sect places a strong emphasis on perfecting hatha yoga, overcoming death and attaining the state of Shiva. Even today, it is a very vibrant sect and evolved souls who have come to this tradition are known as the Naths. *Nath* means master. *Adiguru*, the original guru, Lord Shiva, is therefore known as *Adinath*. Different sects have accepted the existence and the teachings of Adinath. In the Jain tradition, the first among the twenty-four tirthankaras is Adinath himself.

In the hatha yoga tradition, there were a number of Naths. After Adinath, the tradition continued with Matsyendranath. Gorakhnath was the disciple of Matsyendranath, and in this way, the Nath tradition evolved. The teachings given to Mother Parvati by Lord Shiva were spread around the world through the Nath tradition. The Nath sect owes its origin to the Pashupata tradition.

Birth of Kartikeya

While Shiva was imparting these teachings to Mother Parvati, the devatas banished by the demon Tarakasura had convened a meeting. The devatas said, "Lord Shiva has got married and he is busy imparting secret spiritual teachings to Mother Parvati in solitude, in the forest. Here, Tarakasura is continuously expanding his empire. He is attacking the lokas and conquering them. No one is able to stop him. He is aiming for the domination of the three lokas. As per the boon given by Brahma, it is Shiva's son who will be able to annihilate him and nobody else. We have to do something so Lord Shiva stops teaching Parvati and gives us a son who will be able to kill Tarakasura."

With this objective in mind, the devatas sent Agni, the god of fire, to Rudradeva, who was teaching Parvati about yoga, tantra and spiritual life in a dense forest. Agnideva reached the forest and approached Shiva. He offered him his pranams and said very humbly, "O Lord! The entire creation is severely troubled by the demon Tarakasura. The whole world is awaiting the birth of Shiva's son, who will free the three worlds from his tyranny and relieve the suffering and torment of the devatas." Shiva said, "What you have said is correct. Here, take my *tejas*, my vitality, in the form of fire." Saying thus, Shiva put his tejas in the hands of Agni.

However, Agni could not bear the heat which emanated from this tejas, and in great fright, he dropped the tejas into the river Ganga. The moment the tejas fell into the Ganga, it transformed into a baby, which started crying.

At that time six *krittikas*, heavenly damsels, had come to the Ganga for their daily bath. They were attracted by the sound of a child's cry and noticed the baby floating in the water. They picked him up and each one started demanding the right to nurse him. An argument followed. The baby, born from the vitality of Shiva, was not an ordinary boy; he was a manifestation of Shiva. Hearing the argument, he sprouted six mouths through which he suckled from six women and accepted them all as his mothers. The krittikas took him to their house. Since he was brought up by krittikas, he was known as *Kartikeya*. The six krittikas were given the status of six stars in the constellation Pleiades by Shiva.

It is said in the stories that Mother Ganga declared that since the boy was the son of her sister Parvati, and since she was the first person to take the baby in her lap, she would look after him and make him proficient in all spiritual sciences. She shouldered the responsibility for the child, imparted all the teachings to him and brought him to Shiva when he came of age.

When Mother Ganga reached Kailash with Kartikeya, Shiva and Parvati lovingly embraced him, blessed him with divine qualities and made him immortal. The devatas arrived and said, "Oh Lord, now the time has come for Kartikeya to kill Tarakasura." Shiva handed him over to the devatas, saying, "Take him and make him the commander of your army and he will vanquish Tarakasura." Accepting this direction from Shiva, the devatas immediately made Kartikeya the commander of their army and Kartikeya left Kailash, along with the devatas. Thereafter, a terrible battle raged between Tarakasura and Kartikeya. In the end, Kartikeya killed Tarakasura. On receiving the news, Lord Shiva and Mother Parvati came to the battlefield. They were overjoyed and warmly embraced their son, showering their

blessings upon him. Kartikeya praised his parents with the
following stuti:

Namah shivaayaastu niraamayaaya
namah shivaayaastu manomayaaya;
Namah shivaayaastu suraarchitaaya
tubhyam sadaa bhaktakripaaparaaya.

Namo bhavaayaastu bhavodbhavaaya
namo'stu te dhvastamanobhavaaya;
Namo'stu te goodhamahaavrataaya
namo'stu maayaagahanaashrayaaya.

Namo'stu sharvaaya namah shivaaya
namo'stu siddhaaya puraatanaaya;
Namo'stu kaalaaya namah kalaaya
namo'stu te kaalakalaatigaaya.

Namo nisargaatmakabhootikaaya
namo'stvameyokshamaharddhikaaya;
Namah sharanyaaya namo'gunaaya
namo'stu te bheemagunaanugaaya.

Namo'stu naanaabhuvanaadhikartre
namo'stu bhaktaabhimatapradaatre;
Namo'stu karmaprasavaaya dhaatre
namah sadaa te bhagavan sukartre.

Anantaroopaaya sadaiva
tubhyamasahyakopaaya sadaiva tubhyam;
Ameyamaanaaya namo'stu tubhyam
vrishendrayaanaaya namo'stu tubhyam.

Namah prasiddhaaya mahaushadhaaya
namo'stu te vyaadhiganaapahaaya;
Charaacharaayaatha vichaaradaaya
kumaaranaathaaya namah shivaaya.

Mamesha bhootesha maheshvaro'si
kaamesha vaageesha balesha dheesha;
Krodhesha mohesha paraaparesha
namo'stu mokshesha guhaashayesha.

156

Birth of Ganesha

Everywhere in Kailash there were celebrations for Kumara Kartikeya's victory. The whole atmosphere was joyous and festive. The ganas of Shiva were serving Shiva and Kartikeya, and Mother Parvati was seated with her two attendants Jaya and Vijaya. Jaya said to Parvati, "Oh Mother, there are quite a few of ganas in Kailash, but they are all engaged in the service of Shiva. We are engaged in your service, but we do not have any ganas. All the ganas listen only to Shiva's instructions. When we ask them to do something, they say that they must first ask Shiva's permission. When I tell them that Mother Parvati wants to go out and Nandi should be ready, they say that Shiva's permission is needed before Parvati can go out."

Kailash has the same rules as our Munger ashram. In Munger, one cannot leave the ashram without a gate pass. Similarly, in Kailash you cannot go out without Shiva's approval and Nandi's signature. Jaya and Vijaya resented the fact that all the ganas were devotees of Shiva, and Parvati had no one serving her except themselves. Shiva's ganas were not ready to serve her, so Jaya and Vijaya advised Mother Parvati to manifest ganas who would obey only her orders. Mother Parvati liked this advice and decided to implement it.

One day, Mother Parvati went for her bath. Jaya had placed the clay paste used for bathing next to the pool. Mother Parvati applied the paste to her body and with the leftover clay made the figure of a boy. She then breathed life into this clay figure. Immediately the boy stood up and with palms joined, asked, "Mother, what are your orders?"

The Cosmic Mother is the only power who can make insentient matter sentient or conscious, so this was not a big job for her. She has the capacity to create thousands of ganas, not just one. In truth, there was no need for her to perform this lila, as just by thinking it she could have created any number of ganas. However, she is the primordial Shakti, and she wanted to enact her lila. She told the boy, "You are my son; I have made you. I give you the order to ensure that no one enters this palace without my permission." Ganesha said, "Right, your will shall prevail."

The boy took a stick and stood guard in front of Mother Parvati's palace, and Parvati got into the bath with her companions. Shiva came to the door and was about to head straight in when he saw this new boy standing guard. The boy challenged him and refused to let him in. Shiva said, "Do you know who I am?" The boy replied, "It doesn't matter. You might be the Almighty, but I do not care. I am following Mother's instructions. You cannot enter."

Shiva was incensed at the boy's impertinence and told his ganas, "Go and find out who this boy is who stopped me from entering. Teach him a good lesson, as he does not know who I am." The ganas went and challenged Ganesha, but Ganesha beat them up and they ran back to Shiva. When Shiva saw that his ganas had lost the fight, he himself went with his trident. He fought with Ganesha and cut off his head with the trident.

When Mother Parvati came out of her bath, she saw Ganesha lying in a pool of blood. Lord Shiva was standing by holding his bloody trishul. When Parvati realized that Shiva had beheaded her son, she started trembling with uncontrollable rage. The story says that when Parvati started trembling with rage, the world began to sway in all directions. There was panic all around. Huge flames of fire started emanating from Parvati's body and it seemed that the whole world would perish. She manifested in her terrible form and thundered, "Who has killed my son?"

Shiva was surprised to see this terrible form of Parvati and thought, "What's happened to Parvati? Why is she bent on burning down the entire creation?" He said, "I have killed this gana as he blocked my path." Parvati said, "He is my son; why did you kill him?" The devatas also came to Shiva and pleaded, "Please save us from the wrath of Adishakti. The three lokas are burning with her anger and there is no peace anywhere. Please douse this anger of Mother Parvati."

Shiva said, "There is only one way to pacify Parvati. I have to perform some surgery. Please make arrangements for an operation."

Shiva was an expert surgeon. You will recall that earlier he had fixed a goat's head on Daksha's body. The present situation also called for his services as a surgeon. He ordered his ganas, "Go out and find a newborn baby, cut off his head and bring it to me. I will join that head with this body and infuse life into it. Only then will Mother Parvati cool down."

The ganas spread out in different directions. Shiva had indicated to the ganas they should look for a child who was resting and whose head was pointing northwards. The ganas found a mother elephant sleeping with her calf's head in the northerly direction. They cut off the calf's head and returned immediately to Kailash. Shiva exclaimed, "You didn't get a human child?" The ganas said, "No, only this elephant calf." Shiva said, "All right, bring him to the operating theatre." He attached the elephant's head to the boy's body and infused life into him.

The moment the boy with the elephant's head returned to life, he stood up and bowed to Mother Parvati and then to Shiva. Shiva and Parvati now accepted him as their son. Shiva said, "I am appointing you chief of the ganas and the devatas." Ganesha was given two posts: ganadhyaksha and sarvadhyaksha. Mother Parvati also gave her blessings, saying, "Henceforth your worship will precede any other worship." Brahma, Vishnu, and the other devatas who were there, showered flowers on Ganesha. They congratulated Shiva and, having pacified Mother Parvati, they worshipped her also. This is how Ganesha acquired the boon of being the first god to be worshipped in any ritual.

Annihilation of the three cities

When Kartikeya killed Tarakasura, the three sons of Tarakasura: Tarakaksha, Vidyunmali and Kamalaksha, retired to secluded mountains caves and started performing various rituals, austerities and sadhanas to please Lord Brahma. They had only aim in mind: to gain the boon of immortality from Brahma and thus extract revenge from the devatas for the death of their father. They practised such severe austerities that Brahma was compelled to manifest and ask, "Tell me what you want, I will try my best to fulfil it."

Tarakaksha said, "Lord, please remove the fear of death from us. Let us never be afraid of death. Let us never enter old age. Make us immortal." Brahma said, "I have given this boon a number of times and have been cheated every time. Therefore, I have decided that from now on, I will not give this boon. You should also understand that whoever is in the dimension of Prakriti cannot be free of old age or death. Whoever is born will necessarily age, become sick and die. Birth, sickness, old age and death are the four eternal truths of existence and nobody can be free of them. Therefore, ask for something else."

The three brothers then consulted among themselves and said, "If you are pleased with us then please ask Vishwakarma to make a city of gold for Tarakaksha. The city will move in the sky by itself and the devatas will not be able to enter it. Similarly, for Vidyunmali make a city of silver, which will move independently in the sky, and for Kamalaksha, make a city of iron, which will be very strong and which will also move independently in the sky. Give us the boon that we will die only during the *abhijit muhurta*, the astrological moment once a year when our three cities are in one line and the moon enters the constellation of Pushya. At that time Shiva will be able to pierce through the cities with a special arrow and kill us. This will be the condition of our death and we will not die under any other circumstance." Brahma said, "So be it."

Narayana and Shiva spend all their time correcting the mistakes of Brahma, who cannot say no to anyone. Someone once asked Brahma, "You give all sorts of boons to different types of demons, such as daityas, danavas and rakshashas, knowing very well that they will harass the entire creation.

160

Why do you give these boons knowing that they will misuse them?" Brahma said, "Well, I am the creator and giving boons is part of my job. The rules of the Almighty ordain that we give, so whoever asks me for something, I give it, and if someone misuses my boon then Mahavishnu and Sadashiva are always there to correct my mistakes."

Following the instructions of Brahma, Vishwakarma erected three cities, one of gold for Tarakaksha, one of silver for Vidyunmali and one of iron for Kamalaksha. The three brothers entered the three cities and moved around freely in them, terrorizing the entire creation. When their evil acts started increasing and the devatas failed to conquer them, they went to Brahma and said, "You have given them this boon, so please tell us a way out." Brahma said, "You have to request Lord Shiva to destroy them. Come, let us all go to Lord Shiva. If he agrees to shoot an arrow through their cities, all at one time, then they will be destroyed."

They went to Shiva and prayed to him, "Oh Lord! Please save the world by killing these three demons." Shiva said, "These three are engaged in my worship. They have erected a *Shivalaya*, temple of Shiva, in each of the cities and conduct a daily worship there. How can I kill my own devotees?"

Tarakaksha, Vidyunmali and Kamalaksha were very cunning demons. They thought, "If we worship Shiva in our cities and become his devotees then Shiva will never be angry with us. He will not kill us, as he is very kind to his devotees. We will receive his grace."

Brahma said to Shiva, "Lord, you have to find a way to help us." Shiva then told Mahavishnu, "Vishnu, take the form of a brahmin, go to their impenetrable cities and try to dissuade them from Shiva aradhana. The day they cease to worship me, they will not receive my protection and I will go and kill them."

Following Lord Shiva's instructions, Vishnu went to the three cities. He diverted their minds from worship of Shiva to material pursuits. Some say that the form of Vishnu as the brahmin was that of Charvaka, who propounded a totally materialistic philosophy of sensory indulgence. While opinions on this matter differ, it does appear that this form of Vishnu was of Charvaka, as he told the demons, "Why do you waste your time worshipping a God whom you will never attain? You are all mighty warriors and endowed with great strength. You should look after your interests and amass wealth. Forget this path of renunciation and sadhana, and fulfil the desires and passions that are within you."

Vishnu spent some time with them imparting the teaching that the most important reality is the body and the senses, and that indulgence of the senses is the aim of life. Deluded by this maya of Vishnu, all the three demons ceased the worship of Shiva. The moment they stopped, Shiva said, "Now I am ready to kill them, but I need a chariot and weapons to pierce the cities. Hearing this, Vishwakarma built a beautiful effulgent chariot and the weapon called Pashupatastra.

Brahma brought the chariot and the weapon to Shiva and said, "The chariot and the weapon are ready for your use. Please mount the chariot." Shiva said, "Before I get on the chariot, a condition has to be fulfilled: you have to give me dominion over all the gods and the other beings. They must be declared to be *pashus*, animals, and myself *Pashupati*, the master of all animals."

Brahma was surprised to hear this. He said, "But you are Pashupati. We have received the teachings from you that all the beings of the entire creation are pashus and you are the only master, *pati*, and *Parameshwara*, Supreme God." Shiva said, "Yes, I have said that. However, the gods, the demons and the humans have not voluntarily given me this authority. Until they agree voluntarily that I am Pashupati and they are pashus, I will not fight." Brahma said, "Lord, whatever you desire will be done."

Following the instructions of Brahma, all the three lokas accepted Lord Shiva as Pashupati, and they worshipped him with this *Pashupati Stotram*:

162

Sa paatu vo yasya jataakalaape sthitah
shashaankah sphutahaaragaurah;
Neelotpalaanaamiva naalapunje
nidraayamaanah sharadeeva hamsah.

Jagatsisrikshaapralaya-kriyaavidhau
prayatnamunmesha-nimeshavibhramam;
Vadanti yasyekshana-lolapakshmanaam
paraaya tasmai parameshthine namah.

Vyomneeva neeradabharah saraseeva veechi-
vyoohah sahasramahaseeva sudhaamshudhaama;
Yasminnidam jagadudeti cha leeyate cha
tachchhaambhavam bhavatu vaibhavamriddhaye vah.

Yah kandukairiva purandarapadmasadma-
padmaapati-prabhritibhih prabhuraprameyah;
Khelatyalanghya-mahimaa sa himaadrikanyaa-
kaantah kritaantadalano galayatvagham vah.

Dishyaat sa sheetakiranaabharanah shivam vo
yasyottamaangabhuvi visphuradurmipakshaa;
Hamseeva nirmala-shashaanka-kalaamrinaala-
kandaarthinee surasarinnabhataa papaata.

All the creatures and devatas acknowledged themselves as the pashus of Lord Shiva, and hailed Shiva as Pashupati, the master who can release you from the *pasha*, leash. From that time, Shiva became known as Pashupati, as he had asked for the lordship of the inner pashu or animal nature of every being, and it was given to him willingly.

Shiva then mounted the chariot and stood motionless waiting for the abhijit muhurta, the moment when the three cities would come into alignment while moving in the sky. As the time drew near, the three cities became visible and started approaching. Vishnu said, "Lord, please get ready to shoot as the three cities are shortly going to come into alignment." At the appointed moment, Lord Shiva fired his Pashupatastra to burn all the three cities to ashes. The three demons perished along with their huge armies and, amidst victorious trumpeting by his ganas, Shiva went back to Kailash after completing this assignment for the devatas.

Ganesha's marriage

Time passed, and the two boys, Ganesha and Kartikeya, spent their time playing with each other. Shiva and Parvati felt immense parental bliss watching their games. When the two boys reached marriageable age, they started arguing as to who would get married first. Hearing their interaction, Shiva also started thinking about it. Age seemed to favour Kartikeya, as he was the elder son. He had become the commander of the gods' army at the age of twelve and killed the demon Tarakasura. Ganesha was born after that event, therefore Kartikeya was probably twelve years older than Ganesha. According to tradition, Kartikeya should have been married first. However, Ganesha had been given the post of sarvadhyaksha, chief of everyone, including the devatas. It had been declared that his worship would be performed first in any ceremony. Ganesha was insisting that his marriage take place first, and since he was sarvadhyaksha and ganadhyaksha, his words could not be easily ignored.

When their children started quarrelling over the matter, the parents began wondering how to solve the problem. One idea flashed in Shiva's mind and he told Parvati, "Let us ask them to go around the world three times and whoever comes back first will be married first." He told his two sons about this decision. Hearing this, Kartikeya said, "Great! This is no problem for me. My vehicle, the peacock, has the ability to fly, so I will fly around the world easily." Ganesha became worried. He thought, 'What do I do? I have put on a lot of weight as a result of partying with the devatas and my vehicle is only a small rat. I don't think he'll be able to carry my weight around the world. It seems my brother Kartikeya is destined to win.'

The brothers commenced preparations for the marathon. Their training started in right earnest. In the training sessions, when Kartikeya's peacock had covered half a mile, Ganesha's vehicle, the rat, had covered only ten yards. This made Ganesha rather anxious, for he knew that Kartikeya would return quicker from his trip. However, Ganesha is endowed with super-intelligence and has knowledge of all the scriptures, so he could not accept defeat that readily. He thought, 'There must be some way out.'

The day of the race dawned and Kartikeya and Ganesha stood ready on the starting line. Shiva said, "The moment I strike my trishul to the ground the race will start." Shiva gave the signal and Kartikeya took off on his peacock. Ganesha, however, remained standing. He placed two mats on the ground and said to his parents, "My dear mother and father, please come and sit on these mats."

Shiva and Parvati followed Ganesha's instructions and sat down in their allotted places. Shiva could not help asking, "What are you up to? You should have left by now. Kartikeya must be much ahead. By now he would have crossed Asia and flying over Europe, and you are still in Kailash!" Ganesha said, "This won't take long. Just a minute." He went to his room and brought out all his pooja items, such as incense, light, fruit, flowers, and so on, on a plate. Shiva and Parvati were quietly watching the activities of their son.

First, Ganesha did pooja and aradhana of his parents, and then he walked around them three times. After doing this *parikrama*, perambulation, he came and stood in front of them with his hands joined in prayer. Some time passed. Mother Parvati could not help asking, "Son, you are not doing the parikrama of the world? You are supposed to do three rounds, are you not?" Ganesha said, "Oh mother, I have already finished the parikrama." "How?" asked Parvati. "It is said in the scriptures that doing parikrama of one's parents is equivalent in merit to going around the world. I have done three parikramas, which means I have gone around the world three times. You are Father and Mother, you are the creator, preserver and destroyer, your parikrama

165

is equivalent to that of the earth. I have won the race, so please get me married quickly."

Shiva smiled and said, "Well done, Ganesha! You are very clever. I have not seen anyone as clever as you. Make arrangements for the wedding." He had Ganesha married to two beautiful daughters of Vishwarupa Prajapati, called Riddhi and Siddhi, and Ganesha lived happily in Kailash in their company.

Mallikarjuna in Dwapara Yuga

When Kartikeya returned after completing his parikrama, he saw Ganesha standing quietly beside his parents. Kartikeya wondered, "How could he possibly have reached here before me? I flew off before him, and according to my calculations, he should be somewhere in the plains of the Himalayas. How is he here?"

Kartikeya touched the feet of his parents and asked Ganesha, "When did you come back?" Ganesha said, "I never went, so there is no question of my returning." "You never went, so how come I lost?" asked Kartikeya. Ganesha solved the mystery by saying, "Brother, you were so excited about doing parikrama of the world that you forgot parents are the manifestation of the world; they are God in effect and whosoever does their parikrama does parikrama of the three worlds. Therefore, my brother, I did parikrama of my parents, won the race and got married to two girls."

When Kartikeya heard this, he became wild with rage. He thought, "I have been cheated. My parents and my brother have played a trick on me. I can no longer stay in Kailash. Let me go off to some faraway place." Thinking thus, he turned around, mounted his peacock and went off to Krauncha Mountain in South India. There, he erected a small thatched hut and spent his time in satsang, Shiva aradhana and propagation of Shiva yoga. He never forgot that Shiva was the ultimate reality and Parvati was the Cosmic Mother. His only gripe was that Ganesha cheated him by going around his parents. Nonetheless, he had complete reverence, faith and devotion for his parents, and he started spreading the teachings of Shiva and Parvati among the different people of the area.

Back in Kailash, Ganesha had two sons from his two wives, named Shubha and Labha. Whenever any auspicious work is undertaken, the swastika mark is drawn, and 'Shubha' and 'Labha' are written next to it to receive the blessings of Ganesha's sons.

When Kartikeya immersed himself in Shiva aradhana in Krauncha Mountain, Lord Shiva and Mother Parvati fondly remembered him and said, "He is very angry with us. Let us go appease him and bring him back."

Shiva and Parvati arrived at Krauncha Mountain and entreated Kartikeya to come back, but he refused. Shiva and Parvati went on insisting, saying, "This is no good. You live here, far away from us, and we keep remembering you every day in Kailash." Kartikeya got more annoyed and said, "My dear mother and father, I have renounced my home, so what is the point of repeatedly asking me to come back? Now that you have come to know that my residence is here on this Krauncha Mountain, it seems I will not no longer find peace here; I will get constant messages from you. Let me leave this place." Saying this he left Krauncha Mountain and built a small hut at a distance of twenty-four miles.

When Shiva and Parvati realized that Kartikeya was in no mood to return, they decided to remain on Krauncha Mountain in their effulgent state. That effulgent state of Shiva and Parvati came to be known as Mallikarjuna. Mallika is another name of Parvati and Arjuna is another name of Sadashiva. *Mallikarjuna* means the place where Shiva and Parvati exist together. It seems that Shiva and Parvati keep on visiting this place to be near their son, as there is an event that keeps on happening to this day. On the special day of Sivaratri, two white pigeons, one male and the other female, come to Mallikarjuna. They stay for a day and then fly away. Nobody knows from where they come or where they go. In this way, once a year Shiva and

Parvati come to visit their son Kartikeya in the form of two white pigeons.

Who knows in what form you will have darshan of God? It is not necessary that he manifests in human form and you see him standing in front of you. He is a master player, the *liladhara*, and he can come in any form. Even if he comes as a bird, take it as your good fortune that the Lord has given you darshan in that form.

Andhakasura

Shiva and Parvati spent their time in Kailash pursuing different activities and going on excursions. One day, Mother Parvati asked, "Lord, before creation, you created an *avimukta kshetra*, realm of liberation. Now after creation has begun, where is this area situated?" Shiva said, "That avimukta kshetra, which is a city of five square kosas, is known as Kashi. It is situated at the confluence of two rivers, Vara and Asi; therefore, it is also known as Varanasi. However, this Varanasi is the gross form; the subtle form exists within it."

Mother Parvati said, "Lord, I have a strong desire to see this place." Shiva said, "All right, let's go. We will spend some time there and enact some lila." Shiva and Parvati then went to Kashi. Appointing Bhairava the guard of the city, Shiva told him, "As long as I am here, you remain here as the protector."

Shiva spent some time in that area with Mother Parvati. Then, during their travels, they came to a place called Mandarachala, which in near Banka in Bihar. Shiva decided to rest there for some time and sat on a rock. Mother Parvati wanted to play and she crept up from behind and covered Shiva's eyes with her hands.

The moment his eyes closed, darkness descended everywhere and nothing was visible. At that point, a few drops of sweat appeared on Shiva's forehead and fell to the ground. The moment those drops hit the ground, a weird creature emerged. It had no eyes and was extremely fair in complexion. If someone is not exposed to the rays of the sun, their skin loses its tan and becomes white. It was exactly like that. When Mother Parvati saw this deformed creature, she became frightened and removed her hands from Shiva's eyes. She asked, "Lord, what is this strange creature that has taken birth?"

Shiva said, "Parvati, this is your son, and I am calling him *Andhakasura*, the blind demon, as he was born in darkness. When you playfully covered my eyes, darkness spread everywhere, for one of my eyes is Surya, the sun, the second is Soma, the moon, and the third is Agni or fire. Surya, Soma and Agni: all three are givers of light. When you closed my eyes, all the three worlds were immersed in total darkness. As he was born during that time, this creature is blind and his skin is also abnormal. You are responsible for his birth, so please take care of him. As instructed, Mother Parvati accepted that blind boy as her son.

At this time, Hiranyakashyap's brother Hiranyaksha had come to the same forest of Mandarachala and was engaged in Shiva aradhana and severe austerities with the intention of begetting a son. Shiva was pleased with his tapasya and manifested before him, asking, "What do you want? Why are you practising such severe austerities?" Hiranyaksha said, "Lord, I am doing this tapasya with the intention of begetting a son." Shiva said, "There is no son in your destiny and from your seed no son will come forth. However, since you are asking for the boon of a child, I will give you my son." He placed Andhakasura in front of Hiranyaksha. Hiranyaksha was immensely pleased and said, "It does not matter any more that the son is not from my seed; I have got a son!" He took Andhakasura and went home.

Sometime later, Hiranyaksha lifted the entire earth and hid it in the depths of the ocean. Mahavishnu took the form of a boar and entered the ocean. He fought with Hiranyaksha, killed him, recovered the earth and placed it back in its rightful place. He then crowned Andhaka as the emperor of the asuras. Andhaka ruled for quite a long time; however, when he received the information that his uncle Hiranyakashyap had been killed by Mahavishnu in the form of Narasimha avatar, his man-lion form, and that he had installed Hiranykashyap's son Prahlad as the king, he became wild with rage.

Andhaka's gripe was that all the devatas were bent on harassing the asuras: they would always deprive the asuras of their rights and ensure that they did not progress. With this sentiment in mind, he started thinking, 'With whom do I fight so that I can extract revenge for the deaths of my father and uncle?' As he was angry, he had completely forgotten that he was Shiva's son, nurtured by Mother Parvati. He developed hatred towards all the devatas, and especially towards Mahavishnu. He thought, "Since Mahavishnu and Shiva support each other, why not fight directly with Shiva. Let me first fight with Shiva, defeat him and then I will fight Mahavishnu." With this intention, he attacked Kailash with his huge army.

The army of Andhakasura had a terrible battle with the ganas of Shiva. Andhakasura was a mighty warrior, as he was born from the sweat of Shiva. He was a part of Shiva himself! Faced with this powerful onslaught from Andhakasura, the ganas of Rudra scattered and ran away. At that point, various forms of Shakti manifested and helped Rudra's ganas. The war was so terrible that the sound of the battle drew Shiva to the battlefield and he started fighting against Andhakasura. Andhaka was being helped by the guru of the asuras, who was a siddha; any demon killed in the battle would be revived by him and sent back to the battlefield. When Shiva saw that it was because of this guru that the army of the demons was not reducing, he swallowed him alive.

At that point, Mother Parvati came in the terrible form of Kali, massacred the entire army of the demons and drank their blood. Shiva hurled his trident at Andhaka. The trident pierced his body, yet he did not die; he was, after all, Shiva's son. Hit by the trident, all the blood flowed out of his body and only the skin and bones remained. However, when the blood flowed out of his body, Andhaka's mind became purified, and dangling from the trident he praised Shiva with the following stuti:

Kritsnasya yo'sya jagatah sacharaacharasya
kartaa kritasya cha tathaa sukhaduhkhahetuh;
Samhaaraheturapi yah punarantakaale tam
shankaram sharanadam sharanam vrajaami.

Yam yogino-vigatamoha-tamorajaskaa
bhaktyaikataana-manaso vinivrittakaamaah;
Dhyaayanti nishchaladhiyo'mitadivyabhaavam tam
shankaram sharanadam sharanam vrajaami.

Yashchendu-khandamamalam vilasanmayookham
baddhvaa sadaa priyatamaam shirasaa bibharti;
Yashchaardha-dehamadadaad giriraajaputryai tam
shankaram sharanadam sharanam vrajaami.

Yo'yam sakridvimalachaaru-vilolatoyaam gangaam
mahormivishamaam gaganaat patanteem;
Moordhnaa'dade srajamiva pratilolapushpaam tam
shankaram sharanadam sharanam vrajaami.

Kailaasashaila-shikharam pratikampyamaanam
kailaasashringa-sadrishena dashaananena;
Yah paadapadma-parivaadanamaadadhaanastam
shankaram sharanadam sharanam vrajaami.

Yenaasakrid ditisutaah samare nirastaa
vidyaadharoragaganaashcha varaih samagraah;
Samyojitaa munivaraah phalamoolabhakshaastam
shankaram sharanadam sharanam vrajaami.

Dagdhvaadhvaram cha nayane cha tathaa bhagasya
pooshnastathaa dashanapanktimapaatayachcha;
Tastambha yah kulishayukta-mahendrahastam tam
shankaram sharanadam sharanam vrajaami.

Enaskrito'pi vishayshvapi saktabhaavaa
jnaanaanvayashruta-gunairapi naiva yuktaaah;

171

Yam samshritaah sukhabhujah purushaa bhavanti tam
shankaram sharanadam sharanam vrajaami.

Atriprasooti-ravikotisamaanatejaah santraasanam
vibudhadaanava-sattamaanaam;
Yah kaalakootamapibat samudeernavegam tam
shankaram sharanadam sharanam vrajaami.

Brahmendrarudramarutaam cha sashanmukhaanaam
yo'daad varaamshcha bahusho bhagavaan maheshah;
Nandim cha mrityuvadanaat punarujjahaara tam
shankaram sharanadam sharanam vrajaami.

Aaraadhitah sutapasaa himavannikunje
dhoomravratena manasaa'pi parairagamyah;
Sanjeevanee samadadaad bhrigave mahaatmaa tam
shankaram sharanadam sharanam vrajaami.

Naanaavidhairgajabidaala-samaanavaktrairdakshaadhvara-
pramathanairbalibhirganaughaih;
Yo'bhyarchyate'maraganaishcha salokapaalaistam
shankaram sharanadam sharanam vrajaami.

Kreedaarthameva bhagavaan bhuvanaani sapta
naanaanadee-vihagapaadapa-manditaani;
Sabrahmakaani vyasrijat sukritaahitaani tam
shankaram sharanadam sharanam vrajaami.

Yasyaakhilam jagadidam vashavarti nityam
yo'shtaabhireva tanubhirbhuvanaani bhunkte;
Yah kaaranam sumahataamapi kaaranaanaam tam
shankaram sharanadam sharanam vrajaami.

Shankhendu-kundadhavalam vrishabhapraveeramaaruhya
yah kshitidharendra-sutaanuyaatah;
Yaatyambare himavibhooti-vibhooshitaangastam
shankaram sharanadam sharanam vrajaami.

Shaantam munim yamaniyogaparaayanam
tairbheemairyamasya purushaih pratineeyamaanam;

172

Bhaktyaa natam stutiparam prasabham raraksha tam
shankaram sharanadam sharanam vrajaami.

Yah savyapaani-kamalaagranakhena devastat
panchamam prasabhameva purah suraanaam;
Braahmam shirastarunapadmanibham chakarta tam
shankaram sharanadam sharanam vrajaami.

Yasya pranamya charanau varadasya bhaktyaa
stutvaa cha vaagbhiramalaabhiratandritaabhih;
Deeptaistamaamsi nudate svakarairvivasvaam stam
shankaram sharanadam sharanam vrajaami.

Pleased with this stuti, Shiva asked, "What do you want?"
Andhaka said, "Lord, I have only one prayer. Let me be
forever pierced by this trident so that the heat of the trident
will burn away the impurities of my body and I will acquire a
pure body." Shiva said, "So be it."

Meanwhile, the guru of the asuras, who had been
swallowed whole by Shiva, was wandering around inside his
stomach. He was trying to find an exit from Shiva's body.
In his search for an exit, he came out from his penis, in the
same manner that sperm does. When he came out, Shiva
said, "From today your name will be Shukracharya." *Shukra*
means the male seed or sperm. Shiva then asked, "Now you
are my son, what can I give you?"

Shukracharya was from the *kula* or lineage of the
demons. He said, "Lord, you are Mahadeva, and you are
the only person who can impart the vidya of *mrita sanjivani*,
reviving the dead." Therefore, Shiva gave him the knowledge
of mrita sanjivani vidya and went back to Kailash.

Gajasura

In the meantime, Mother Durga killed the demon Mahishasura. Mahishasura had a son called Gajasura, whose body
was like an elephant. When Gajasura came to know that his
father had been killed by the Devi, he engaged in severe
tapasya and pleased Brahma, who granted him his request

that his death should not come by any man or woman who is in the grip of passion: "If I have to be killed, it must be by someone who has conquered passion."

After receiving this boon, Gajasura went about like an elephant on the rampage and started attacking and conquering the whole world. One day, he attacked Kashi. A terrible fight ensued between him and Bhairava, yet Gajasura did not die. The harassed devatas went to Lord Shankara and said, "Lord, Gajasura has been spreading terror throughout the earth and it is time he is killed. However, he has been given a boon by Brahma that he will only be killed by someone who has conquered passion. Since you have conquered passion you are the only person who can execute this job."

Shiva prepared himself and came and fought with Gajasura. After a long fight, Shiva pierced Gajasura's body with his trident. When the trident pierced Gajasura, his impure mind was purified and bhakti awakened within him. He said, "Lord, I am so grateful to have received liberation at your hands. I have a request: please wear this skin of mine as it has now been purified by the touch of your trident." Shiva covered himself with the huge skin of Gajasura and from then on he received the name of *Krittivasa*, wearer of skin.

Banasura

Meanwhile, Sri Krishna had been born on the earthly plane. He had come to Dwaraka and settled there. At the time when Sri Krishna's son Aniruddha was born, Banasura ruled over the kingdom of Shonitpur. Banasura had a daughter called Usha, who had reached a marriageable age. She had a desire to marry the most handsome and perfect person. Every day her companions would draw the pictures of different princes, place them before her and inform her about them.

One day, Usha's companion drew the picture of Krishna's son Aniruddha. She was immediately attracted to the picture. She told her companion, "I have to meet this prince." That

174

night, when Aniruddha went to sleep, Usha's companion used her yogic powers to airlift him, along with the entire bed, to Shonitpur. The next morning, when Aniruddha opened his eyes, he found himself in a new place. A girl was waiting before him with folded hands. He asked her, "Who are you? Where am I? How did this happen?" Usha then told him everything and slowly affection started developing between them.

King Banasura had several hands and he was always immersed in the worship of Shiva. His worship was similar to that which Ravana conducted in an earlier age. He was a great sadhaka. Shiva was so pleased with him that he gave him the boon that he would forever protect his city and would live there with his ganas.

When Usha's companion Chitralekha abducted Aniruddha from Dwaraka, brought him to Shonitpur and united him with Usha, the news reached Banasura that an alien male was living in the princess' palace. He went there, fought with Aniruddha and tied him up with a serpent leash. Aniruddha became a prisoner of Banasura.

When this news reached Lord Krishna, he came with his army and attacked Shonitpur. There followed a terrible war between Krishna's army and Banasura's army. Nobody was winning or losing; it was an indeterminate battle. When Krishna drew his *sudarshan chakra*, discus, to kill Banasura, Shiva himself entered the battlefield with his ganas, as he had vowed to protect Banasura's city. Therefore, the battle continued between the two armies and also between Krishna and Shiva.

When, even after fighting for a very long time, there appeared no clear winner, Krishna asked Shiva, "Lord, please tell me some way through which I can win." Shiva then indicated to Krishna to use *jrimbhanastra*, an arrow that causes yawning. When Krishna used this weapon, Shiva felt drowsy and went off to sleep. Krishna then started using his sudarshan chakra to cut off the hands of Banasura and Banasura started crying aloud in agony.

When Krishna was ready to cut off Banasura's head, Shiva thought, "Enough of this lila." He woke up, stood up and said, "Krishna! As long as I am alive, I am bound by oath to save this city. Therefore, do not cut off his head." Shiva brokered a truce between Banasura and Krishna. It was announced that there would not be any war and Krishna went back to Dwaraka along with Aniruddha and Usha. Banasura pleased Lord Shiva by performing the *tandava nritya*, the dance of creation, and worshipped him with a stotra.

Vande suraanaam saaram cha suresham neelalohitam;
Yogeeshvaram yogabeejam yoginaam cha gurorgurum.

Jnaanaanandam jnaanaroopam jnaanabeejam sanaatanam;
Tapasaam phaladaataaram dataaram sarvasampadaam.

Taporoopam tapobeejam tapodhanadhanam varam;
Varam varenyam varadameedyam siddhaganairvaraih.

Kaaranam bhuktimukteenaam narakaarnavataaranam;
Aashutosham prasannaasyam karunaamaya-saagaram.

Himachandana-kundendu-kumudaambhoja-sannibham;
Brahmajyotihsvaroopam cha bhaktaanugrahavigraham.

Vishayaanaam vibhedena bibhrantam bahuroopakam;
Jalaroopamagniroopamaakaasharoopameeshvaram.

Vaayuroopam chandraroopam sooryaroopam mahatprabhum;
Aatmanah svapadam daatum samarthamavaleelayaa.

Bhaktajeevanameesham cha bhaktaanugraha-kaataram;
Vedaa na shaktaa yam stotum kimaham staumi tam prabhum.

Aparichchhinnameeshaanamaho vaanmanasoh param;
Vyaaghracharmaambaradharam vrishabhastham digambaram.

Trishoolapattishadharam sasmitam chandrashekharam;
Kathitam cha mahaastotram shoolinah paramaadbhutam.

Shiva was pleased with him, so he included him in his family and gave him the post of Mahakaala.

Nageshwara in Dwapara Yuga

There lived a demon couple named Daruka and Darukaa, who were devotees of Mother Parvati and had received blessings and boons from her. However, they were demons, and it is not easy to overcome the demoniac nature. The most difficult thing in this world is to change one's nature. It is like a dog's tail: always curled up. If you ever want to know your own nature in an unbiased way, then look at a dog's tail. Your nature is exactly the same. If you want to straighten a dog's tail, what will you do? Put it in a pipe, and as long as it is in a pipe, it will remain straight. Similarly, when you are in the company of the guru, you behave well, yet the moment you are outside the ashram gate, your head-trips begin. In the ashram you say everything is nice; however, when you go out, you stop at the first tea shop, have tea, samosa, jalebi, snacks and sweets, smack your lips and say, "That was great! In the ashram all we got was dry chappatis."

When a disciple is in the company of the guru, he tries his best to keep his tail straight, yet the moment he is away from the guru, the tail curls up again and he goes back to his usual nature. Changing your nature is the most difficult thing in this world. If a demon becomes a *bhakta* or a devotee, his nature will remain that of a demon, for bhakti has nothing to do with the *vrittis* or modifications of the mind. The bhakti tradition has spoken of different *bhavas* or feelings with which you can connect yourself to God. These bhavas include *vaira bhava*, enmity; *madhurya bhava*, love; *sakhya bhava*, friendship; and *dasya bhava*, the attitude of a servant.

People think that Kamsa and Ravana were wicked people. Yes, I agree they were wicked, yet they were bhaktas. Krishna had pervaded Kamsa's mind, even before taking birth. Every day, Kamsa would remember him at least once and wonder where he was, thinking, 'Whether alive or dead, he is my nemesis.' When God is remembered constantly with the feeling of fear or hatred, that is also bhakti. Even if you have hatred or enmity towards God, you remember him by these feelings. This is why bhakti has no specific rules.

In bhakti, it is not necessary for you to be a saintly person. You can offer your faith, devotion and worship in any form. In the Puranas we come across stories of people who did not change their depraved lifestyle, yet when they called out to God just once with a pure heart, they received His blessings. This is why, according to the rishis and munis, the path of bhakti is the best and simplest method in this Kali Yuga. It does not have to be taught to anyone. Did you need to go to school to learn how to get angry and cultivate hatred or jealousy? These abilities come to you spontaneously. Similarly, you do not have to ask anyone how to practise bhakti.

People keep asking me, "How do I practise bhakti? How do I intensify my feelings, my *bhavana*?" If you need to intensify your bhavana, you must become aware of that bhavana, not the anushthana. You can practise any anushthana; however, if your mind and feelings are not connected with the anushthana, it is of no use.

Daruka and Darukaa were staunch devotees of Mother Parvati and had her blessings. They were the chiefs of their tribe and Parvati had given them a plot of land, over two hundred kilometre in size, on the west coast of India, in what is currently the state of Gujarat. They used to reside there and later it became known as Darukavana. They would perform different demoniac acts there: harassing people, robbing and looting them, beating them up, killing people, and so on. They carried on with their nefarious activities totally undeterred, as they had the blessings of Mother Parvati.

Harassed by Daruka and Darukaa, some people approached Maharshi Aurva and told him how the demons were terrorizing the saints, householders, everyone, and thus were creating anarchy in society. Hearing this, Aurva placed a curse on the demons that henceforth, if they troubled any good person or tried to destroy a yajna, they would die right there and then. The two were in trouble. The gods were very glad to hear this news. They said, "We must immediately capitalize on this opportunity and attack them. If they fight with us and try to kill us, they will immediately die." The demon army came to know of this plan and went to Daruka with the information. Hearing this, Darukaa said, "Do not worry. Mother Parvati has given me another boon, through which I can transport this land anywhere on earth. Before the devatas come, we will go and hide in the ocean."

Darukaa lifted the entire forest and placed it in the depths of the ocean, and they remained there in hiding for a long time. One day, the demons saw a number of boats with a lot of people in them passing through that area. They thought, 'This is a good opportunity. These people have come here on their own; let us catch them.' They captured them, brought them to Darukavana and locked them up in a prison. Among the merchants caught in that group was one named Supriya, who was a great devotee of Shiva, and chieftain of the group. In order to practise his daily worship, Supriya built a small Shivalingam and started his aradhana inside the prison cell, immersing himself in japa of his ishta.

Shiva was pleased with Supriya. Through his powers, he built pillars, a roof, and a full-fledged temple inside the jail for Supriya. The moment this news reached Daruka, he became very angry and came with his attendants to kill him. When they reached the jail, they saw a beautiful temple with an effulgent Shivalingam in the middle, emitting a divine radiance. As Shiva was pleased with Supriya, he manifested in his divine form with the Pashupata weapon and finished off Daruka and his companions. He also gave the boon that henceforth, the forest would be inhabited by saints and that the demons with a predominance of tamas would have no place there.

When Darukaa saw all this she became frightened and realized that they would all die, including her husband. She immediately appealed to Mother Parvati with a heartrending prayer. She prayed to her for the safety of her husband and herself. After listening to her, Parvati went to Lord Shankara and said, "Lord, Daruka and Darukaa are my devotees and both have appealed to me to save them. I have a request: let Daruka and Darukaa remain in this forest as king and queen of the demons, and let us also stay here in order to control them." Shiva said, "As you wish. You are my own self, so how can I negate your wishes?"

In that forest, there was a big burrow. Shiva took the form of a snake and entered that hole. Parvati followed him as a female snake. In this way, they established themselves as Nageshwara and as Nageshwari in Darukavana.

Omkareshwar in Dwapara Yuga

While all these events were taking place in Darukavana, Narada was performing a Shiva anushthana in Gokarna. This went on for a very long time. After completing the anushthana, Narada came to the Vindhya mountains. When he entered the area, the mountain manifested in its divine form and welcomed him. Narada said, "Vindhyachala, you are a great range, but you should do Shiva aradhana, attain his blessings and become taller than the Meru mountains. I want you to worship Shiva and receive the boon that you become taller than the Meru mountains and touch the sky!"

Narada has always been doing the enjoined work of the devatas. Narada has never done any work that was not needed or was against the will of the Almighty. If sometimes he had created discord between two people, it would have been as per the dictates of the Almighty. Therefore, Vindhya agreed with Narada and prepared to perform worship of Shiva.

Narada went to the place that presently is known as the island of Omkareshwar. He constructed a Shivalingam and began his worship. Shiva was pleased with him and manifested there and offered him a boon. At that time, Narada, as well as other devatas, rishis and munis gathered there and requested Shiva, "Oh Lord, please reside here

180

permanently as Omkareshwar." Shiva said, "So be it." The Shivalingam in this place, which was initially installed by Vindhyachala, split into two forms: one called Omkareshwar and the other Amleshwar. Thus, the one Shiva is seen here in two forms.

It is in this Omkareshwar area that Adiguru Shankaracharya had darshan of his guru Govindapada and performed seva. He also practised sadhana here. When Shankaracharya arrived in Omkareshwar, his guru Govindapada was meditating inside a cave. At that time, the Narmada river flooded over. The water level started rising and infiltrating the cave. Shankaracharya saw that his guru's meditation would soon be disturbed by the rising water. He did not want his guru's samadhi to be disturbed, so he placed his *kamandalu*, the water pot of a sannyasin, near the entrance of the cave and directed the rising water to that pot. Govindapada's cave exists even today. You get a very strange feeling inside the cave. The stotras of Shankaracharya still resonate here. The shakti of the guru is still present in an awakened form.

Mahakaala in Dwapara Yuga

There was a demon named Dushana. He attacked the city of Avantika with his demonic forces and his army started ravaging and plundering the city. At that time, a brahmin named Vedapriya lived in the city along with his four sons, Devapriya, Priyamedha, Sukrita and Subrata. He was immersed in Shiva aradhana and was unaware of the demon attack and subsequent rampages.

When the demons came to Vedapriya's house in the course of their looting and killing spree, they saw him engaged in Shiva worship along with his four sons. The moment Dushana raised his hand to strike the Shivalingam with his sword, a thundering sound of *Hum* arose. The earth split open and caved in, and in that hole in the ground, Shiva manifested as Mahakaala and, with his roaring sound, destroyed the demon and his entire army.

When Shiva manifested as Mahakaala, Brahma came forth to chant the Mahakaala stuti.

Namo'stvanantaroopaaya neelakantha namo'stute;
Avijnaatasvaroopaaya kaivalyaayaamritaaya cha.

Naantam devaa vijaananti yasya tasmai namo namah;
Yam na vaachah prashamsanti namastasmai chidaatmane.

Yogino yam hridahkoshe pranidhaanena nishchalaah;
Jyoteeroopam prapashyanti tasmai shreebrahmane namah.

Kaalaatparaaya kaalaaya svechchhayaa purushaaya cha;
Gunatrayasvaroopaaya namah prakritiroopine.

Vishnave sattvaroopaaya rajoroopaaya vedhase;
Tamoroopaaya rudraaya sthiti-sargaantakaarine.

Namo namah svaroopaaya panchabuddheendriyaatmane;
Kshityaadipancharoopaaya namaste vishayaatmane.

Namo brahmaandaroopaaya tadantarvartine namah;
Arvaacheena-paraacheenavishvaroopaaya te namah.

Achintya-nityaroopaaya sadasatpataye namah;
Namaste bhaktakripayaa svechchhaavishkrita-vigraha.

Tava nihshvasitam vedaastava vedo'khilam jagat;
Vishvabhootaani te paadah shiro dhyauh samavartata.

Naabhyaa aaseedantariksham lomaani cha vanaspatih;
Chandramaa manaso jaatashchakshoh sooryastava prabho.

Tvameva sarvam tvayi deva sarvam
sarvastutistavya iha tvameva.
Eesha tvayaa vaasyamidam hi sarvam
namo'stu bhooyo'pi namo namaste.

After singing his praise, Brahma requested Shiva to reside in Avantika as Mahakaala. Mahadeva had burnt all the demons to ashes with his mantra *Hum,* and smeared the ashes over his entire body and head. That tradition continues until today; the worship of Shiva is performed with ashes from the funeral pyre, not with ashes made from cow dung cakes. In this way, Lord Shiva established himself as Mahakaala in Avantika city, which is known as Ujjain today.

There is another story connected with Mahakaala. The king of Avantika, Chandrasena, was a friend of Shiva's courtier, Manibhadra. Manibhadra had gifted a precious jewel to King Chandrasena, which he had received as a blessing from Shiva. The jewel had the power that the place it was kept in would never lack anything: the rains would come on time, the crops would be harvested on time, there would be no poverty or shortage of anything. The state was indeed prosperous and happy; however, when the kings of the surrounding states came to know that King Chandrasena had a jewel that fulfilled all his wishes, they gathered together and attacked Ujjain.

When the city was being attacked from all sides, King Chandrasena went straight to Mahakaala, surrendered to him and started his worship. When the king began performing his aradhana, all his subjects gathered there to witness it. A cowherd boy, barely five years, named Srikara had also come to witness this aradhana. This boy lived at home with his widowed mother. The boy was so fascinated with what he saw that when his mother told him to go play while she cooked his food, he ran outside, put a stone under a tree and replicated what he had seen the king doing. He started offering flowers, fruit, water, milk, and so on, and completely forgot himself. He became so absorbed in his aradhana that he even forgot what he was doing.

His mother repeatedly called out to him, "Srikara, come inside, the food is ready." However, Srikara was so immersed in his Shiva aradhana that he did not hear anything. His mother came outside and saw what he was doing. She became very angry because she had been calling for a long time and here he was offering flowers, fruit, water and milk to a stone! In her anger, she kicked the Shivalingam and all the items he had been using in his worship, and dragged him inside.

Srikara started crying, "Mother I was doing pooja and you have destroyed everything." He was a small boy and he did not understand what was happening. Still crying, he went off to sleep. The next morning when he woke up, he saw that a beautiful temple had appeared at the place where he had done his pooja. He ran outside and saw a Shivalingam inside the temple. He embraced the lingam and started crying. He called out to his mother, "Ma, ma, come and see this miracle!" Mother said, "Yes, I can see it! The ramshackle hut we used to stay in has been converted into a palace. The place under the tree where you were doing pooja has been transformed into a divine temple. Son, I could not gauge the depth of your feelings yesterday and I destroyed everything. Please forgive me." The son said, "What's to forgive? Whatever God wanted has happened."

The news of this miracle spread like wildfire and King Chandrasena also came to see how the little boy had received the grace of Mahakaala. When he saw the beautiful temple that had manifested overnight, he accepted the little boy as a child of the divine. The kings who had surrounded the city and were preparing to attack also received this information through their spies. They forgot their enmity and joined King Chandrasena in his Shiva aradhana.

King Chandrasena brought Srikara to the palace and declared that he would be the king of all the cowherd boys of his kingdom. Hanuman also arrived there and gave his blessings, saying, "Srikara! King Chandrasena has made you the king of all the cowherds. In your lineage, in the eighth succeeding generation, the famous Nanda will be born and Mahavishnu will incarnate as his own son." After making this prophecy, Hanuman disappeared. Sure enough, after eight generations, Srikara was born as Nanda to enjoy the divine company of Krishna as his son.

Satsang 6

19 February 2009

Paramshiva is the beginningless God, the beginningless element. His presence pervades all three dimensions of time. You can see him in whatever form you desire. He can be seen in a form that is beyond the gunas, or sometimes in the bondage of the gunas; sometimes as a tapasvi, or as a yogi, or an ideal mother or father. His *sakara*, with form, and *nirakara*, formless, manifestations are complementary to each other. Whether we talk about his sakara or his nirakara manifestation, it is all the same, as that same formless Paramshiva assumes a form to enact the lilas in this world.

Once, Sri Krishna had fought with Jambavana in the forest in order to attain the jewel called 'syamantaka mani'. At that time, after surrendering to him, Jambavan handed over his daughter Jambavati to Sri Krishna. After coming back to Dwaraka, Sri Krishna married her according to prescribed rituals. However, Jambavati did not have any children and this made her very upset. She mentioned this to Sri Krishna, who said, "Worship of the gods and the blessings of a saint are the only means of liberation in this world and hereafter. Let us go to Maharshi Upamanyu in the Himalayas and seek his blessings and grace."

Sri Krishna and Jambavati went to Maharshi Upamanyu, who imparted the teachings of the Pashupata system to them. Maharshi Upamanyu cleared all the doubts Sri Krishna had about the Pashupata system and said, "Krishna, your thinking is correct. One can have a child through the grace of guru and God. Begetting a child can also bestow liberation in this world and hereafter. In order to attain a child, observe Pashupata dharma with Jambavati."

Maharshi Upamanyu then described Pashupata dharma, Shiva tattwa and the unique manifestation of Shiva with five forms.

Shivalingam

In the Shaiva agamas it is said that Shiva's nirakara form is that of the Shivalingam. The Shivalingam is a symbol not only of Shiva, but it is the joint symbol of Shiva and Shakti. Shakti resides in Shiva, as Shakti is born of the Self of Shiva. Therefore, the Shivalingam has both Shiva and Shakti established in it. It has been called a lingam because during *laya* or dissolution, the entire creation merges and dissolves back into the lingam. The cause of laya is called the *lingam*.

The Shivalingam has a part that extends upwards, and this is the symbol of the Shiva tattwa. The other part, the base called peeth or *argha*, is the symbol of Shakti. Shakti also manifests herself in the Shivalingam in two other forms. In the lingam, she manifests as *kalaa*, creative expression of the intellect, and in the argha as *bhakti*, creative expression of emotions. Shiva also exhibits two forms in the lingam: the destroyer and the base of creation. The argha is the symbol of the foundation of creation and the lingam is the symbol of its dissolution. In this way, the Shivalingam is the symbol of both Shiva and Shakti; it is not only a symbol of Shiva, which is how it is normally understood. It has the form and the image of both Shiva and Shakti. It is the symbol of the nirakara or the formless nature of Shiva and Shakti. In the end, the formless also has to be experienced, and how is it possible to experience it without a symbol?

Our guru, Swami Satyananda, says that in order to climb up to the roof, you need a ladder. Once you have reached the roof, throw the ladder away, as it is no longer needed. In the same way, in order to experience the nirakara or the formless, in the beginning it is necessary to have a sakara symbol. Sri Swamiji says that the foundation of Indian culture is worship of images or idols. On account of this, India has been attacked by different cultures that believe idol worship should not be performed, as God is formless and should not be portrayed by a form, an idol. However, Sri Swamiji says that if you accept only the formless God and do not accept the different forms, it is an insult to the omniscience and omnipresence of God. If God is omnipresent and omniscient then he is everywhere, whether with form or without. If you accept God only as nirakara and negate his sakara aspect then that God cannot be *poorna*, complete.

All the methods and techniques of upasana or aradhana all over the world are essentially sakara. If you are focusing on your breath then that breath is sakara: it is a form on which your mind is focusing. If you are meditating on a mantra then that mantra is sakara: it is the support for your mind. If you meditate on a form then you connect yourself with that form. Aradhana or upasana cannot be a nirakara method.

How can the sakara mind accept the nirakara? Take the example of a water pot whose mouth is closed. When this pot is dipped in water, no water will enter it. However, when the mouth is open, water will immediately enter it. When a person contemplates on the formless or nirakara God and does not accept God with form, that is like a pot in the water with its mouth closed. The water cannot go inside, and so remains outside. That person is not able to experience God in his life. This is why in the Indian tradition and philosophy, sakara has been accepted as more important than nirakara, as this is the path that can take you to your ishta. It is for this purpose that Shiva and Shakti have manifested their nirakara form as the Shivalingam.

Shiva's nature
Shiva is a god who is very fond of the number five. Shiva has five faces: four faces look in the four different directions and

the fifth face looks upward. Each face has given birth to a different letter of the alphabet. The first face has given rise to the first and primordial letter, A. The second mouth has given birth to U, which is the fifth vowel. The third mouth has given rise to M, which is the fifth letter of the fifth group of letters called *vargas*. The fourth mouth has given rise to *bindu*, the source of all vibrations. The fifth face has given rise to *nada*, psychic sound.

A, U, M, bindu and nada: these five manifest as mantras and they combine to form *Aum*. *Aum* has been accepted as the mantra of Shiva's nirakara or formless entity. Just as the Shivalingam is the visual symbol of Shiva's nirakara form, *Aum* is the mantra of Shiva's nirakara form, known as the shabdabrahman. Here Brahman means the beginningless, infinite reality that is God, and the experience of that ultimate reality as sound is called *shabdabrahman*.

Sadashiva

Sadashiva has a form with five faces: a sakara form. Each face has three eyes, ten hands and a complexion as white as camphor: this is the form described as Sadashiva. The mouths of Sadashiva, called *sadakhya*, each represent one of the five *bhootas* or elements: *akasha* or space, *vayu* or air, *agni* or fire, *jala* or water and *prithvi* or earth. The mantra of these five elements is *Namah Shivaya*. Thus, the essential mantra of Sadashiva is *Namah Shivaya*, which is also referred to as the *panchakshari* or five-syllabled mantra.

The aradhana of Shiva's sakara form is performed with the mantra *Namah Shivaya* and that of the nirakara form, with *Aum*. If *Namah Shivaya* is a gross aradhana then *Aum* is a subtle aradhana. If *Namah Shivaya* is manifest, sakara, then *Aum* is the unmanifest, formless, nirakara. These mantras invoke Shiva. Whether you use *Aum* or *Namah Shivaya*, both have been called Pranava. Normally *Aum* is understood to be the Pranava mantra; however, in the Shaiva agamas it is said that the gross form of Pranava is *Namah Shivaya* and the subtle form is *Aum*.

188

Pranava

Pra means *prapancha* or 'the illusion of the world', *na* means 'non-existent' and *va* means 'for you'. Thus, *pranava* means 'the illusory world does not exist for you'. For the person who perfects the sadhana of Pranava, the illusory world no longer exists. *Pra* also means 'the ocean of existence created by Prakriti' and *nava* means 'a boat'. Therefore, 'with this boat of Pranava, you can cross this ocean of existence': this is the second meaning. Additionally, one who worships Pranava has all his karmas eliminated and thereby receives a new lease of life. In this context, *nava* would mean the 'new' reality which is free of maya. Pranava makes a sadhaka a *navin*, or a 'new' person, whose nature is that of Shiva.

In this way, commentators have tried to explain the Pranava in various ways; however, the Shaiva agamas have simply said, "For you there is no prapancha, no illusion of the world." When one takes refuge or shelter in Shiva, and becomes immersed in Shiva aradhana, then one is freed from all the illusions of this transient existence and attains permanent peace and happiness.

Aum is the *akshara*, the non-decaying, subtle form of Pranava, and *Namah Shivaya* is the gross form. Where the five letters are manifest, that is the gross form and where the five letters are not manifest, that is the subtle form. This is the teaching of Pashupata dharma, which was given to Sri Krishna by Maharshi Upamanyu. The maharshi then advised Krishna, "If you want to please Mahadeva, try to see that your mind and intellect, your knowledge and wisdom, are in a state of balance."

Maharshi Upamanyu further said, "Normally, when a person is born, it is accepted that he is born with a physical body only; however, in truth, this is not so. This physical body is linked with six sheaths or *koshas*, three of which are given by the mother and three by the father."

Normally, a yogi or a yoga teacher who has not gone into the depths of yoga will say that the body has five sheaths or *koshas*: annamaya, pranamaya, manomaya, vijnanamaya and anandamaya. However, Maharshi Upamanyu says that there are six koshas, not five. He explains that the body, the prana and the mind, the *annamaya*, *pranamaya* and the *manomaya* koshas, are obtained from the father, while the vijnanamaya, anandamaya and atmamaya koshas are obtained from the mother. In the vijnanamaya kosha, one is freed from the *kleshas* or afflictions, and thus experiences the bliss and joy, *ananda*, of the anandamaya kosha. In the atmamaya kosha, one merges oneself with *Ishwara*, the non-decaying principle or God element. In this context, 'mother' refers to the Shakti, or energy element, and 'father' refers to *Purusha* or consciousness.

One is born with these koshas and engages oneself in all the worldly transactions. However, simultaneously, one also has the potential and ability to advance in the spiritual path. In this world, the human being is the only creature who can maintain a proper balance between the material and spiritual life. All the other beings in this creation are solely guided by material instinct and that is why it is said in the scriptures: *Bade bhaga manusha tana pava* -"You are very fortunate to have received the human body."

You are fortunate to have received the human body. There is tremendous possibility for your evolution in this body. When you receive the human body, you are on your way to becoming a god. This is why it is said that receiving a human body is a great blessing from God. You will no longer be going around in the lower strata of creation; it is certain that now you will be going forward. Therefore, march ahead on the path of God-realization.

Even while involved in *bhoga* or enjoyment of the senses, it is possible for you to attain yoga; this possibility is exists in human life. Maharshi Upamanyu conveyed this teaching to Sri Krishna. He said that the world is *Panchabrahma swaroopa*, like a fivefold Brahma. Panchabrahma is related to the five faces of Shiva. *Purusha* or consciousness, *srotra* or hearing, *vani* or speech, *shabda* or sound, and *akasha* or space manifest from Sadashiva's Ishana face. *Ishana*

190

also means the sun. Therefore, this is the face that has illuminated the whole world.

Prakriti or energy, *tvacha* or skin, *pani* or hands, *sparsha* or touch and *vayu* or air, have all emanated from the face of Shiva called Purusha. In this context, the word 'purusha' indicates another truth stated in the scriptures: *Puri shete iti purushah* – "One who resides in the 'puri' is Purusha." The body has been called a *puri* or city. *Nava dware pure dehi* –"This body is the city with nine gates." That ultimate element called Purusha is a resident in this city of nine gates. This body is an area or *kshetra* and the knower of that area, the *kshetrajna*, resides within it.

A person who resides in Munger is called a 'Mungerian', whatever his name may be. Similarly, whichever city you reside in, you are known by that city. Similarly, whoever resides in the city of the body is identified with the body. The kshetrajna is known by the kshetra. Purusha is that element which resides or sleeps in this city of nine gates. In this context, purusha is not a person, but the ultimate element. That ultimate element has no gender; it is neutral. It is neither male nor female, yet it can assume different forms and is immanent in all forms. This is why it is said that prakriti, tvacha, paani, sparsha and vayu have emanated from the Purusha face of Sadashiva.

Ahamkara or ego, *netra* or eyes, *paira* or feet, *roopa* or form, and *agni* or fire emanate from Sadashiva's third face, which is known as Aghora. *Ghora* means 'terrible'; *aghora* means 'that which is not ghora' or 'that which is peaceful or sober'.

Buddhi or intellect, *rasana* or sap, *payu* or the anus, *rasa* or juice, and *jala* or water emanate from Sadashiva's Vamadeva form or his fourth face.

Mana or mind, *nasika* or nose, *upastha* or the genitals, *gandha* or smell, and *prithvi* or earth emanate from Sadashiva's face known as Sadyojata.

The five faces of Shiva constitute the entire creation as per the Shaiva agamas. This creation in the form of the *panchabrahman* is propelled by the sound body, mantras.

191

This is why in the Pashupata philosophy it is said that when you are doing mantra sadhana, you should make your mind one-pointed and dwell on the mantra. Mantra is one of the main components of the Pashupata system.

Krishna's upasana in Dwaraka

While imparting the teachings of Pashupata dharma as described above, Maharshi Upamanyu told Sri Krishna, "Krishna, you came here with the desire of begetting a son. I advise you to follow Pashupata dharma along with Jambavati and appease Mahadeva Shiva. When you receive his grace, you will also get a son." Sri Krishna immersed himself in the aradhana of Shiva, along with Jambavati. Shiva was pleased with his aradhana, appeared before him with Parvati, and asked, "Krishna, what is your desire? You are Narayana himself and you must have performed this aradhana to establish a system in the world."

Krishna said, "Lord, I do not have any personal desire, but Jambavati wants a son." Shiva said, "There is no son written in her destiny." Krishna said, "I know that. This is why we performed this aradhana, for you are the one person who can change destiny. To this, I add one more request of my own: let this son be like you." Shiva said, "Think carefully before you ask for this boon, because wherever I go there will be destruction. The purpose of my birth is destruction. The purpose of Brahma's birth is creation, that of Narayana is sustenance. If I take birth in your family as your son then your lineage will be destroyed."

Krishna said, "Lord, this is what I want, as in the near future, my people will consider themselves invincible and start terrorizing others. I want these people to depart before I leave." Shiva said, "As you wish. A part of me will take birth in Jambavati's womb and his name will be Samba."

The stories of Sri Krishna tell that Samba had joked in bad taste with the rishis. He had tied an iron club to his torso and asked the rishis, "Please tell me who is in my womb, a boy or a girl?" This club was later ground to dust and the

192

iron powder was sprinkled on the ocean banks. This iron powder later became sharp grass and was the cause of the destruction of the entire Yadu clan. This was as per the curse from the rishis, yet this was also Shiva's lila.

After Shiva had assured Sri Krishna that he would take birth in his family, Mother Parvati said, "Krishna, you did such an excellent aradhana, all the three worlds are overjoyed, and I am so happy with it that I would also like to give you a boon. Please ask and I will give it to you happily."

Krishna said, "Mother, if you are truly pleased with my aradhana and want to give me something then give me not one but five boons. Firstly, please give me the boon that I shall bear no ill-will towards any good person. When I come across a person who is greater than me, who is more learned and more prosperous, let me not harbour jealousy or hatred towards that person. Secondly, let me always worship the brahmins properly. Let there be no shortcoming in this respect. Thirdly, let no one be unhappy with whatever work I do; let everyone be glad with whatever I do. Fourthly, let me have equal vision towards everyone wherever I go. Let me not see anyone as being high or low. Lastly, let me conduct different types of yajnas, which will satisfy the devatas and give me excellent sons with your blessings. In summary, let me always respect and welcome saints and sannyasins, let my love for them remain unwavering, and let me always remain content."

This is the prayer Sri Krishna made to Parvati. She was very happy to hear these requests and said, "Until now people have asked for either position, or power or immortality. Nobody has ever asked for the boon, 'Let me not be negative towards anyone.' Therefore, Krishna, victory to you, *Jaya Ho!*" Saying this, Mother Parvati and Shiva both disappeared.

After that, Sri Krishna came to Maharshi Upamanyu's ashram and informed him that with his blessings his aradhana had proved fruitful. He told him about the boon received from Shiva. Upamanyu said, "In this world, who is a greater benefactor than Shiva? When Shiva becomes angry, it becomes unbearable, yet when Shiva performs daan, tapas and sadhana, he displays such one-pointedness and proficiency that it has no parallel. There is no one greater than Shiva in this world. Thus, you should always dwell on Shiva's glories." Saying this, he bade farewell to Sri Krishna, who went off to Dwaraka.

Prapancha

People say that this world is *prapancha*, an illusion. The expansion of the *pancha bhootas*, the five elements, is called prapancha: *pancha* means five and *pra* is a prefix meaning expansion. The five elements are earth, water, fire, air and space. Space has only one quality: *shabda* or sound. Air has two: sound and touch, *sparsha*. Fire has three: sound, touch and form, *roopa*. Water has four: sound, touch, form and taste, *rasa*. Earth has all five: sound, touch, form, taste and smell, *gandha*. However, the basic quality of earth is smell. When there is full expansion of the qualities of all the elements, that is called prapancha. This world is the full form of prapancha, as all the elements and their qualities have manifested and spread out here.

As a result of prapancha, one is influenced by the *indriyas* or sense organs, and their objects. The indriyas have five objects: shabda, sparsha, roopa, rasa and gandha; sound, touch, form, taste and smell. The sense organs like to receive these objects. The eyes like to see something nice. The skin likes to feel something nice. The ears like to hear something nice. The nose likes to smell something good. In this way, the sense organs are keen to receive the objects in the form of prapancha. One becomes entangled in maya due to these five objects of the senses. If you see a beautiful flower, you would like to have it. If you see tasty food, you would like to eat it. The senses like to receive that which is pleasant and reject whatever is unpleasant.

There is a story connected with Mahatma Buddha. A beautiful woman became a *bhikshuni*, a female mendicant, took initiation from him and became part of his group of disciples. As she was a beauty queen, thousands came just to see her. There were some among those visitors who started wondering, "Why not take diksha and enjoy the company of this beauty?"

When this lady realized that people were coming to see her and not to imbibe the teachings of Buddha, she asked the assembled disciples in front of Buddha, "Why have you come here?" They all replied, "We have come here to appreciate your beauty." The bhikshuni said, "If this is so, then stay here as a bhikshu." Saying this, she threw a bottle of acid on her face. The acid disfigured her, and those who were infatuated with her beauty no longer looked at her. A lot of people had taken initiation with the hope that this beautiful woman would not be able to withstand the rigours of the bhikshu life for long, and when she left, she might agree to come with them!

This example drives home the point that human beings always run after the objects of the senses. The more you chase the sense objects, the more you bind yourself to the world, and when you bind yourself to the world, you distance yourself from Shiva and Shakti.

Shakti

Shakti manifests in every Shivalingam in two forms: kalaa and bhakti. In the kalaa form, she is again manifest in five sub-forms: kalaa, vidya, raga, kaala and niyati. These are the *pancha kalaa*, the five limiting aspects of energy. In the Shaiva agamas, these kalaas have also been called the five *kanchukas* or coverings because they veil the real nature of the being. Just as cloth covers the body, these five kalaas cover the being, the consciousness. They prevent one from realizing the true nature of consciousness.

The Shakti that manifests as the five elements is known as *kalaa*. That Shakti which becomes the cause of karmas, and through which karma is fulfilled, is called *vidya*. That Shakti through which you become attached to the sensory objects is called *raga*. *Kaala* is that which makes you emotionally attached to different beings, mistaking them for Brahman or the reality. That Shakti of God, which is responsible for the control and management of the entire creation, is called *niyati*. Thus, the five kalaas – kalaa, vidya, raga, kaala and niyati – are established in the lingam as Shakti. In the base or argha, the same Shakti is established as bhakti.

Bhakti

The need for bhakti is release from the *kleshas* or afflictions and attainment of divine wealth. In our scriptures, bhakti has been accepted as the means for ending suffering, not jnana or karma. Karma becomes a cause for suffering and jnana has no effect on the human mind. If I ask in a month's time what has been discussed here, nobody will remember anything. Jnana is like water flowing over the head. People hear it, yet they are unable to imbibe it. Knowing fully well what is *dharma* or *adharma*, righteousness or unrighteousness, people are still unable to forsake the path of adharma.

The same problem was faced by Duryodhana. Before the start of the Mahabharata war, Lord Krishna went to Hastinapur with peace proposals. He said that the war should not be allowed to take place, as it would cause great destruction. However, Duryodhana said clearly that without a war, he would not give the Pandavas even five villages, not even land equivalent to a needle's eye.

Krishna asked, "Duryodhana, don't you know what is *satya* and *asatya*, truth and untruth, dharma or adharma?" Duryodhana replied, *Janami dharmam na cha me pravrittih* – "I know very well what is dharma, but I do not have any inclination or liking for it." *Janami adharmam, na cha me nivrittih* – "I know what is adharma and I cannot free myself from that. I cannot forsake the path of adharma. I do not know which devata is seated inside me, compelling me to do all these works."

The point to be noted here is that Duryodhana had full knowledge of adharma and dharma, what is correct and incorrect. However, he was so overwhelmed with and bound by hatred that he took up the path of adharma, not dharma. Therefore, even when the mind knows very well what is correct, one's behaviour may not be in accordance with dharma or natural justice.

Until *jnana* or wisdom is imbibed, it cannot be a means for achieving liberation. This is the reason why neither jnana nor samadhi alone can give you liberation. In this world, there is only one means to liberation and that is bhakti. You can sit for thousands of years in samadhi. You might even forget yourself and the world, and colour your mind with that element, yet you will not attain liberation. The person who does not follow the path of bhakti does not attain liberation or *mukti*, and is called a *yoga bhrashta,* a yogi who has deviated from the path. The sadhana remains incomplete, whatever lofty sadhanas one might have done.

Our guru, Swami Satyananda, has said, "Although I have thoroughly studied all the shastras and texts of the tradition, my path became clear only after I gave a place to bhakti in my life. As long as I had not given a place to bhakti, my path was not clear." This is why bhakti is referred to as an incarnation of Shakti. However, these days, people are chasing maya, forgetting bhakti.

In my childhood, I used to hear a story about two sisters, Bhakti and Maya. Bhakti was very beautiful; she would wear pretty clothes and people were attracted to her. Maya was ugly, and her clothes were tattered and torn; she had no ornaments and nobody looked at her. Maya would always lament that Bhakti was prettier. She was jealous because people would gravitate to Bhakti and not to her. "I don't have good clothes or jewellery, whereas Bhakti has everything" she lamented. Therefore, she devised a plan.

One day, when Bhakti and Maya had gone to the river for the morning bath, Maya finished her bath quickly, came out, put on Bhakti's clothes and disappeared as fast as possible. She was ugly, but she covered her face with all

197

the fine clothes, so that it was not really visible. People now started chasing her, deluded by her dazzling appearance.

Meanwhile, although Bhakti was very pretty, people would not go near her, as she was forced to don the torn and tattered clothes of her sister. People said, "She might be pretty, but she is a beggar and she cannot attract us."

In this Kali Yuga, people chase maya and turn their backs on bhakti. In Satya Yuga, it was the opposite. People give importance to maya or bhakti according to their mentality. If they give importance to bhakti then we bow down to them, as bhakti is the refuge of a human being, and that which takes one to the Ultimate.

Shiva's incarnation as Sureshwara avatara in Dwapara Yuga

Maharshi Upamanyu, who had imparted the teachings of Pashupata dharma to Sri Krishna, was the son of Vyaghrapada Muni. Vyaghrapada Muni lived a very sattwic and austere life. He lived in a small hut, in which there was nothing to eat or drink. The cooking fire would not be lit for days on end. Whenever Upamanyu became tormented by the pangs of hunger, his mother would mix some flour with water and give it to him saying, "Son, drink this milk and go to sleep."

Upamanyu noticed that the milk consumed by the children of other munis and rishis was clear, white and clean. When he compared the milk in his pot with that of the other children, Upamanyu realized that the milk that was being given to him was not real. He cried, and his mother said, "Son, in this world, whatever anyone receives in life comes through the grace of Lord Shiva. If you want milk then perform his aradhana and please him." Upamanyu accepted his mother's words and went off to the Himalayas. At that time, he was around twelve years old, and he never came back to his parents.

Upon reaching the Himalayas, Upamanyu made a small temple with eight bricks. Inside it, he made a small Shivalingam out of earth, and immersed himself in Shiva aradhana. Hungry and thirsty, he remained engrossed in his sadhana, with the simple faith, "I am doing aradhana of the God who gives everything." *Parameshwara*, the ultimate transcendent reality, was so pleased with the sadhana of this little boy that he came down in the form of Indra and said, "Upamanyu, you are very young. Your body is soft and gentle, and this severe tapasya does not suit you. What do you want? I will give you whatever you want." Upamanyu looked at Paramshiva in the form of Indra and said, "I have not worshipped you. I have been worshipping Lord Shiva. But if you want to give me something then give me bhakti of Lord Shiva. After that, you can go back, as I have not called you: do not come between me and my God."

Shiva was testing him, so he said, "What can Shiva give you? I am the king of the heavens. I have all the wealth and prosperity. All the devatas listen to me. Shiva does not have anything of his own. In truth, he is a beggar. He doesn't even know from where he will get the day's food. What use is this Shiva worship? Whatever you want, ask me and I will give it to you." Upamanyu said, "I do not want anything from you." Saying this, he took a sankalpa to beat Indra up as he was slandering his aradhya. When the Lord saw that the child was making a resolve to attack Indra, he decided to help him. The child had closed his eyes and was praying, "Lord, please remove this Indra from here as he is creating a disturbance in my aradhana." At that point, the weapon called Aghorastra came to Upamanyu's hands. *Aghorastra* might sound terrible, yet its nature is very gentle; it means that weapon which is not *ghora* or terrible, but peaceful.

The lila of the Lord is unique. This weapon was given to Upamanyu so that the anger he was feeling towards Indra would quieten down. Upamanyu became quiet and peaceful. He felt that whatever was happening was divine, so he turned his back on Indra and, sitting in front of the Shivalingam, became immersed in his aradhana of Shiva.

At that point, Shiva manifested along with Parvati. In the story it is said that Shiva and Parvati blessed Upamanyu with eternal youth and promised that he would not be touched by disease, old age or death. Shiva said, "I appeared as Indra in order to test your devotion. Remember that I am your father and Parvati is your mother." Shiva instructed his assistants to take care of Upamanyu's needs so that he could remain forever in the Himalayas.

From that time onwards, Upamanyu stayed in the Himalayas, immersed in Shiva aradhana. He has been accepted as the greatest tapasvi of this age and at his place of worship Narayana himself, in the form of Sri Krishna, imbibed the teachings of Pashupata dharma.

Shiva's incarnation as Kirata avatara in Dwapara Yuga

The time for the great battle of Mahabharata was drawing close. The Pandavas were living in the forest for the period of their exile. They agreed among themselves that this was the opportune moment for Arjuna to do tapasya of Shiva and attain the weapon called Pashupatastra. Maharshi Vyasa came and said that in the ensuing battle, the weapons should be divine; therefore, Arjuna should first please Ashutosha or Shiva, and with his blessings all the weapons of the devatas would automatically come to him.

After receiving this instruction from Maharshi Vyasa, Arjuna went to the mountain called Indrakila on the banks of Ganga and immersed himself in Shiva aradhana. When Duryodhana came to know through his spies that Arjuna was performing Shiva aradhana to obtain divine weapons, he sent his demon friend Muka to disturb the worship. Duryodhana told him, "Muka, I cannot send any other warrior or soldier for this work, as then the whole world will come to know that it is our doing. I want this job to be done secretly. The saying is 'Let the serpent die and the stick remain intact'. Therefore, you go and disturb his aradhana, and if possible kill him."

As instructed by Duryodhana, Muka reached the Indrakila mountain and took the form of a huge boar with big, sharp teeth. Arjuna was in deep meditation, engrossed in his aradhana, and he was not at all aware that this conspiracy was being hatched. Lord Shiva saw that Muka had come to break up Arjuna's aradhana and told Parvati, "Come, let us enact a lila."

Shiva became a *kirata*, a tribal hunter, Parvati became the hunter's wife, and the ganas became his assistants. He came to the forest where Arjuna was doing his aradhana, just as Muka was advancing towards Arjuna, killing other animals on the way. Shiva decided to kill the demon and at the same time test Arjuna.

The boar now started grunting so loudly that Arjuna's meditation was disturbed, and he opened his eyes to see a huge boar rushing towards him. Arjuna lifted his bow and shot an arrow towards the boar. Shiva, in the form of Kirata, lifted his bow and shot an arrow at the boar at exactly the same moment. Shiva's arrow was aimed at the back of the boar. It pierced his back, came out through his mouth and disappeared into the ground. Arjuna had aimed at the mouth. It entered the mouth, went through his back and into the ground. Muka, who was hurt badly on both sides, fell down gasping for breath and died.

Arjuna approached the huge boar to recover his arrow. Enacting his lila, Shiva sent one of his assistants to recover his own arrow. Arjuna and Shiva's assistant reached the boar at the same time. Shiva's lila was such that both their arrows looked the same. In fact, Shiva's arrow had come back to him after killing the demon and it was Arjuna's arrow which was lying there. When Rudra's assistant lifted the arrow, Arjuna shouted, "Stop, this is my arrow. Give it back to me." The assistant said, "No way, this arrow is my master's. How can I give it to you? I am taking it back to him."

Arjuna said, "How can this arrow be your master's? All the signs that are there on the arrow indicate that it is mine, so please give it back to me." They started quarrelling. Shiva and Parvati in the form of the hunter and his wife reached there and asked, "What's the problem? Where is my arrow? Give it to me quickly as I have to leave immediately." The gana said, "Master, this warrior says that the arrow is his and he will not return it. He is quarrelling unnecessarily." Shiva in the form of the hunter said, "How can the arrow be his? I have shot the arrow."

Arjuna said, "I can prove that it is my arrow. I shot the arrow at his mouth and the arrow pierced his mouth and came out through the back. If you had shot an arrow, as you say you have, then it would obviously have entered from the back, as you are coming from that direction. There is no person in the world that can shoot an arrow, pierce through the back and then make the arrow turn around and enter the mouth."

However, Shiva had already decided to enact his lila, so he said, "Look here; this is my sign here." He showed the arrow to Arjuna. Arjuna saw with surprise that the arrow that had previously borne the sign of the Pandavas, now bore the mark of the Kirata. Arjuna could not accept it and said, "Come on, you are trying to take credit for this." In this way, the argument started heating up and eventually they started fighting.

Shiva was testing Arjuna, who was reputed to be one of the best marksmen in the world. Arrows started flying from both directions. Shiva smilingly started intercepting and destroying Arjuna's arrows. Arjuna was surprised to see all his arrows become ineffective. "I am reputed to be the best archer in the world and this Kirata fellow has made all my arrows ineffective. I wonder, maybe this man is Parashurama or Vishwamitra!"

During his life, Arjuna had encountered another great archer, Ekalavya, who had become disciple of Dronacharya. He had made an image of Dronacharya and perfected his aim in front of that image. Once, when Dronacharya had gone to the forest with his disciples, he saw a dog whose mouth was full of arrows. He said to Arjuna, "Who could be the marksman who has filled the dog's mouth with so many arrows, and with such precision, that not a drop of blood is falling on the ground?"

They came to know it was Ekalavya. Dronacharya then asked Ekalavya for his right hand thumb as *guru dakshina*, an offering to the guru. The thumb is used to position the arrow; without his thumb, an archer will not be able to aim properly and thus Arjuna remained the world's number one shooter. This was the thinking behind Dronacharya's strange instruction. Ekalavya gave his thumb, yet he was very talented and he found a way out. This is the technique now used by the archers in the Olympics: the arrow is placed between two fingers and not the forefinger and the thumb.

After their arrows were exhausted, Shiva and Arjuna took out their swords. The swords got shattered. Next, they took out their cudgels and started clubbing each other. These were also shattered in no time. All their weapons were exhausted so they started hurling trees, plants, stones, rocks and boulders at each other. Eventually, they started punching each other with their bare hands. When his hands got tired, Arjuna started kicking, but then Shiva lifted him up and thumped him so hard that Arjuna lay sprawled on the ground.

Arjuna got up fast and made it to the Shivalingam. He thought, "Let me first finish my worship, then I will fight." However, when he saw the Shivalingam he received a great shock: all the injuries that he had inflicted on the Kirata were clearly seen on the lingam. Amazed, he looked at the Kirata, who was still standing there, and then again at the lingam. All the injuries on the Kirata's body were there on the lingam. Again he looked at the Kirata, who was now smiling. Now Arjuna recognized him, "Oh heavens! He is my aradhya, Lord Shiva!"

Arjuna ran towards Shiva, fell at his feet and said, "Lord, please forgive me. I have committed a great offence; I have failed to recognize you. I have shot arrows at you, attacked you, punched you and kicked you, and you accepted everything." Smiling, Lord Shiva said, "Arjuna, the kicks and punches which you delivered to me were, in fact, my aradhana. Therefore, do not harbour any guilt on that account. You have not insulted me; I have been testing you. The purpose that has brought you here for this aradhana will be surely fulfilled." Saying this, Lord Shiva gave his Pashupata weapon to Arjuna, and left with Parvati for his abode.

The great Mahabharata war then took place. After the war was over, grandfather Bhishma was lying on the battlefield, on his bed of arrows, waiting for the auspicious moment to leave his body. Arjuna, along with his brothers, went to him and asked, "Grandfather, can I clear one doubt of mine?" Bhishma said, "Sure, unburden yourself."

Arjuna said, "Grandfather, the war finished eighteen days ago. Duryodhana has been killed and we have retrieved our empire, yet one question keeps arising in my mind. Whenever I used to fight, I would see an effulgent figure walking ahead of my chariot, which was driven by Krishna. He had a trident in his hand, and with that he was destroying the Kaurava army. Until today I have not been able to figure out who this divine figure was."

Bhishma said, "This divine figure was none other than Lord Rudra himself. He was giving direction to your arrows and ensuring that not one of them was wasted. The other warriors wasted a lot of their arrows. Some went to the ground, some flew up to the sky, but in your case, wherever you aimed, it would reach that target because Rudra himself was guiding it. Wherever Krishna, Narayana, Parameshwara Shiva, and you yourself, Arjuna, are present, victory is assured."

Ghushmeshwar in Kali Yuga

In South India there is a mountain known as Devagiri. A brahmin called Sudharma used to live near that mountain with his wife, Sudeha. Both of them were very keen devotees of Shiva. Although they had all the comforts and facilities of life, they used to keenly feel the absence of a son.

One day Sudeha told her husband, "It seems that no child will be born from my womb. I suggest that you get married to my sister Ghushma. The son we will get from her will continue our lineage and will also perform our funeral rites." Sudharma was initially reluctant to accept this idea, but later agreed and married Ghushma.

Ghushma used to follow a daily routine. She would have an early morning bath in the river, make a small Shivalingam out of earth, worship it, and then immerse it again in the river. She continued with this routine even after marriage. After some time, Ghushma gave birth to a virtuous boy, yet when the boy was born Sudeha became jealous, thinking, "My husband will now take care of Ghushma and her son and will no longer pay any attention to me. He will forget me." This fire of jealousy started burning within her.

Ghushma's son started growing up. In the course of time, he got married, and the daughter-in-law came to live in the house. With the arrival of the daughter-in-law, Sudeha could not control herself any longer. At night, when the son was sleeping in his bed, she took a knife, cut his body into pieces, put them in a sack and drowned them in the river. After committing this crime, she went off to sleep without any worry. In the morning, when the son was not found in bed, people assumed that he had gone to the river for a bath. Ghushma also started her daily routine without any worry. As usual, she went for a bath in the river, did the pooja of the Shivalingam and immersed it back in the river. However, as she immersed the lingam, Shiva manifested and said, "Ghushma, I am very pleased with your bhakti and I have come here to give you a boon." Ghushma said, "Lord, I do not want anything. My worship was not based on any desire, only on faith."

The Lord said, "That is all right. You may not want anything, but I want to give you something. I am giving you your son." Ghushma was surprised and asked, "My son? I don't understand what you mean." Shiva said, "Burning with jealousy, Sudeha butchered your son and dumped him in the river. He died, but I have come here to return him back to you because your bhakti is exemplary and of the highest order."

The moment Shiva uttered these words, Ghushma's son came out of the water, whole and hearty, as if he had just finished his bath, and bowed down to Shiva and his mother. Shiva then said, "Ghushma, there is one thought in my mind." Ghushma said, "What is it Lord?" Shiva said, "I want to punish your sister." Ghushma said, "No, no, Lord, please do not do that. If she had not done this, I would not have had your darshan. She has done me a good turn. She is fit to be worshipped by me, so if possible, forgive her and let her attain the state of Shiva." Shiva said, "Ghushma, I am very pleased with your bhakti and the pure feeling that you have just expressed."

Understand this very clearly. When God comes before you, there should be no *vikara* or impurity in your mind. Purity is what he accepts very easily.

Shiva told Ghushma, "Now, ask for a boon for yourself." Ghushma said, "If you are pleased with me then please stay here forever for the welfare of all, and be known all over the world in my name." From that time onwards, Shiva has been known as the God of Ghushma, *Ghushmeshwar*.

With the story of Ghushmeshwar, the narrative of the twelve jyotirlingams is concluded. Below is a short description of the twelve jyotirlingams.

Twelve jyotirlingams
1. **Kedareshwar** – This is Shiva's first jyotirlingam in the Himalayas. Nara and Narayana had performed their sadhana here. Kedareshwar is situated to the west of Kedar mountain on the banks of Mandakini river.
2. **Somnath** – The second jyotirlingam is situated in Saurashtra. This is in the state of Kathiawada in the area known as Prabhasa.
3. **Mallikarjuna** – This is located on the Srisailam mountain, on the banks of Krishna river, in the Krishna district of the region of Chennai. Srisailam is also known as the Kailash of the South.

4. **Mahakaaleshwar** – This temple is in the state of Malwa, in the city of Ujjain, on the banks of the Kshipra river. Lord Shiva exists here as Mahakaala.
5. **Omkareshwar** – The two separate lingams of Omkareshwar and Amleshwar are situated at the pilgrimage centre of Omkara, on the banks of the Narmada river. These two jyotirlingams have been accepted as the two forms of the same jyotirlingam.
6. **Bhimashankar** – This is situated on the banks of the Bhima river, at the source of the river at Sahya mountain, around 190 kilometres from Nasik.
7. **Vishwanath** – Vishwanath is in the famous city of Kashi or Varanasi, which is a part of the avimukta kshetra or Anandavana. Kashi is not destroyed during the *pralaya* or the great dissolution, as Shiva has established himself here in Vishwanath.
8. **Tryambakeshwar** – The Tryambakeshwar temple is located in Nasik district, 29 kilometres from Nasik Panchavati, at the source of Godavari River, near Brahmagiri.
9. **Baidyanath** – In the Puranas, the Deoghar area is known as *chitabhoomi*, the funeral grounds, as this is where Lord Shiva burnt Sati's body. It is also the place where Sati's heart fell. The Ravaneshwar lingam, known as Baidyanath Mahadeva, is also located here. In the Shaiva agamas it is called Chitabhoomau or Deoghar.
10. **Nageshwar** – Nagesh jyotirlingam is located in Daru-kavana, about twenty kilometres from Gomati Dwaraka. For this reason, some people call it Dwarakavana instead of Darukavana. Some people accept the lingam located in Audagrama, in the state of Hyderabad, as the Nageshwar jyotirlingam. However, according to the description in the Shaiva agamas, it is near Dwaraka.
11. **Rameshwaram** – This is in Setubandha, in the Ramanada district of the Chennai area.
12. **Ghushmeshwar** – This is in Shivalaya, in the state of Hyderabad, next to Daulatabad station in Berul village.

God has established himself in his own form in these twelve jyotirlingams. Even today, if you do aradhana, sadhana and archana in these places, Lord Shankara showers his blessings on you.

God is omnipresent, yet we search for him here and there. *Devalaya* or temples are the accepted centres of God. A temple is a place where, through the power of faith, God manifests as a conscious entity. Where the consciousness of God is not manifest, that place is *samsaralaya*, the residence of the worldly. In these twelve jyotirlingams, we experience the presence and divinity of God. Over thousands of years, millions of people have worshipped God in these places, with faith and devotion, and have awakened the power of God in those areas.

Science explains this phenomenon. One of the modern scientists of the west, Izhak Bentov has proved that if you bring a stone, which is an insentient object, into your home and start worshipping it, after some time the shakti in that stone becomes sentient, conscious. I am telling you about the opinion of a western scientist because their mentality is predominantly materialistic, not spiritual. If they can come to this conclusion through research and study, then for them that can be called truly revolutionary, but not for Indian culture. Today science has accepted the fact that through the power of faith, an insentient object can become conscious and have the capacity to fulfil your deep-rooted desires. The power of faith can fulfil all your desires.

Bhakti: the means of attaining Shiva

Bhakti frees you from bondage and takes you to the state of Shiva. You are free to do different practices like asana, pranayama, exercise, tapasya, vratas, anushthanas, mantra japa, yet always keep aside ten minutes for bhakti. Bhakti removes one's infatuation with the world. Humans are infatuated with the world and its objects. Bhakti has the power to free one from the shackles of infatuation with the world. This is why bhakti is also said to take the form of

208

nivritti, renunciation of the world. Bhakti is also referred to as *urdhwamukhi,* uplifting, *nirmaya,* negating maya, and *shuddha,* pure: these are different names for bhakti. Bhakti is known to be of six different types: shraddha bhakti, nishtha bhakti, avadhana bhakti, anubhava bhakti, ananda bhakti and samarasa bhakti.

1. *Shraddha bhakti*: In this type of bhakti there is difference between the *upasya,* the deity or the one who is worshipped, and *upasaka,* the worshipper. There is the feeling of 'I' and 'You'. With this feeling of duality, the shraddha or faith, and the intensity of the feeling that is awakened, is known as *shraddha bhakti.* 'I believe in God': that is the essence of shraddha bhakti.

This bhakti is possible only when the feeling of 'I' and 'You' exists, and the awareness is there that I am the worshipper and this is my aradhya or worshipped one.

2. *Nishtha bhakti*: Shraddha bhakti transforms into nishtha bhakti. When the shraddha becomes very intense and strong, it is called nishtha bhakti. Shraddha bhakti increases love or *prem,* and nishtha bhakti further deepens it.

We can compare shraddha bhakti with milk and sugar when they are separate. When the sugar mixes with the milk and its sweetness merges with the milk, then that state is comparable to nishtha bhakti.

3. *Avadhana bhakti*: The fully ripe state of nishtha bhakti is called avadhana bhakti. This becomes possible through one-pointedness of mind. When the mind becomes attached to something and does not vacillate from that focus, that is the state of *ekagrata* or one-pointedness, the state of *avadhana bhakti.*

4. *Anubhava bhakti*: Avadhana bhakti transforms into anubhava bhakti. When the sadhaka's mind becomes completely centred on the aradhya, on whatever or whoever one is devoted to, and does not wander here and there, then one becomes aware of one's own *Shiva swaroopa,* one's essential Shiva nature. Experiencing this state of Shiva as the supreme blessing is called *anubhava bhakti.*

5. *Ananda bhakti*: Anubhava bhakti transforms into ananda bhakti. When you become one with Shiva, you experience the bliss, the ananda, that is beyond this world. Experiencing this transcendental bliss as Shiva's blessings is *ananda bhakti*.

6. *Samarasa bhakti*: Ananda bhakti transforms into samarasa bhakti, which is the ultimate stage of bhakti. One is relieved of the feeling of being a separate entity and merges in God. This is samarasa bhakti.

These six forms of bhakti, which are described in the Shaiva agamas, indicate that bhakti is a process wherein one first connects with God and then tries to increase one's faith. How you go about increasing your faith or shraddha is up to you. This is not taught anywhere; it is a spontaneous expression of life. These six forms of bhakti are not to be seen separately; rather, they are complementary to each other. They are the steps that a human being has to take in life. In the Indian tradition, it has been said that this is the sadhana that takes one towards moksha or liberation.

The four efforts of artha, kama, dharma and moksha complete the cycle of a *jiva*, a bound soul. Only a soul entrapped in the world needs to perform these four actions or anushthanas. The jiva or the pashu has to clean his impurities through sadhana and give the final polish with bhakti. If you have to sell an old utensil in the market, first you clean it by scrubbing it vigorously, and after all the dirt marks are removed, you use a metal cleaning solution like Brasso to give it the shine that will attract customers. Only then will you get a good price for the item. If it is not shining clean, people will not value it. This is why one has to clean all the dirt and impurities of life through sadhana and give it a shine through bhakti yoga.

Creation and dissolution

According to the Indian tradition, twenty-seven *manvantaras*, days of Brahma, have passed. The first manvantara was Swayambhu Manu's and currently the twenty-seventh is

Vaivasvata Manu's. The great dissolution or *mahapralaya* has occurred twenty-seven times, and likewise, new creation also occurred twenty-seven times. This is not only talked of in the scriptures; it is now being accepted by the scientific community. They formulated a theory called the 'Big Bang' theory. According to it, creation started with an explosion. In the very beginning, there was nothing in space, then there was an explosion, the Big Bang, and energy spread in all directions. That energy later solidified into planets, constellations, galaxies, and so on, and after a long passage of time, animate creation came into existence.

In earlier times, scientists used to think that the Big Bang occurred only once, but now they have started to accept the possibility that the Big Bang, the cosmic explosion that is the cause of creation, has occurred more than once. They have not been able to arrive at a fixed figure. Their opinion is that when there is an explosion in space, then a sound vibration or *nada* spreads out into space, like circular ripples spreading out in water from a central point where a stone has been thrown in. When you throw in a second stone, again the ripples will spread out. If you can measure the spread of the ripples, and count them, then it is possible that you will come to know how many stones were thrown in the water.

The quality related to *akasha tattwa* or space is sound. The waves of the Big Bang explosion that took place in space are still there, because the quality of space is sound, and the sound of this explosion can be heard even now through high quality instruments.

When this fact of science is compared with the events described in the *itihasa*, or history, and the Puranas, the ancient scriptures, we come to realize that what is written in the Puranas is true. They are not flights of imagination from somebody's fertile mind. Scientific truths, the eternal truths, have been inscribed in the Puranas. If you think that the scriptures contain random speculation, you should revise your opinion.

211

The question that arises is: when the creation is destroyed, what happens to the earth, the moon, the planets, the stars, the constellations? Where do they go? Has anyone thought about this? This creation is not eternal; it is the creation cycle that is eternal, and that cycle involves creation and destruction. The creation that is born is certain to be destroyed. Where does it go? Where is it dissolved? Science is presently trying to investigate this.

At the time of dissolution, there is not even a ray of light in existence, let alone the planets. What happens? Where does everything go? Is the entire creation burnt to ashes? It has been said in the Shaiva agamas that at the time of dissolution, everything merges in the lingam.

Three aspects of the lingam

The lingam is of three kinds: gross, subtle and transcendental. The lingams established in the temples in which we worship them, are the gross lingams. They are made of matter, be it stone or metal. This gross lingam has been called the *ishta lingam*: that which is our ishta, our beloved, that which we worship and accept as our God. When faith is attached to the lingam then that insentient lingam becomes conscious, and manifests divinity and blessings. However, the devotee must have the capacity of sadhana, upasana and sankalpa.

The Puranas tell the story of Markandeya. He was only sixteen years old, yet he was destined to die at this age. When the fateful night came, he sat in front of the Shivalingam and meditated on Shiva. When Death arrived, put the noose around his neck and wanted to take him away, Shiva manifested from the lingam, revived Markandeya and told Death, "Please go away. You cannot touch someone who has surrendered to me." Markandeya was not an extraordinary person, but he had *sankalpa shakti,* or willpower, as well as faith, sincerity and devotion.

A saint or an evolved soul does not just drop down from the heavens, but is born of parents who are ordinary people. A saint is born of ordinary parents, yet with God's grace he carries good samskaras, and this gives him the right direction later on in life. However, do remember that in whichever direction your life goes, you have *iccha shakti*, the power of desire, *kriya shakti*, the power of action, and sankalpa shakti, the power of will, within you. When there is balance between iccha, kriya and sankalpa, then a person becomes capable of doing the impossible.

In the life of Markandeya or other pure souls, iccha, sankalpa and kriya do not have separate identities. It is possible for everyone to give these three one identity. If you have sincerity and dedication then your ishta lingam manifests divinity and energy. God manifests and gives his blessings, and with that blessing, one frees oneself from the *kleshas* or afflictions of the world.

The next type of lingam is subtle. This subtle lingam is the prana lingam, which is within our body. In the yogic texts and the Shaiva agamas, it is said that in our body the lingams exist in the chakras. One of them is the black lingam, one is the smoky lingam and the third is the *jyotirlingam* or the luminous lingam.

One becomes aware of the black lingam in mooladhara chakra, when one enters into deeper states of meditation. By entering into the deeper states of meditation through sadhana, one awakens the dormant shakti within, known as *kundalini*. When the kundalini is awakened, one experiences the smoky or *dhumra* lingam, which is not so clear. The black lingam appears solid and is made of stone, whereas the dhumra lingam is made of smoke. If we put smoke inside a glass, the smoke moves around inside the glass in circles. This is exactly the experience of the dhumra lingam, which is located in the heart.

According to the Shaiva agamas and yoga philosophy, all the human experiences of the mind, such as the deep-rooted desires or *vasanas* and the impressions of chitta, as well as *prana*, the life force, exist in the manifest dimension and correspond to the mooladhara, swadhisthana and manipura

213

chakras. The symbol of the black lingam in our body, which has the kundalini wrapped around it in spirals, controls and guides these three chakras. Where one leaves behind the material world and enters and stabilizes oneself into the world of pure feelings or *bhavas*, the smoky lingam manifests. This dhumra lingam becomes clear in anahata.

The third lingam, the jyotirlingam, is in sahasrara. Sadashiva resides here and his nature is that of effulgence. According to yoga and tantra, it is said that when, in the process of evolution, kundalini attains Sadashiva, the covering of maya is removed from human life and one becomes a *siddha,* a perfected being, a *Buddha,* an enlightened being, and a *mukta,* a liberated soul.

The first type of lingam, the gross lingam, is called the ishta lingam. The second type of lingam, which is subtle, is called the prana lingam. The third type is the jyotirlingam, which is transcendental, unmanifest, beginningless, infinite, and the source and support of everything.

The jyotirlingam, the transcendental lingam, is also called *bhava lingam.* When the sadhaka starts spontaneously chanting *Shivoham, Shivoham,* and experiences the Shiva tattwa within, then that bhava lingam, the *paratpara* or ultimate lingam, manifests. At that point, all the duality of the world ceases and a person experiences *Shiva sayujya,* merger with Shiva.

In the scriptures it is said that a human being is a part of the non-decaying principle or *Ishwara.* According to the scriptures, a part of God exists within us. Yet, at the same time, we are not God, as our lives do not have the completeness and wealth of God. A person who has completeness in life is called *Ishwara*; otherwise, you are a normal human being.

Imagine a matchstick. The fire element is hidden inside and when you rub the match it lights up, but only for a few moments, then it burns out. Similarly, you may experience flashes of divinity once in a while, yet afterwards you return to your normal state and previous behaviour. This is why

214

it is not possible to experience the Shiva within by merely thinking about the jyotirlingam or the prana lingam or the ishta lingam. In order to experience the Shiva within, one has to live one's life as a *sadhaka*, a spiritual aspirant.

Sadachara or good conduct

When Shiva was talking to Mother Parvati about Pashupata dharma, he also said that if a person practises appropriate behaviour, one does not have to do any other practice. He said that one of the main observances of Pashupata dharma is good conduct, as that makes a person fit to attain Shiva. A person with good conduct will not have an impure mind and his heart, feelings and thoughts will be pure. Therefore, good conduct is accepted as the first step in attainment of God.

If you practise meditation, but do not practise good conduct, then your attainment from meditation will not be complete; it will be partial. When life's goodness, its simplicity and sattwic quality become manifest in your life, then this spontaneously becomes *sadachara* or good conduct. This is why it is said in the scriptures that when one is worshipping God, one should tie all hatred, jealousy and anger up in a bundle and keep it aside. As long as you are involved in sadhana, they must not create obstacles in your path.

Normally, when performing an anushthana, people pay a lot of attention to the body and get carried away by food restrictions: this should be eaten, that should not, and so on. However, nobody has paid any attention to mental behaviour: we should not think this or that. You worry about food all day long, but has anyone thought, 'What is the appropriate behaviour while I am doing an anushthana?' In reality, that is the most important part of the anushthana.

Of what use is a clean body with an impure mind? You scrub your body vigorously with soap and clean it. You seek out the prescribed food and digest it. Your body begins to feel light and energetic; however, if in that body your mind

215

is polluted, it is of no use. In spiritual life, your attainments will be on account of your feelings, faith and dedication, not on account of the body. This is why the teaching of restraint is given so much importance in the Shaiva agamas and the yogic texts.

In yoga, what is suggested before you practise asanas? In Sage Patanjali's *Yoga Sutras*, it is said that you must first practise yamas, then niyamas, then asanas and the other sadhanas. What is the use of niyamas like shaucha, santosha, tapas, swadhyaya and Ishwara pranidhana, and yamas like satya, ahimsa, asteya, aparigraha and brahmacharya in yoga? They bring about a transformation in the mental modifications or *vrittis*.

When the mind becomes peaceful, then you enter spiritual life. You cannot have spiritual attainment with a restless mind. This is why in the system of sadhana, so much importance is given to yamas and niyamas. One may belong to the Shakta tradition, the Vaishnava tradition or any other tradition, it does not matter; it is essential for every person to take care of the mind. It is necessary to practise yamas and niyamas for managing the restless mind.

The yogic and tantric texts, including the Shaiva agamas, clearly state that in this life, the process of transformation starts only when one takes shelter in truth. This is why in the yamas the first position goes to *satya*, truth. The five yamas are satya, ahimsa, asteya, aparigraha and brahmacharya. One begins the yamas when one takes shelter in truth. The yamas and niyamas are practised in order to balance a distorted mind. Once the distorted mind is balanced, then one automatically takes to the path of *sadachara* or good conduct.

Pranava japa

The sadhana of Pranava dhyana has to be regular. There are twenty-four hours in a day. People perform worldly transactions all the twenty-four hours, dealing with family, possessions, friends, enemies, and so on. Make a resolve to devote ten minutes to your own self-evolution and the other twenty-three hours and fifty minutes to the world. Take ten minutes out from your day, sit peacefully, focus on the eyebrow centre, and do your Pranava sadhana.

This sadhana may be related to the gross or the subtle. The gross sadhana of Pranava is meditation on the panchakshari mantra, *Namah Shivaya*. Mantra has one basic purpose, which is to free the mind from bondage, from thoughts: *Mananat trayate iti mantrah*.

When we connect our *bhavana* or feelings to our ishta through mantra, the ishta awakens within us. This is why Pashupata dharma has given a clear directive to connect the mind to the mantra every day, after withdrawing it from worldly matters. The mantra may be *Aum, Aum Namah Shivaya, So-Ham,* or any other mantra: it does not matter. However, it is essential to practise japa.

During japa one must feel oneness with one's chosen deity. That is why, in the scriptures, the mantra *So-Ham* is given. *Sa* plus *aham*, 'That' plus 'I am', meaning 'I am That'. Some say this is a statement of Vedanta. It does not really matter whether this thought belongs to Vedanta, Samkhya or tantra; any idea or concept may relate to a system of philosophy, yet fundamentally it is related to the sadhaka and his life, if he wants to attain it. Therefore, forget the idea that this belongs to Vedanta, Shaiva, Vaishnava, Shakta, or some other philosophical system; the techniques of sadhana do not belong to any religion or to any sect or philosophy. Sadhana can be performed by any person, and a person chooses his religion, tradition or sect based on his feelings.

Whatever thought system suits you, imbibe that. However, when you are doing sadhana, you must follow the sequence set by the tradition. You might go to a doctor hoping for a sweet pill, but if he gives you a bitter pill, will you refuse it? What is your objective? Did you go there to have sweets or to get rid of your disease? That decision is yours. If you have to cure your disease, you have to listen to the doctor. Likewise, the system prescribed by the *parampara*, the tradition, has to be followed in sadhana.

You should not change a sadhana to suit your desires or your conveniences. Often people change the structure of sadhana in order to suit their convenience, yet instead of changing the sadhana, why don't they change their lifestyle? This is where you fail and do not attain any experience, as you keep dabbling here and there.

Once, a pandit sat in a boat and started rowing the boat, without untying it. The pandit enjoyed rowing the boat throughout the night; however, the boat did not move. All of you are in the same condition, yet when you do not attain any experience in the sadhana, you grumble and say, "This sadhana is of no use; the sadhus are misleading us. It is a scam for them to earn a living." A real sadhu does not mislead anyone; rather, you are poisoning your own mind. You want to make everything convenient for yourself so you don't follow the discipline of a tradition or a system of sadhana. If you follow the tradition, the system and its disciplines, then you will attain happiness, peace and prosperity in life. There is no doubt about this.

Shiva

I have talked a lot about Shiva, but in reality, who is he? What is the explanation? The word *Shiva* is made up of three letters: *sha, e* and *va*. In this context, *sha* stands for *nitya sukha* or eternal happiness and *ananda* or bliss. *E* means *purusha* or consciousness and *va* means Shakti in the form of *amrita* or nectar. When we utter 'Shiva', we refer to both Shiva and Shakti. It is very important to remember that the nectar form of Shakti and the transcendental Purusha, who is auspicious, benevolent and bestower of ananda, is called Shiva.

The word 'Shiva' points towards both Shiva and Shakti, and it is the most benevolent and auspicious element in creation. Shiva is jnana and Shiva is the ultimate experience. If Shiva is the goal, then bhakti is the means. Once again, ask yourself, "Who was there before creation and who will be here afterwards?" You will receive the answer, "Before creation, Shiva was there and he will be there after creation, and Shiva and Shakti are not different from each other."

Shiva is not male, nor is Shakti female; they are the eternal elements of the manifest and unmanifest creation, which expand into the world and accompanying life. The glory of Shiva is infinite. The credit for whatever I have said goes to Mahadeva and my guru, Swami Satyananda, through whose inspiration this discourse took place.

Hara Hara Mahadeva

Kṣamā Prārthanā

1. Mantrahīnaṃ kriyāhīnaṃ bhaktihīnaṃ sureśvara.
   Yatpūjitaṃ mayā deva paripūrṇaṃ tadastu me.
2. Āvāhanaṃ na jānāmi na jānāmi tavārchanam.
   Pūjāṃ chaiva na jānāmi kṣamasva parameśvara.
3. Pāpo'haṃ pāpakarmā'haṃ pāpātmā pāpasambhavaḥ.
   Trāhi māṃ pārvatīnātha sarvapāpaharo bhava.
4. Aparādhasahasrāṇi kriyante'harniśaṃ mayā.
   Dāso'yamiti māṃ matvā kṣamasva parameśvara.

Om śāntiḥ śāntiḥ śāntiḥ. Hariḥ om

220

Glossary

Abhaya mudra – 'mudra to dispel fear'; a gesture of benediction; gesture of fearlessness; see Mudra

Abhijit muhurta – astrological moment signifying victory

Acharya – one knowing or teaching the *acharas* or rules; teacher, preceptor, spiritual guide

Adharma – unrighteousness; unnatural or inappropriate behaviour; disharmony; not fulfilling one's natural role in life; wickedness, injustice, guilty or wicked deed, sin; all that is contrary to dharma and the law; demerit

Adhibhautika – suffering which proceeds from extrinsic causes such as other people, beasts, birds or inanimate objects; in Samkhya philosophy, one of the threefold causes of misery, viz. 1. adhyatmika, 2. adhibhautika and 3. adhidaivika

Adhidaivika – pertaining to heaven or celestial beings; extrinsic sufferings due to supernatural causes; in Samkhya philosophy, one of the threefold causes of misery, viz. 1. adhyatmika 2. adhibhautika 3. adhidaivika

Adhyatmika – pertaining to the *atma* (soul); relating to oneself or to the law of life; that which proceeds from intrinsic causes, such as disorders of the body and mind; in Samkhya philosophy, one of the threefold causes of misery, viz. 1. adhyatmika 2. adhibhautika 3. adhidaivika

Adi – beginning, commencement; first, primary

Aditi – boundlessness, immensity; mother of the gods known as Adityas

Advaita – non-duality; not divided into two parts; monistic vision of reality; of one or uniform nature; that for which there is no other, especially referring to Brahman/Atman; union of soul and matter; union with the supreme existence or Brahman; see Vedanta

Agama – historical sacred literature, 'that which has come down', 'to carry on' or 'to go forward'; the philosophy and scriptures of tantra where Lord Shiva teaches his consort Parvati; esoteric tradition of tantra suitable for the present age of Kali yuga; testimony or proof of an acceptable authority because the source of knowledge has been checked and found trustworthy

Aghora – that which is not ghora; that which is peaceful; 'one for whom nothing is abominable'; one who is totally in tune with their nature, having mastered the elements; totally innocent; in the Shaiva agamas Sadashiva's third face is known as aghora

Agni – fire; the god of fire; fire of the stomach, digestive faculty; metabolism; the third mahabhoota in Samkhya philosophy

Ahamkara – ego; egoism or self-conceit; the self-arrogating principle 'I', self-consciousness; the principle responsible for the limitations, division and variety in the manifest world; in yoga, the rajasic state of consciousness limiting awareness of existence

Ahimsa – absence of violence from within; non-violence; harmlessness, abstaining from killing or giving pain to others in thought, word or deed; general attitude of welfare for the entire world; one of the yamas as described in Sage Patanjali's *Yoga Sutras*

Ahimsa loka – the highest of the fifty-six lokas which exist above the twenty-eight lokas of Rudra according to the Shaiva scriptures. The city of Jnana Kailash, residence of Sadashiva, is in this loka

Aishwarya – inner wealth; regal or divine qualities; in the tantra agamas it means a balanced, awakened, intuitive, discriminative and sattwic state of mind endowed with all the divine qualities; material or spiritual wealth;

supremacy, sovereignty, power; divine attributes like wisdom, renunciation and others

Ajna chakra – the third eye, the command or monitoring psychic/ pranic centre; guru chakra. Physically, the concentration point is situated at the medulla oblongata at the top of the spinal column in the midbrain, corresponding to the pineal gland; see Chakra

Ajnana – lack of knowledge or wisdom; ignorance, non-cognizance; unawareness

Akasha – element of ether, space, sky; to shine, to appear; in Samkhya philosophy: the first mahabhoota; that which fills all space; the three internal spaces most often used in meditation are chidakasha, daharakasha and hridayakasha; see Pancha mahabhoota

Akshara – literally, indestructible, non-decaying refers to the letters of the Sanskrit alphabet; letter, form; quality of a mantra; syllable; sounds which do not die; fixed, firm

Amrit – nectar; literally 'deathless'; immortal; life; the nectar of immortality which descends from bindu; also called soma

Amurta sadakhya – the second face or aspect of Shiva as the one who is facing north, its brilliance is equivalent to one million suns. Its shape is that of a luminous pillar; it is responsible for the creation of *prapancha*, the delusion of the world, and also for its dissolution

Anahata chakra – psychic centre in the region of the heart, the vibration or 'beat' of which regulates life from birth to death; corresponds to the cardiac plexus in the physical body; corresponds to hridayakasha in meditative practices; centre of emotions which, when developed, gives the psychic force to materialize desires; centre where Shiva and Shakti unite; see Chakra

Ananda – peace, joy and fulfilment; pleasure, happiness; pure unalloyed bliss; state of consciousness; in Vedanta, one of the three attributes of the ultimate principle; a name of Shiva

Anandavana – literally the garden of bliss, another name for Kashi (Varanasi)

Anatmaka – the cessation of all *kleshas* or afflictions

Anugraha – divine grace, kindness, assistance; the ability to be established in the state beyond tirobhava; the fifth of Shiva's five basic actions: sustenance; see Panchakritya

Anushthana – a resolve to perform a mantra or other sadhana with absolute discipline for a requisite period of time; a fixed course of sadhana; systematic performance of religious practices undertaken usually for some definite period of time, for example, forty days

Apana – one of the five energies (pancha pranas), moving downwards from the navel to the perineum, governing the lower abdominal region and responsible for elimination and reproduction; downward moving breath; see Pancha prana

Aparigraha – freedom from covetousness; abstention from greed; non-receiving of gifts conducive to luxury; without possessions or belongings; one of the five yamas described by Sage Patanjali in the *Yoga Sutras* as a preliminary discipline of yoga; see Yama

Aradhana – worship, tapasya, sadhana; to be fully immersed in worship of the deity

Aradhya – the object of adoration and worship

Arati – rite of worship involving the waving of lights before a deity

Archana – offering of flowers or other items at the time of worship; honouring; reverence or respect paid to deities and superiors; the sixth step of navadha bhakti

Ardhanarishwara – the androgynous or half-male, half-female form that is Shiva and Shivaa combined; the concept of ida and pingala nadis in yogic philosophy

Argha – a symbol of Shivaa or Shakti; the horizontal part of the shivalingam where the vertical lingam is placed; see Peetha

Artha – wealth; security; accomplishment; attainment in all spheres of life; material need; see Purushartha

Asat – non-existent; untrue; not being or existing, not manifest; in Vedanta, the passive aspect of the ultimate principle, Brahman

Asatya – untruth

Ashwamedha yajna – horse sacrifice; an elaborate vedic ceremony undertaken by kings to attain sovereignty

Asteya – honesty, not stealing; one of the yamas of Sage Patanjali's *Yoga Sutras*; see Yamas

Astra – weapon; projectile weapon such as an arrow, a spear or a missile

Asuras – demons; inhabitants of other dimensions usually in opposition to the gods; evil spirit

Atmamaya kosha – in which one merges oneself with the God element; see Kosha

Atmanivedana – absolute surrendering of one's Self to the Divine; the ninth step of navadha bhakti

Atmasamarpan – absolute offering of one's self to the Divine; the ninth step of navadha bhakti

Aum – universal mantra. In Sage Patanjali's *Yoga Sutras*, repetition of Aum and meditation on its meaning is the practice resulting in union with Ishwara. In Vedanta, Aum is regarded as Shabda Brahman and as the seed of the Vedas. In *Mandukya Upanishad*, the 'A' of Aum is explained as the waking state of consciousness, the 'u' as the subconscious, the 'm' as the unconscious and the whole reverberation to represent the superconscious state; the primordial nada, the sound body of Paramshiva

Aum Namah Shivaya – mantra which is also known as the panchakshari mantra; see Panchakshari mantra

Avadhana – attention, devotion, carefulness

Avadhana bhakti – a state of devotion which becomes possible through one-pointedness of the mind

Avadhuta – one who is free from all worldly attachments or mental illusions; an ascetic who has renounced the world and is usually naked; the sixth order of sannyasa; the highest state of asceticism or tapas

Avidya – ignorance; lack of conscious awareness; mistaking the non-eternal for the eternal; confined cognition; the chief of the five kleshas or sources of trouble and confusion described in Sage Patanjali's *Yoga Sutras*. In Vedanta, it is a mistake that considers the non-eternal, impure, evil and non-atman to be eternal, pure, good and atman; illusion personified or Maya; one of the five restricting cloaks of maya; see Kanchuka

Avimukta kshetra – realm of liberation (Kashi)

Baidya (Vaidya) – a therapist or a doctor

Bael – common name for the sacred bilva tree. Its leaves are often used in ritual worship; its fruit is invigorating. It is associated with Lord Shiva

Bhagavad Gita – *Gita*: 'divine song'; Lord Krishna's discourse to Arjuna delivered on the battlefield of Kurukshetra during the great Mahabharata war. It is one of the source books of Hindu philosophy containing the essence of the Upanishads and yoga

Bhagavan – the Lord; God

Bhajan – devotional song, praise, hymn; adoration, worship

Bhakti – devotion; worship of God; the means for self-transformation; complete devotion to the higher reality of life; love for all beings; devotion as service; channelling of emotion to a higher force

Bhava – feeling; love; condition; state, inclination or disposition of mind

Bhavana – emotion; feeling of devotion

Bhikshuni – a female bhikshu, beggar, mendicant or monk

Bheel – a tribal community

Bhoga – experience and craving for pleasure, enjoyment, delight through objects of pleasure

Bhogi – the experiencer; a person in love with the world

Bhoota – element; existing, real; an element or elemental; state of existence, being; what has come into being; an entity as opposed to the unmanifested; any of the five elementary constituents of the universe: earth, water, fire, air, space; see Mahabhoota

Bhutala – the realm of earth

Bhuvana – a being; mankind; world, earth, abode, residence; dimension, plane of existence; also called loka; see Loka

Bilva – a sacred tree. Its leaves are often used in ritual worship; its fruit is invigorating. It is associated with Lord Shiva. Commonly known as the bael tree

Bindu – point; seed, source, drop; the basis from which the first principle, maha tattwa, emanated according to the tantra; psychic centre located in the brain at the top of the head, where Hindu brahmins wear a tuft of hair; the most important psychic centre in nada yoga; semen

Brahma – the god of creation; created by Lord Shiva according to the Shaiva agama

Brahmacharya – conduct suitable for proceeding to the highest state of existence, especially continence or absolute control of sensual impulses. One of the yamas described by Sage Patanjali in the *Yoga Sutras* resulting in virya, indomitable courage, virility, power and energy

Brahmajnana – supreme knowledge; realization or immediate knowledge of Brahman

Brahman – the one existent reality, which is called Shiva in the Shaivite scriptures; supreme consciousness

Brahmana – integral part of the Vedas which elucidates the path of ritual to be followed by householders and explains the meaning and use of vedic hymns

Brahmanda – literally 'Brahma's egg', the cosmic egg, the macrocosmos

Brahmin – of the priestly caste; a person whose life is dedicated to the study of the Vedas and dispensation of the knowledge of Brahman and is thus qualified to act as a priest in vedic rituals; one of the four guilds or divisions of the caste system in India

Bhrashta – fallen from the way of yoga or spiritual life

Buddha – enlightened soul

Buddhi – intellect; discerning, discriminating aspect of mind; the faculty of valuing things for the advancement of life

Chaitra – first lunar month of the year corresponding to March/April according to the Hindu almanac, and containing the Chaitra Navaratri festival

Chandra – moon; shining, bright; representing mental energy

Chappati – Indian flat bread

Charitra – narrative; character, personality

Chaturyuga – the cycle of four yugas: Satya Yuga, Treta Yuga, Dwapara Yuga and Kali Yuga

Chintan – contemplation; thinking, thought; care, anxiety

Chiranjeevi – one who does not grow old

Chitta – individual consciousness, including the subconscious and unconscious layers of mind; thinking, concentration, attention, enquiry; the stuff of the mind; storehouse of memory or samskaras; one of the four parts of the total mind

Dal – a savory dish made of pulses

Dacoit – gangster

Daitya – demon; child of Diti

Daksha – celebrated lord of created beings (Prajapati), one of the ten sons of Brahma; able, competent, expert, skilful; suitable; upright, honest

Dakshina (Dakshinaa) – offering to the guru, teacher or deity

Dakshin (Dakshina) – the right side; the right hand or arm; situated to the south, southern; sincere, straightforward, honest; epithet of Shiva or Vishnu

Damaru – an hourglass-shaped hand drum; one of the accoutrements of Lord Shiva

Danu – wife of Kashyapa who gave birth to the *danavas* (demons)

Darbar – the king's court

Darshan – a glimpse, seeing, observing; sight, vision; knowing, understanding; philosophical system of the vedic tradition based on revelations or truths that were 'seen' in a higher state of consciousness

Dasya bhava – cultivating the inner attitude of being a servant of God; the fifth step in navadha bhakti

Devadatta – one of the minor pranas which provides for the intake of extra oxygen in a tired body by causing a yawn; name of the conch-shell of Arjuna

Devalaya – 'residence of God'; a place where, through the power of shraddha or faith, God manifests as a conscious entity

Devarishi – a rishi or seer able to travel through the divine lokas or dimensions

Devata – god; form of divine dignity or power; divine being representing the higher state of evolution; illumined form; divinity, deity; the presiding deities or illumining powers of the five sense organs

Dhananjaya – minor prana responsible for decomposition of the body after death; another name of Arjuna

Dharma – enjoined duty, the natural role one plays in life; ethical law; duty; the laws or fundamental support of life; usage, practice, custom; religion; virtue, righteousness, good work; regarded as one of the four aims of human existence; see Purushartha

Dhyana – spontaneous state after deep concentration or meditation; the seventh of the eight steps described in raja yoga; the intermediate internal process where the power of attention becomes so steadily fixed upon the object of meditation that other thoughts do not enter the mind; natural expression of the sattwic state

Diti – mother of all the demons or daityas

Divya – divine; divine power

Drashta – witness, uninvolved observer, onlooker, seer; the consciousness which knows what is going on; atman or purusha

Dravana – to dispose of

Dukha – grief, pain, suffering; illness

Dukhanta – cessation of suffering

Duryodhana – the eldest of the one thousand Kaurava princes and arch enemy of Arjuna

Dvaita – dual; duality

Dwija – 'twice born'; a person who has had a rebirth through knowledge or initiation; a brahmin; used also for a person of the kingly and warrior caste, *kshatriya*, or the merchant caste, *vaishya*, whose investiture with the sacred thread makes up a second birth

Dwapara Yuga – the third aeon of the world, consisting of 864,000 years according to *Suryasiddhanta*

Ekadasha Rudra – eleven Rudras named Kapali, Pingala, Bhima, Virupaksha, Vilohita, Shasta, Ajapada, Ahirbudhnya, Shambhu, Chanda and Bhava. When Brahma's manasputras refused to join in the work of creation, he fainted, and Paramshiva manifested from Brahma's forehead in the form of Rudra and created eleven more beings similar to him. Rudra is a full manifestation of Paramshiva and is also called Shiva. The eleven pranas in the human body are the eleven Rudras according to the Shaiva scriptures. They were also reborn as the sons of Kashyapa's cow, Surabhi, in order to save heaven from the demons

Ekagrata – one-pointedness of mind where pure sattwaguna dominates enabling concentrated or meditative states of mind

Ekakshara – literally having one letter or one syllable, usually referring to the mantra *Aum/Om*

Gaja – elephant

Ganadhyaksha – chief of the ganas; epithet of Ganesha

Ganas – close assistants, attendants and companions of Lord Shiva; crowd, group; troop; the army of Ganesha

Gandha – smell

Gandharva – celestial musician; celestials who engage in musical arts, dancing and singing; singer in general

Ganga – the river Ganges, the most sacred river in India; the Ganges personified as a goddess; the eldest daughter of Himavat, king of the mountains

Garbha – womb; belly; embryo; act of conception; inside, middle or interior of anything; offspring of the sky

Ghat – river bank; place of cremation (by a river bank)

Ghata – mud pot

Ghora – terrible; dreadful; violent

Guna – quality; subordinate or constituent part; attribute, characteristic or property contained within all of creation consisting of varying amounts of the three different aspects called gunas, viz. sattwa, rajas and tamas. The three gunas undergo transformation from the unmanifest, *avyakta*, to the manifest, *vyakta*, state, produce matter and control it, thus creating the whole cosmos. They relate directly to the human character; strength

Guru – 'one who dispels darkness', caused by ignorance; teacher; preceptor; teacher of the science of ultimate reality who, because of extended practice and previous attainment of the highest states of meditation, is fit to guide others towards evolution

Hamsa – swan, goose, duck, flamingo; vehicle of Brahma and Saraswati. In poetic convention it is represented as being able to separate milk from water as it possesses the ability of subtle discrimination

Hiranyagarbha – 'golden womb'; cosmic subtle body; the golden egg or womb of creation; golden seed of the unity of life. Hiranyagarbha is the first formation from the formless, the beginning of all time and space. The history of the universe and of human beings is unwinding from this everlasting, all pervading timeless centre

Hiranyakashipu – celebrated demon king and father of Prahlada. He was slain by Vishnu to save Prahlada, a great devotee of Lord Vishnu

Iccha shakti – the power of desire; creative force or desire which is the first manifestation of the greater mind; omnipotent desire, force

Indra – king of the vedic gods, the ruler of heaven; lord of the senses; the mind or the soul; the rain god

Indriya – sense organ; power, force; physical power or virility; power of the senses

Ishana – divinity; Surya or the sun; a face of Shiva; Purusha, consciousness; srotra, hearing; vani, speech; shabda, sound and akasha or space, manifest from Sadashiva's Ishana face; ruler, master, lord; name of Shiva; the Sun as a form of Shiva; name of Vishnu

Ishta (devata) – chosen deity; object of desire; the chosen ideal; the particular form of God one is devoted to; worshipped, reverenced, beloved; liked, favourite, dear; a sacrificial rite

Ishwara – higher reality; unmanifest existence; non-changing principle or quality; a state of consciousness beyond the physical and mental realms governing the entire physical universe; Supreme Being, lord, master; one who rules; powerful, able, capable

Ishwara pranidhana – cultivation of faith in the supreme or indestructible reality; one of the niyamas described by Sage Patanjali in the *Yoga Sutras*; complete dedication of one's actions and will to the Lord

Itihasa – history

Jala – water

Jalebi – usually orange, pretzel-shaped pastry deep fried in sugar

Japa – repetition of a mantra or name of God, to repeat continuously without a break

Jata – the matted hair or locks of hair of sadhus and ascetics

Jathara – digestion; the digestive faculty; gastric fluid; belonging to or being in the stomach; abdominal area

Jatharagni – the digestive fire

Jrimbhanastra – an arrow to cause yawning

Ji – a suffix denoting respect

Jiva – a being, a spirit, a bound soul, a soul entrapped in the world; principle of life, vital breath; individual or personal soul; life, existence; creature, living being; living, existing, vivifying

Jivan – life; existence; the principle of life; vital energy; water; livelihood, profession, means of existence; enlivening, animating, life-giving

Jivanmukta – a soul who is liberated while living; a person who, being purified by true knowledge of the supreme reality, is freed from future births and all ceremonial rites while yet embodied

Jivanmukti – final liberation in the present state of life; expanded state of awareness

Jnana – knowing, understanding; hearing; consciousness, cognizance; higher knowledge derived from meditation or from inner experience; wisdom

Jnana Kailash – the city in Ahimsa Loka where Sadashiva resides; see Loka

Jnanamaya – composed of wisdom; full of knowledge; the characteristic of the immortal lokas; see Loka

Jnanendriya – sensory organ; five subtle organs of perception, viz. ears, *karna*; skin, twacha; eyes, *chakshu*; tongue, *jihva* and nose, *nasika*

Jyoti – flame; light, brightness

Jyotirlingam – natural oval-shaped stone worshipped as Lord Shiva; there are twelve jyotirlingams worshipped in different parts of India; symbol of pure consciousness; induces concentration of mind, the effulgent Shivalingam in sahasrara symbolizing the illumined state of consciousness

Jyotisha – astronomy; the eye of the Vedas; a tool in yoga to ascertain the auspicious times for different practices; one of the six sciences auxiliary to the Vedas; the Vedanga that deals with astronomical and astrological matters with respect to vedic karma

Kaala – time; fourth of the pancha kalaa. Kaala is that which makes one emotionally attached to different beings, mistaking them for the Brahman or the reality; black or dark blue colour; time (in general); proper time or portion of time; time considered as one of the nine substances; one of the five *kanchuka* (limiting aspects of energy) which creates the dimension of time and restricts the individual within it; one of the eight bhairavas or of states consciousness; the supreme spirit regarded as the destroyer of the universe; epithet of Shiva as a personification of the destructive principle or law of existence; Yama, the god of death; the planet Saturn; the weather

Kaalachakra – the immortal dimension beyond the lokas subject to laya and the abode of the Cosmic Self; wheel of time. See Loka; see Jnanamaya

Kama – desire; passion; emotional need for fulfilment; wish, object of desire; affection, love; semen, virility; desire for sensual enjoyments, considered as one of the four ends of life; the god of love

Kailash – name of a mountain peak of the Himalayas; residence of Shiva and Kubera

Kalaa – one of the five *kanchuka* (limiting aspect of energy) which restricts the creative power of individual consciousness and body; the manifest universe of time and space; ray or force which emanates from the nucleus of bindu due to vibrations caused by nada; part of a letter or word; art; the shakti which manifests as the five *bhootas* or the elements; see Pancha kalaa

Kalasha – pot; copper vessel

Kali – goddess of destruction and wife of Lord Shiva; epithet of Parvati or Durga; divine mother; primal manifestation of Shakti who destroys time, space and object (i.e. ignorance); yogic state of consciousness; blackness, night

Kali Yuga – the age of Kali, which some sources say lasts 432,000 years and is the fourth and current era (yuga) of the world now more than 5,000 years old, the 'iron' age, dark, evil, difficult and full of strife; see Yuga

Kalpa – ritual, ceremony; one of the six auxiliary sciences (Vedanga) of the Vedas; the *Kalpa Sutras* are manuals that provide meticulous details of the processes and rules of yajna; according to *Suryasiddhanta*, a kalpa lasts 4,320,000,000 years and consists of many mahayugas. Two kalpas make a day and a night of Brahma

Kanchuka – 'sheath' or 'envelope'; veil or covering of consciousness; invisible cloak of maya which limits or restricts consciousness and creates the notion of duality; five in number, viz. 1. kalaa: limits the power to do all 2. vidya: limits the power to know all 3. raga: creates like and dislike 4. kaala: limits perpetual existence by creating the notion of time 5. niyati: limits freewill; see Pancha kalaa

Kanya – young girl; virgin

Kanyadana – the handing over of one's daughter in marriage

Karana – the unmanifested potential cause that, in due time, takes shape as the visible effect; material cause of the universe remaining during the period of dissolution; the generative cause, creator, father; the origin; ground, motive; reason

Karma – action and result; action in the manifest and unmanifest dimension; work, deed; duty; in vedic parlance, karma means a sacrificial rite, *yajna*; law of cause and effect that operates inexorably throughout the universe and shapes the destiny of each individual with actions inevitably bearing their fruit; it also implies devoted action to alleviate the suffering of the afflicted; each individual spirit, *jiva*, is under the influence of karma

Karmamaya – getting attached to karmas; the dimension in which one is involved in the wheel of karma. It is this dimension which a human being evolves through according to the Shaiva scriptures.

Kamandalu – a water pot

Karma yoga – the process of freeing oneself from karmas by renouncing the fruits of actions; the yoga that reveals the secret of action; action performed with meditative awareness; dynamic spirituality; yogic path of selfless service; yogic discipline based on the law of cause and effect; gaining immunity to karma by dedicating one's actions to God; actions performed unselfishly for the welfare of others

Karmendriya – motor organs, five physical organs of action, viz. vocal chords, *vach*; hands, *hasta*; feet, *pada*; genital organs, upastha, and anus, *payu*

Karya – action; effect (correlate of karma); the physical body is described as the karya, whereas the causal body is described as the *karana* (cause); the world; what ought to be done or performed, duty

Kashi – Shiva's city, the modern Varanasi, also known as Anandavana and also as Avimukta kshetra

Kashyapa – name of a rishi who was the father of gods and demons. He was the son of Marichi, who was a son of Brahma and bore an important share in the work of creation. It is said that Kashyapa married the thirteen daughters of Daksha. Through Aditi he begot the twelve gods (adityas) and by Diti the demons (daityas). With his other wives he had numerous and diversified progeny such as serpents, reptiles, birds and nymphs of the lunar constellation. The father of the gods, demons and all living beings, he is therefore often called Prajapati, the progenitor

Kathakara – storyteller

Kedareshwara – the first Shivalingam on earth, manifested as a result of the austerities of sages Nara and Narayana

Khechari mudra – 'the attitude of moving in space'; tongue lock; a hatha yoga practice in which the elongated tongue passes back into the pharynx to stimulate the flow of life-giving nectar (amrit), whereas in the milder raja yoga form the tongue is inserted in, or folded backwards towards, the upper cavity of the palate

Kinnara – celestial musicians

Kirata – a tribal hunter

Kirtan – singing God's names; the second step of the ninefold path of devotion; see Navadha bhakti

Kleshas – five afflictions or causes of suffering described in Sage Patanjali's *Yoga Sutras*, viz. ignorance, *avidya*; ego or sense of doership, *asmita*; attraction, *raga*; aversion, *dwesha,* and fear of death, *abhinivesha*

Kop bhavan – the quarters reserved for the lady of the house when she is annoyed

Kosa – a unit of measurement equal to about three kilometres

Kosha – sheath; body or realm of experience or existence; covering of the self which limits manifestation of the ultimate reality; the human being is usually said to have five koshas: annamaya, pranamaya, manomaya, vijnanamaya and anandamaya. Rishi Upamanyu also teaches of a sixth kosha, atmamaya kosha

Krikala (Krikara) – name of one of the subsidiary pranas, whose function is to prevent substances going up the nasal passages and into the throat by bringing on sneezing and coughing, also induces hunger and thirst

Kripa – blessing; grace; mercy

Kritya – action to be done; duty

Krishna – black, dark; eighth incarnation of Vishnu who took birth in Dwapara Yuga as the son of Dewaki. He was brought up in Vrindavan by Yashoda, and loved Radha.

His activities are recorded in the *Bhagavata Purana*. He later reclaimed his inheritance and married the princess Rukmini. To uphold dharma he orchestrated the Mahabharata war. His teachings to his friend and disciple Arjuna during that war are immortalized in the *Bhagavad Gita*. He is perhaps the most celebrated hero in Indian culture

Kriyatmaka yoga – the systematic and organized forms of yoga practices as categorized in the Shaiva agamas

Kriya shakti – the power of action

Kriyoparama yoga – the state where all the systematic practices of yoga end or culminate and one becomes established in yoga; see Kriyatmaka yoga

Kshama loka – the lowest of the fourteen lokas of Vishnu and the highest of the fourteen lokas of Rudra according to the Shaiva scriptures

Kshatriya – one of the four divisions of the caste system in India, the kingly or warrior caste; one who protects others from injury

Kshetra – field, area; ground; place of origin, womb; sphere of action; the body; the mind; dimension; field of influence; place; chakra trigger points

Kshetrajna – knower of the field, body or dimension; the divine consciousness which resides within; the immanent aspect of the Supreme Self

Kubera – treasurer of the gods

Kula – family; lineage

Labha – benefit; one of Ganesha's sons

Lakshmi – the goddess of wealth and prosperity, and wife of Vishnu; good fortune; loveliness, grace; success, accomplishment; creative power of manipura chakra

Laya – dissolution; disappearance, extinction, destruction; union, fusion, melting

Lila – 'play'; diversion, pleasure; activity of Prakriti and its three gunas; the five actions of Paramshiva; see Panchakritya

Lingam – symbol; mark, sign, characteristic; sign of gender, male organ; idol of Shiva; a naturally formed oval stone;

often means the Shivalingam, an archetypal symbol; organ of creation

Loka – open space, place, region; plane of existence, dimension; the world, earth; people, humankind; of the twenty-eight planes of consciousness or regions, the highest seven are called loka, viz. bhuh, bhuvah, swah, mahah, janah, tapah and satya lokas; the Shaiva scriptures describe fourteen lokas of Brahman (Patala to Satya), fourteen lokas of Vishnu (Satya to Kshama), twenty-eight lokas of Rudra (Kshama to Shuchi), and fifty-six more lokas (Shuchi to Ahimsa). All these lokas are subject to *laya* or dissolution. Above them is Kaalachakra, the abode of the Virat Purusha, which is eternal

Madhurya – sweetness

Madhurya bhava – attitude of lover and beloved towards the Lord

Maha – big; great; noble

Mahabhoota – the elements of *akasha*, space; *vayu*, air; *agni*, fire; *jala*, water and *prithvi*, earth

Mahaprana – prana in its cosmic unmanifest aspect

Maharshi – 'great seer'; a great rishi, sage or saint; singer of vedic hymns

Mahatma – 'great soul'; saint; used with reference to a person who has destroyed the ego and realized the self as one with all; high-souled, high-minded, magnanimous, noble;

Mahat – great; greater mind; the great principle; the total mind which includes manas, buddhi, chitta and ahamkara; universal intellect (also called buddhi); in Samkhya philosophy mahat is the first evolute from Prakriti's process of manifestation; big, large, vast; abundant; epithet of Shiva

Maha tattwa – 'the great element', the third of twenty-five principles of Samkhya; of great essence; see Mahat

Mahavidya – ten forms of shakti representing the subtle teachings of Shakta tantra: Kali, Tara, Bhuvaneshi, Shodashi, Sri Vidya, Bhairavi, Chinnamasta, Dhumavati, Bagalamukhi and Kamala

Mahima – glory; greatness; glory, majesty, dignity; might, power; high or exalted rank or position; one of the eight major siddhis, the power of increasing size at will

Mala – rosary; garland, necklace; in yoga a mala may be made of beads of various substances such as tulsi, rudraksha, sandalwood or crystal. One function is to aid mantra repetition

Manana – focusing the mind on one thought; thinking, cognition, reflection, intelligence, understanding; inference arrived at by reasoning; meditation on the eternal verities

Manasputra – a son born through will or sankalpa; mentally conceived

Mandap – the central platform created to conduct a ceremony or ritual

Manikarnika – famous cremation ghat in Varanasi

Manipura chakra – manipura: 'city of jewels'; psychic/pranic centre situated behind the navel in the spinal column, corresponding to the solar plexus and associated with vitality and energy; centre of willpower

Manishi – thinker

Mantra – a word or sentence propounded by liberated souls to help spiritual aspirants and ordinary people in gaining perfection, health or supernatural powers; vedic hymn; a sacred text; word of power; divine power transmitted through word; incantation; subtle sound vibration; tantric tool which liberates energy and expands the consciousness

Manu – the first law-giver; name of a celebrated personage regarded as being the representative and father of the human race, sometimes regarded as one of the divine beings; name of the fourteen successive progenitors or sovereigns of the earth, the third Manu is supposed to be a type of secondary creator who produced the ten Prajapatis or Maharishis and to whom the code of laws known as *Manu Smriti* is ascribed

Manvantara – era of each creation; the first Manvantara was Swayambhu Manu's and now the twenty-seventh is

Vaivasvata Manu's. The great dissolution or *mahapralaya* occurs after each manvantara

Maryada – the spontaneous correct response to any situation, an attribute particularly notable in Sri Rama

Maryada purushottama – a person with the highest ideals

Maya – power of illusion; partial understanding; wrong or false notions about self-identity; cause of the phenomenal world; in Vedanta philosophy, the two powers of maya are: 1. the power of veiling (*avarana shakti*) 2. the power of projection (*vikshepa shakti*); in Samkhya philosophy, pradhana or Prakriti (nature)

Moksha – liberation, freedom, release; state of existence; in yoga, final emancipation, liberation from the wheel of birth and death, the aim of yogic practices; see Purushartha

Mooladhara chakra – the basic psychic and pranic centre in the human body, situated in the perineum in men and the cervix in women; connected to the coccygeal plexus; the seat of *kundalini* (the primal evolutionary energy in human beings)

Mrita sanjivani vidya – science of reviving the dead

Mrityu – death

Mudha – dullness; a dull state of mind; perplexed, confounded; foolish, stupid; a forgetful state of mind; state of ignorance or forgetfulness of one's real nature in which tamas predominates and the mind is in such a dull state that at times thinking also ceases to manifest

Mudra – 'gesture'; physical, mental and psychic attitude which expresses and channels cosmic energy (technically bandhas are also a type of mudra); psycho-physiological posture, movement or attitude; a movement or position made or taken by the fingers or limbs in meditation as a result of the circulation of kundalini shakti; a seal, a sealing posture; also means 'grain', one of the panchamakara (five M's) of tantra; see Panchamakara

Mukta – liberated soul

Mukti – release, liberation; according to Vedanta, liberation is due to right knowledge or intuition of truth; final absolution of the self from the chain of birth and death

240

Muni – a mendicant, sage, ascetic; one who contemplates; one who has conquered the mind; one who maintains silence or stillness of mind

Nada – subtle sound vibration created by the union of Shiva and Shakti tattwas; subtle sound vibration heard in the meditative state; voice, sound, cry, roaring; primal sound or first vibration from which all creation has emanated; the first manifestation of the unmanifested absolute; Aumkara (Omkara) or Shabda Brahman

Naga (Naagaa) – militant sannyasa sect; an order of sadhus distinguishable by their nakedness

Naga (Naaga) – snake; fabulous serpent-demon or semi-divine being with the face of a man and the tail of a serpent; elephant; of the five minor pranas, it relieves abdominal pressure by causing one to belch, also responsible for hiccupping

Nakshatra – constellation; star, asterism, heavenly body; star of birth; one of twenty-seven lunar mansions

Nara – water; name of an ancient sage said to be a companion of Narayana; decaying principle; matter; man, male, person, hero; supreme being, original or eternal man

Narayana – another name of Lord Vishnu; 'companion of man'; name of an ancient sage said to be a companion of Nara; the supporter of life; the life force

Nasadiya Sukta – a creation hymn from the *Rigveda Samhita*

Nata – dancer; performer

Navadha bhakti – ninefold bhakti; different elements are given in different texts, in the *Shiva Purana* they are listed as: shravana, kirtana, smarana, sevana, dasya, archana, vandana, sakhya and atmanivedana or atmasamarpan

Navami – the ninth lunar day

Netra – eye

Nidra – fourth basic instinct: deep sleep; isolation from mind and senses; unconscious state; shutting off; sloth; one of the five vrittis listed in Sage Patanjali's *Yoga Sutras*

Nilakantha –'blue-throated one', an epithet of Shiva

Nirakara – without form, formless; unmanifest

Nirguna – without any qualities; without attributes, formless

Nirmaya – negation of maya

Nishkala – beyond the limitations of form

Nitya – eternal; continual, perpetual

Nivritti – the path of renunciation of the world; lack of vrittis

Niyama – rule; observances or rules of personal discipline to render the mind tranquil in preparation for meditation; the second step of ashtanga yoga mentioned by Sage Patanjali in the *Yoga Sutras*. His niyamas include: 1. purity, *shaucha* 2 contentment, *santosha* 3. austerity, *tapas* 4. self-study, *swadhyaya* 5. dedication to the highest principle, *Ishwara pranidhana*; vedic text or explanation; doctrine

Niyati – power of God responsible for the control and management of the entire creation; destiny; that which is fixed

Om – See Aum

Palana – maintaining creation in an orderly state; sustenance; second of Shiva's five basic actions; see Panchakritya

Pani – hand; one of the five organs of action (*karmendriyas*)

Payu – the anus; the organ of excretion, one of the five organs of action (*karmendriyas*)

Padasevana – literally worship of the guru's feet; humbly obeying the guru and applying the guru's teachings in daily life; the fourth stage of navadha bhakti in the Ramacharitamanas

Pancha – five

Panchagni – five fires; sadhana of sitting in the middle of four fires with the summer sun acting as the fifth fire

Panchakritya – Shiva's five basic actions: *srishti* or creation, *palana* or sustenance, *samhara* or destruction, *tirobhava* or veiling, and *anugraha* or grace

Panchabhootas – the five elements; see Pancha mahabhootas

Panchakshari mantra – literally the five-syllable mantra, it is 'Namah Shivaya' in the mantra *Aum Namah Shivaya*

Pancha kalaa – one of the two manifestations of Shakti from the Shivalingam. The five kalaas are: kalaa, vidya, raaga, kaala and niyati. They are also known as kanchuka; see Bhakti

242

Pancha kosha – five sheaths, bodies or realms of experience and existence, viz. 1. physical dimension, *annamaya kosha* 2. mental dimension, *manomaya kosha* 3. energetic dimension, *pranamaya kosha* 4. intuitive dimension, *vijnanamaya kosha* 5. blissful dimension, *anandamaya kosha*

Pancha mahabhootas – the five gross or atomic states of nature, consisting of ether or space, *akasha*; gases or air, *vayu*; light or fire, *agni*; liquids or water, *apas*, and solids or earth, *prithvi*. They are an extension of the tanmatras in the physical world

Panchamakara – five elements used in tantric ritual sadhana, all of which begin with the letter 'M', viz. *mudra* (psychic attitude), *mamsa* (flesh), *maithuna* (physical union), *matsya* (fish) and *madya* (wine). The category of aspirant determines the symbolic interpretation

Pancha prana – five major divisions of pranic energy in the physical body, viz. apana, prana, samana, udana, vyana

Pandava – a son or descendant of Pandu; the five brothers: Yudhishthira, Bhima, Arjuna, Nakula and Sahadeva who held an inter-family feud against the Kauravas as recorded in the *Mahabharata* epic

Pandit – priest; learned man; scholar; man of wisdom

Panigrahana – 'accepting the hand'; the ritual of marriage

Para – used in the *Bhagavad Gita* to indicate the supreme goal of life; other, different; distant, removed, remote; beyond; subsequent; higher

Parabrahman – the transcendental reality; absolute supreme reality

Paraloka – the dimension beyond; see Loka

Param – the highest point or pitch, culminating point; the supreme being; final beatitude; extreme, farthest; last, worst; best, excellent; conspicuous

Parampara – tradition

Parikrama – circumambulation

Pasha – leash, noose; snare, net for catching birds

Pashu – an animal, beast; a being who is bound; the bound soul; brute; in tantra it refers to a person living at the instinctive animal level of consciousness

Pashupata – 'master of animals'

Pashupata tantra –the philosophy and techniques that allow a person to master their animal tendencies and become liberated

Patala loka – the lowest of the fourteen lokas of Brahma according to the Shaiva scriptures; abode of serpents and demons; instinctive or animal realm; hell; seven planes of consciousness or regions described as being below mooladhara chakra, viz. atala, vitala, sutala, rasatala, talatala, mahatala, patala

Patanjali – author of the *Yoga Sutras*; an ancient rishi who codified the meditative stages and states of samadhi into the system of raja yoga and is famous as the propounder of ashtanga yoga

Pati – master, God or Ishwara; lord, ruler, husband

Peeth – seat; the horizontal part of the Shivalingam where the vertical lingam is placed. Also called argha, a symbol of Shivaa or Shakti; see Argha

Pitri – ancestor; departing ancestor; a divine hierarchy consisting of deceased progenitors and ancestors; father

Pooja – an honouring, showing respect; rites; worship

Poorna – complete; full, filled; whole, entire; accomplished; strong, powerful

Poornata – fulfilment

Poorva Phalguni – name of the eleventh lunar mansion

Prajapati – 'lord of created beings'; the god presiding over creation; an epithet of Brahma; epithet of the ten lords of created beings; a father; see Kashyapa

Prakriti – nature; individual nature; manifest and unmanifest nature; cosmic energy; the active principle of manifest energy; nature or primordial matter (source of the universe); according to Samkhya philosophy, Prakriti consists of three aspects or qualities called gunas: sattwa, rajas and tamas

Prana – vital energy force, essence of life permeating both the macrocosmos and microcosmos; the sum total of all energy residing within the universe, both in the unmanifest states and in manifest nuclear states; breath, respiration; principle of life; vital energy that functions in various ways for the preservation of the body and is closely associated with the mind; one of the *pancha prana* (five energy fields), which operates in the region of the heart and lungs; according to the Shaiva scriptures the eleven pranas are the eleven Rudras living inside each person. There are five pranas: prana, apana, samana, udana and vyana. There are five upapranas or sub-pranas: kurma, krikara, naga, devadatta and dhananjaya. There is also one master of them all, Mahaprana, who enters into the womb before birth, and when it leaves, the body dies

Pranam – bending, bowing, reverential salutation, obeisance, prostration; stopping

Pranam mudra – the attitude of prayer, a hand gesture in which the palms are joined together and the hands placed in front of the chest with the thumbs lightly touching the heart centre

Pranava – another word for the sacred syllable *Aum* (*Om*), the primal sound vibration; a kind of musical instrument; epithet of Vishnu. *Pra* means *prapancha* or 'the illusion of the world', *na* means 'non-existent' and *va* means 'for you'. Thus pranava means 'the illusory world does not exist for you'

Pratyabhijna – knowing; recognition or recovering consciousness; recollection

Pravritti – conduct, behaviour; employment, occupation, activity; continued effort, perseverance

Pravritti marga – path of extroversion; path of action of life in worldly society; the path of involvement with the world

Prapancha – the illusion of the world

Prem – love; affection

Prithvi – earth, literally 'the broad one'; the solid state of matter, in Samkhya philosophy it is the fifth mahabhoota

Purana – ancient scriptures; past event; ancient, old; name of a class of sacred texts believed to be composed by Rishi Vyasa

Purusha – 'who dwells in the city'; the body being the dormant receptacle of consciousness, the soul; the totality of consciousness; male, mankind; the supreme being,

God; in Samkhya philosophy, Purusha designates pure consciousness, undefiled and unlimited by contact with Prakriti or matter; consciousness; in the Shaiva scriptures, energy, skin, hands, touch and air, have all emanated from the face of Shiva called Purusha

Purushartha – human attainment; the four goals to be fulfilled in life: 1. wealth, *artha*; 2. desire, *kama*; 3. duty, *dharma,* and 4. liberation, *moksha*

Raga – attraction to what is pleasant; love, affection; passion, amorous feeling; likes; attitude of mind toward the object of your love; attachment, anything which colours the mind; colours, especially the colour red; one of the five causes of affliction (*kleshas*) described in Sage Patanjali's *Yoga Sutras* as being attracted or attached to what gives pleasure; musical scale; in the Shaiva agamas it is the third of the pancha kalaa

Rajas – one of the three constituent qualities or *gunas* of nature and all matter; dynamism; state of activity; creativity combined with ego involvement; emotion; restlessness; oscillation; as a personality trait it is expressed by the desire to dominate

Rakshasa – demon, evil spirit, goblin

Raksha – watch; protection; care

Rakshya – to protect

Rama – the hero of the epics *Ramayana* and *Ramacharitamanas*, the seventh incarnation of Vishnu as the son of Dasharatha and Kaushalya and the most dutiful disciple of Vishvamitra. He married Sita after performing the wonderful feat of bending Shiva's bow. On the eve of his coronation as king of Ayodhya, he was exiled for fourteen years through the scheming of his father's favourite wife, Kaikeyi. During his exile he killed the demon Ravana, thus fulfilling the main purpose of his incarnation; pleasing, rejoicing, delighting; beautiful, lovely, charming; obscure, dark-coloured, black; white

Ramacharitamanas – a version of the *Ramayana* written in a Hindi dialect by Tulsidas

Ramarajya – the time of Rama's reign, when no one lacked anything anywhere; contentment, happiness, fulfilment, absence of any want

Ramayana – literally 'the path of Rama', one of the most famous ancient Indian epics, composed by Valmiki, containing about 24,000 verses in seven chapters

Rasa – juice; serum found in the body tissues; taste

Rasana – sap

Richa – collection of mantras; single verse or stanza from the Vedas expressing shades of universal truth

Rishi – inspired poet, ascetic, anchorite, seer; realized sage; one who contemplates or meditates on the self; one who experiences other dimensions

Roti – Indian flat bread

Rudra – the aspect of Paramshiva entrusted with *samhara* or destruction; see Ekadasha Rudra; howling energy; deity of manipura chakra; name of Lord Shiva in the *Rigveda* meaning 'he who proclaims himself aloud'; signifies transformation through dissolution

Ruta dravana – an epithet of Rudra, literally, the one who disposes of sorrow

Satmaka – the end of all kleshas or afflictions and also attainment of bhakti and jnana

Sabji – vegetable

Sadachara – good conduct

Sadakhya – the five faces of Shiva (Sadashiva) in the Shaiva agamas: Shiva sadakhya, amurta sadakhya, murta sadakhya, kartri sadakhya and karma sadakhya

Sadashiva – 'always auspicious' or 'the eternal Shiva'; the five-faced Shiva is the manifest form of Paramshiva. He has ten hands, in which he holds a pot, a half-moon shaped sword, a bow and arrow, a spear, a trident, a conch, a discus, a *damaru* or small drum, a lotus, and his last hand is held in *abhaya mudra*, gesture of benediction. His body is white like camphor and all the faces have three eyes, matted locks and snakes garlanding the throat

Sadhana – spiritual practice; fulfilment, accomplishment, complete attainment of an object; expedient tool, implement, means of accomplishing anything; worship, adoration; propitiation; practice or discipline performed regularly for the attainment of inner experience and self-realization

Sadhu – sage, saint, ascetic; excellent, perfect; fit, proper, right; enough; righteous, honourable; kind; virtuous or holy person

Sadhya – the goal

Sadyojata – Sadashiva's form or face from which emanate *mana*, mind, *nasika*, nose, *upastha*, the generative organ, *gandha*, smell, and *prithvi*, earth

Saguna – with qualities or attributes (*guna*)

Sahasrara chakra – the thousand-petalled lotus; abode of Shiva or super-consciousness; highest chakra or psychic centre, which symbolizes the threshold between the psychic and spiritual realms and is located at the crown of the head

Sahasranama – thousand names

Sakala – complete, which implies manifestation with form; together with the parts, all, whole, entire

Sakara – with form; manifest

Sakhya – friendship; friendship with God is the eighth step of the ninefold path of devotion; see Navadha bhakti

Samabhavana – possibility; feeling of equality

Samadhi – culmination of meditation; state of unity with the object of meditation and the universal consciousness; final step of raja yoga; self-realization

Samana – one of the pancha prana, it is essential for digestion; a sideways moving flow of energy situated between the navel and diaphragm, which augments the pranic force of manipura chakra; the balancing force with the function of uniting prana and apana, an essential step in the awakening of kundalini; see Pancha prana

Samhara – destruction; destruction of duality; one of Shiva's five basic actions; see Panchakritya

Samkhya – number; one of the six systems of Indian philosophy (*shaddarshana*) and attributed to the sage

248

Kapila. Samkhya is a spiritual science dealing with the twenty-five elements of creation; relating to numbers, calculating, enumerating; discriminative, deliberating, reasoning; a reasoner; the philosophical basis of the yoga system

Samosa – hot pastry with savoury filling

Samriddhi – prosperity; success, wealth, abundance

Samsara – the world; illusory world, the manifest gross world; cycle of birth, death and rebirth, transmigration, metamorphosis, metapsychosis; passage; the course or circuit of worldly life, secular life, mundane existence; curse

Samsaralaya – the residence of the worldly

Sanga – company

Sankalpa – will, volition, positive resolve; purpose, aim, intention; determination, conviction; desire, wish; thought, idea, reflection, fancy, imagination

Sankalpa shakti – willpower

Sannyasa – dedication; complete renunciation of the world; abandonment of the temporal

Sannyasin – one who has taken sannyasa initiation; a yogi; one who is not dependent on the results of action

Santosha – contentment, satisfaction; one of the five niyamas enumerated by the *Yoga Sutras* of Sage Patanjali

Saraswati – goddess of knowledge, speech and learning represented as the daughter of Brahma; speech, voice, words; name of a river; see Vagdevi

Sarga – the creation of the world; see Srishti

Sarovar – lake

Sarvadhyaksha – lord of all; a title of Ganesha

Sarveshwara – ruler of all

Sat – existence; truth

Sati – Kali as Rudra's consort according to the Shaiva scriptures; a name of the goddess Durga; Sati, the daughter of Daksha Prajapati, immolated herself for her father's insult to her husband, Shiva, and was then reborn as Parvati, the daughter of Himalaya (or Himavanta). She married Shiva and became the mother of Kartikeya, the god of war, and Ganesha, the god of learning, wisdom and good luck. Sati's self-immolation was regarded so virtuous that women sometimes immolated themselves upon the death of their husband as an alternative to lifelong widowhood. Such a woman was called a sati. Gross abuse of this custom led to its being outlawed in the 19th century

Satsang – gathering in which the ideals and principles of truth are discussed; spiritual association; association with the wise and the good, along with the resolve and effort to express this in life

Sattwa – in Samkhya, one of the three constituent qualities or gunas of Prakriti and all matter; state of luminosity, harmony, equilibrium, steadiness; being, existence, reality, true essence; purity, balance or goodness; life, spirit, breath, principle of vitality; consciousness, mind, sense

Satya – true, real, genuine; honest, sincere, truthful, faithful; virtuous, upright; absolute truth; reality; one of the yamas described in Sage Patanjali's *Yoga Sutras*

Satya loka – one of the seven higher dimensions of consciousness; also called Brahma loka or the dimension of truth; the divine plane; the highest of the fourteen lokas of Brahma, and the lowest of the fourteen lokas of Vishnu according to the Shaiva scriptures

Satya Yuga – the age in which piety and righteousness predominated and the first of the four aeons (*yugas*) of the world, the 'golden' age lasting for 1,728,000 years according to *Suryasiddhanta*, the age of truth and purity; also called Krita Yuga; see Yuga

Sayujya – merging; abiding in the absolute

Senapati – lord of the army; commander in chief

Sevak – a servant

Sevana – service; the fourth step of the ninefold path of devotion; see Navadha bhakti

Shabda – the word; sound; object of the sense of hearing and property of space, *akasha*; musical note of birds, the human voice and the like; sound of a musical instrument; significant word; see Mantra

Shabdabrahman – the Vedas; spiritual knowledge conveyed in words; knowledge of the supreme existence or the spirit; the eternal sound that is the first manifestation of reality and lies at the root of all subsequent creation; the form or the sound body of Paramshiva; see Aum

Shadakshara – 'six syllables', refers to the mantra, *Aum Namah Shivaya*

Shaiva – one who worships Shiva as the supreme reality

Shakta – one who worships the various manifestations of Shakti in the form of Kali, Durga, Lakshmi, Saraswati and others; a sect in which Shakti (Devi or Ma) is worshipped as the supreme reality

Shakti – energy; primal energy; manifest consciousness; power, ability, capacity, strength, the power of composition, poetic power or genius; in Samkhya, the power inherent in a cause to produce its necessary effects; the female aspect of creation and divinity worshipped by the Shakta sect; power that is eternal and supreme and of the nature of consciousness; counterpart of Shiva; the moving power of nature and consciousness; in Hindu mythology Shakti is often symbolized as a divine woman

Shaktipeeth – 'seat of Shakti'; the sixty-four centres of Shakti worship across India. According to legend, when Sati immolated herself, Shiva was wild with grief and roamed the worlds with Sati's corpse on his shoulder. To pacify him, Vishnu cut up the corpse with his discus and the body parts fell at different places; each of these came to be known as a Shaktipeeth

Shankha – conch

Shanti – pacification, allayment, removal; peace, calmness, tranquillity, quiet, ease, rest; cessation, end; absence of passion

Sharanagati – surrender; seeking shelter

Shastras – scriptures, sacred book; any department of knowledge, science

Shatarupa – 'one hundred forms'; the name of the first female who was formed from the left side of Brahma, a tapasvini and accomplished yogini

Shiva – 'auspicious one' or 'good'; name of the god of the sacred Hindu trinity who is entrusted with the work of destruction; destroyer of ego and duality; the first or original yogi; cosmic consciousness, counterpart of Shakti; the manifest form of Paramshiva who first appeared as Sadashiva; see Sadashiva; see Rudra;

Shivaa – the female counterpart of Shiva, Shakti

Shivalaya – Shiva temple

Shivalingam – black oval-shaped stone of which those occurring naturally in the Narmada river are especially revered; symbol of Lord Shiva; symbol of consciousness; nishkala symbol of Lord Shiva; see Jyotirlinga

Shiva sadakhya – the first face or aspect of Shiva; the state of constant purity where there is no incompleteness, mark or darkness. The pure Shiva sadakhya is also the form of Sadashiva.

Shiva swaroopa – the nature of Shiva

Shiva yoga – the yoga described in Pashupata tantra

Sivaratri – the lunar day upon which Paramshiva manifested himself as Sadashiva; fourteenth night of the dark lunar fortnight in the month of Phalguna, which falls in February or March, on which a rigorous fast is observed in honour of the marriage of Shiva and Shakti

Shraddha – faith; trust, belief, confidence; belief in divine revelation, religious faith; sedateness, composure of mind; respect, reverence

Shravana – ear; the act of hearing; that which is heard or revealed, the Veda; hearing of the shrutis or scriptures; study; listening; the first stage of the ninefold path of devotion; see Navadha bhakti

Shubha – auspiciousness; one of Ganesha's sons

Shuchi loka – the pure radiant plane; the highest of the fourteen lokas of Vishnu, and the lowest of the twenty-eight lokas of Rudra according to the Shaiva scriptures

Shuddha – pure

Shudra – one of the four varnas or divisions of the caste system in India; one whose consciousness is least developed, due

252

to which one remains in ignorance; in the *Rigveda*, it refers to the soul yet to be purified by samskaras; one with a services-oriented tendency of mind or one engaged in such a profession

Shukra – sperm; the planet Venus; name of the preceptor of the demons (asuras) who by means of his magical powers restored the lives of demons killed in battle; name of fire

Shoonya – void; state of transcendental consciousness; state of darkness prior to enlightenment, referred to as 'the dark night of the soul'; mental vacuum; empty-hearted; vacant glance; listless; absent; non-existent, empty, deserted, wholly destitute; solitary; state of nothingness, zero

Siddha – master, one who has perfected sadhana; perfected being; sage, seer; semi-divine being of great purity and holiness; accomplished soul particularly characterized by eight supernatural faculties called siddhis

Siddhanta – spiritual theory; the established end; the demonstrated conclusion of an argument, established view of any question, the true logical conclusion; an established text book resting on conclusive evidence; a proven fact

Siddhi – paranormal or supernatural accomplishment; control of mind and prana; psychic abilities; eight supernatural powers obtained by yogis as a result of long practice. They are associated with opening the chakras and the resultant power over the elements, viz. 1. anima 2. laghima 3. prapti 4. prakamya 5. mahima 6. ishitvam 7. vashitva 8. garima; other siddhis include the power of entering other bodies, the ability to read another person's thoughts, clairvoyance, clairaudience, omniscience, effulgence, vanishing from sight, and more. They are considered to be obstacles on the path to realization because they maintain interest in samsara; see Samsara

Soma – name of a plant that was the most important ingredient in ancient sacrificial offerings; juice of a potent plant drunk during religious ceremonies to experience divine intoxication; the moon, which in mythology is represented as having sprung from the eye of the sage Atri or as having been produced from the sea at the time of churning; nectar of the gods, amrita;

Someshwara – a Shivalingam manifested due to the austerities of the moon god, Chandradeva or Soma

Smarana – remembrance or contemplation; the third step of the ninefold path of devotion; see Navadha bhakti

Sparsha – touch

Srishti – creation, manifest universe; manifestation, emanation; letting go

Srotra – hearing

Sthiti – state; sustenance; maintaining creation in an orderly state; condition; see Palana

Stotra – group of mantras sung in praise of a deity

Stuti – a hymn of praise; singing the praises of God

Sudarshan chakra – *sudarshan*: 'auspicious vision' or 'correct understanding' of reality, *chakra*: wheel; the name of the weapon, discus, of Lord Vishnu

Sukha – happiness, delight, joy, pleasure; prosperity; wellbeing, welfare, health; heaven; suitability, comfort

Surya – the sun; vital pranic energy; the sun god; symbol of the atma

Sutra – a brief statement which explains the ancient spiritual texts; thread, string, line, cord, fibre; short rule or precept; aphorism or condensed statements strung together to give an outline of a philosophy as in Sage Patanjali's *Yoga Sutras*

Swadhisthana chakra – literally 'one's own abode'; psychic/pranic centre situated at the base of the spinal column in the lumbar region (level of the generative organs), associated with the sacral plexus, and the storehouse of subconscious impressions

Swadhyaya – self-study; continuous conscious awareness of what one is doing; one of the niyamas in Sage Patanjali's *Yoga Sutras*; education of the self; study of the scriptures and texts of yoga; self-knowledge

Swarga loka – heavenly dimension; heaven

Swastika – mystical mark on a person or thing denoting good luck; lucky object; meeting of four roads; mansion or temple of a particular form

Swayambhu Manu – literally the self-illumined Manu; the name of the first male who was formed from the right side of Brahman. He was a sadhaka of the highest order

Swayamvara – selection of a husband by a woman in a public ceremony

Tamas – one of the three constituent qualities, *gunas*, of Prakriti and all matter; stability, stillness; ignorance, darkness; the gloom or darkness of hell; mental darkness; illusion, error; in yoga it is characterized by inertia, laziness, mental dullness, unwillingness to change

Tandava – dancing in general; particularly the powerful dance of Shiva, symbolizing the destruction of the universe; the art of dancing

Tanmatra – subtle nature; quality or essence of the elements, *mahabhootas*, and the associated five senses called jnanendriyas, viz. 1. sound, *shabda* 2. touch, *sparsha* 3. form, *rupa* 4. taste, *rasa* 5. smell, *gandha*

Tantra – most ancient universal science and culture which deals with the transition of human nature from the present level of evolution and understanding to a transcendental level of knowledge, experience and awareness; loom, thread, warps of thread extended lengthwise in a loom; main point, principle doctrine, rule; theory, science; scriptures devoted to spiritual techniques in the form of a dialogue between Shiva and Shakti forming a set of rules for ritual worship, discipline, meditation and the attainment of supernatural powers; a particular path of sadhana laying great stress upon mantra japa and other esoteric upasanas; from the roots *tanoti*, to expand, and *trayate*, to liberate

Tantric – related to tantra

Tapas – austerity; process of burning the impurities; warmth, heat, fire; pain, suffering; penance, mortification; meditation connected with the practice of personal self-denial; tapas in yoga means a burning effort which involves purification, self-discipline and austerity, a process in which the inner impurities covering the inner personality are completely eliminated

Tapasya – practice of austerity

Tapasvi (n) – ascetic, one who practises austerity or penance; devout

Tapasvini – female tapasvin

Tattwa – 'that-ness'; the truth about something, or the thing-in-itself; an element, a primary substance; essence, truth, reality; principle, category; the five basic elements: earth, water, fire, air and space; in Samkhya twenty-five tattwas are mentioned

Tejas – 'golden light or flame'; luminosity; edge or tip of a flame; fire, heat; light, brilliance, splendour; might, majesty; fire as an element or mahabhoota

Teertha – passage, road, way; fort; descent into a river; place of pilgrimage, a shrine dedicated to a holy object especially on or near the bank of a sacred river

Tirobhava – veiling; diversionary tactics to divert or stop the ascent of an individual to the source, and keep him engaged in material life; fourth of Shiva's five basic actions; see Panchakritya; see Anugraha

Tirthankara – a preceptor of the Jain sect

Treta Yuga – the second of the four aeons of the world, lasting for 1,296,000 years according to *Suryasiddhanta* and leading up to Satya Yuga; an aeon where goodness is on the rise

Trishula – trident often used as a symbol of the gunas or some other triad

Tulsi – the holy basil plant of India, sacred to Lord Vishnu and venerated by the Vaishnavas as most divine

Tvacha – skin; the power to feel, one of the five abstract knowing senses or jnanendriyas

Udana – one of the five pranas (energy fields), it is located in the extremities of the body: arms, legs and head. It rises up the throat and enters into the head

256

Upasya – one who is worshipped, the deity; that which is the object of upasana, namely God

Upasaka – the worshipper

Upadesha – advice; instruction; teaching

Upa pranas – five minor pranas, viz. krikara (or krikala), devadatta, dhananjaya, naga and kurma responsible for such actions as sneezing, yawning, decomposition, belching and blinking respectively

Upastha – the generative organ

Urdhwamukhi – moving upwards

Vagdevi – 'goddess of speech'; consort of Lord Brahma, goddess of wisdom and learning; see Saraswati; see Vak

Vaikuntha – epithet of Vishnu; epithet of Indra; heaven

Vaira – enmity

Vaishnava – those who worship Vishnu in the form of Rama, Krishna, Narayana and others; the sect that reveres incarnations of Vishnu as the supreme reality

Vaishya – one of the four divisions of the caste system, *varnas*; In India, those who specialize in trade or undertake the responsibility of caring for society

Vajra – thunderbolt

Vak – word, sound, speech

Vanaprastha ashrama – third stage of life, traditionally from fifty to seventy-five years of age, where one retires from worldly life in order to practise sadhana in relative seclusion

Vanaprasthi – one who retires to the forest

Vandana – prayer, worship; literally bowing down before God; actually living like the being you are worshipping and letting go of your ego; the seventh of the nine steps of bhakti

Vani – speech

Vamadeva – name of a form or face of Shiva. *Buddhi*, intellect, *rasana*, sap, *payu*, anus, *rasa*, serum found in body tissues, and *jala*, water, emanate from Sadashiva's Vamadeva form or face

Varadana – benefaction; the bestowal of a boon

Varga – a class, category; group of letters in the Devanagari alphabet

Varna – caste; the four main castes recognized as part of society are brahmin, kshatriya, vaishya and shudra; colour, hue; paint; complexion, beauty; class of men, tribe, race, kind, species; groups of letters in the Sanskrit alphabet

Vasana – deep-rooted desire; subtle desire; knowledge derived from memory; fancy, imagination, idea; false idea, ignorance; wish, inclination; mental disposition; a tendency created in a person by performing an action or by enjoyment, which then induces the person to repeat the action or to seek a repetition of the enjoyment; subtle impressions acting like seeds in the mind capable of germinating or developing into action; the cause of birth and experience in general

Vayu – god of wind; wind, air; vital air

Vedanta – 'the last part of the Vedas'; the Upanishads; Vedanta teaches the ultimate aim and scope of the Vedas. It states that there is one eternal principle, Brahman

Vedi – altar; platform; place near the fire pit in a *yajna* (sacrifice)

Vidhi – method; doing; performance, practice, an act or action; manner, way, means, mode; rule, commandment, any precept which enjoins something for the first time; sacred precept or rule

Vidya – spiritual knowledge; second of the pancha kalaa. That shakti which becomes the cause of karmas and through which karma is fulfilled, is called vidya; from the root 'vid' or inner knowledge; higher knowledge, learning, lore, science

Vikara – impurity; modification or change, generally with reference to the modifications of the mind

Virat – 'enormous'; the sum total of the entire manifest universe; macrocosm; the physical world that we perceive; the Lord in the form of the manifest universe

Virat purusha – the cosmic person who lives in Kaalachakra, beyond dissolution; the deity presiding over the universe; the cosmic or universal aspect of the deity

Vishnu – vedic deity; preserver of the universe; supreme consciousness; the second deity of the Hindu trinity, entrusted with the preservation of the world, a duty which obliges him to appear in several incarnations; deity often associated with water

Vishuddhi chakra – literally 'centre of purification', the psychic/pranic centre located at the level of the throat pit or the thyroid gland and associated with the cervical and laryngeal plexus at the base of the throat. It is the psychic centre connected with purification and communication

Vishwakarma – name of the architect and engineer of the gods; epithet of the sun

Vrata – vow; resolution to carry out a particular vow under strict rules, for example, in regard to food, sleep, bathing and the like

Vrittis – mental modifications; a modification arising in consciousness; circular movement of consciousness; the five mental modifications described in Sage Patanjali's *Yoga Sutras* are: 1. right knowledge, *pramana* 2. wrong knowledge, *viparyaya* 3. dream or fancy, *vikalpa* 4. sleep, *nidra* 5. memory, *smriti*; being, existence; abiding, remaining; attitude, being in a particular state or condition; action, movement, function; operation of mind; thought waves

Vyabhicharini – fickle; moving from one object to another searching for pleasure; fluctuating and flirting action

Vyasa – name of a great sage who wrote the *Brahma Sutra* and the *Mahabharata*, which includes the *Bhagavad Gita*, and codified the four Vedas and more; also called Rishi Krishnadvaipayana, Rishi Veda Vyasa and Badarayana, and considered to be an avatara of Lord Vishnu

Vyoma – space; sky or firmament, ether; another term for akasha

Yajna – sacrifice or sacrificial rite; vedic sacrifice; the offering of oblations to the fire; yajna consists of three syllables, 'ya', 'ja' and 'na', which refer to the three processes involved in every act performed and must be balanced – production

259

(*ya*), distribution (*ja*) and assimilation (*na*); yajna has three components: ritual or worship (*pooja*), satsang and unconditional giving (*daan*)

Yajamana – the facilitator of a yajna; one who performs yajna; the master of a sacrifice; person who performs a regular sacrifice and pays for its expenses or who employs a priest or priests to sacrifice on their behalf

Yajurveda – literally 'knowledge of sacrifice'; Veda containing all the rituals, mantras, karmas and resulting fruits or effects of karmas (*karmaphala*) relating to sacrifice. The second of the four principal Vedas, it is a collection of sacred texts in prose relating to sacrifices

Yaksha – nature spirit; name of a certain type of demigod described as attendants of Kubera, the god of riches. They are employed in guarding his gardens and treasures; a ghost or spirit

Yama – self-restraint or rules of conduct which render the emotions tranquil; the first of the eight limbs and a means of attaining samadhi in the ashtanga yoga of Sage Patanjali's *Yoga Sutras*. The five mentioned by Sage Patanjali are: 1. non-violence, *ahimsa* 2. truth, *satya* 3. non-stealing, *asteya* 4. continence, *brahmacharya* 5. non-covetousness, *aparigraha*; universal moral commandments or ethical disciplines transcending creed, country, age and time; forbearance, self-control; restraining, controlling, any great moral or religious duty or observance; god of death

Yati – mendicant; Dravidian ascetics; earliest sannyasins; to control oneself

Yoga – the root is *yuj*, meaning 'to join, to yoke, to concentrate one's attention'; a method of practice leading to conscious union of the individual soul (*atman*) with the universal existence (*Brahman*); practices, philosophy and lifestyle to achieve peace, power and spiritual wisdom as well as perfect health, a sound mind and a balanced personality

Yoga nidra – 'psychic sleep'; practice where the body sleeps and the mind remains aware although its movements are quietened, inducing deep relaxation; a state of complete bodily relaxation and magnetization in which the mind rests in a suspended state; awake yet calm and free from all distractions; sleep of Vishnu during the end of a yuga

Yogi – a practitioner of yoga; a person who lives yoga; a person in love with God; an adept in yoga; follower of the yoga system of philosophy and practice; one connected or endowed with yoga; one possessed of magical powers

Yogini – female yogi

Yoni – the source, the womb, the female reproductive organ; any place of birth; origin; generating cause; spring

Yuga – aeon; according to yogic understanding, advanced civilizations have risen and fallen many times as the universe pulsates through phases of evolution and manifestation (a day of Brahma) and phases of involution or dissolution where there is no manifestation (a night of Brahma). There are four aeons of the world, viz. 1. Krita or Satya Yuga, 2. Treta Yuga, 3. Dwapara Yuga, 4. Kali Yuga. These four yugas combined make one mahayuga, while 1,000 mahayugas make a day of Brahma and 1,000 more make a night

Śivanāmāvalyaṣṭakam

1. He chandrachūḍa madanāntaka śūlapāṇe,
Sthāṇo giriśa girijeśa maheśa śambho.
Bhūteśa bhītabhayasūdana māmanāthaṃ,
Saṃsāra-duḥkha-gahanājjagadīśa rakṣa.

2. He pārvatī hṛdayavallabha-chandramaule,
Bhūtādhipa pramathanātha girīśajāpa.
He vāmadeva bhava rudra pinākapāṇe,
Saṃsāra-duḥkha-gahanājjagadīśa rakṣa.

3. He nīlakaṇṭha vṛṣabhadhvaja pañchavaktra,
Lokeśa śeṣavalaya pramatheśa śarva.
He dhūrjaṭe paśupate girijāpate māṃ,
Saṃsāra-duḥkha-gahanājjagadīśa rakṣa.

4. He viśvanātha śivaśaṅkara devadeva,
Gaṅgādhara pramathanāyaka nandikeśa.
Bāṇeśvarāndhakaripo hara lokanātha,
Saṃsāra-duḥkha-gahanājjagadīśa rakṣa.

5. Vārāṇasīpurapate maṇikarṇikeśa,
Vīreśa dakṣamakhakāla vibho gaṇeśa.
Sarvajña sarvahṛdayaika-nivāsa nātha,
Saṃsāra-duḥkha-gahanājjagadīśa rakṣa.

6. Śrī manmaheśvara kṛpāmaya he dayālo,
He vyomakeśa śitikaṇṭha gaṇādhinātha.
Bhasmāṅgarāga nṛkapāla-kalāpamāla,
Saṃsāra-duḥkha-gahanājjagadīśa rakṣa.

7. Kailāsaśaila-vinivāsa vṛṣākape he,
Mṛtyuñjaya trinayana trijagannivāsa.
Nārāyaṇapriya madāpaha śaktinātha,
Saṃsāra-duḥkha-gahanājjagadīśa rakṣa.

8. Viśveśa viśvabhayanāśaka viśvarūpa,
Viśvātmaka tribhuvanaikaguṇādhivāsa.
He viśvanātha karuṇāmaya dīnabandho,
Saṃsāra-duḥkha-gahanājjagadīśa rakṣa.

Om śāntiḥ śāntiḥ śāntiḥ. Hariḥ om

Śiva Stuti

1. Jaya śivaśaṅkara, jaya gaṅgādhara,
   karuṇākara karatāra hare,
   Jaya kailāśī, jaya avināśī,
   sukharāśī, sukha-sāra hare,
   Jaya śaśi-śekhara, jaya ḍamarū-dhara,
   jaya jaya premāgāra hare,
   Jaya tripurārī, jaya madahārī,
   amita ananta apāra hare,
   Nirguṇa jaya jaya, saguṇa anāmaya,
   nirākāra, sākāra hare,
   Pāravatī pati, hara hara śambho,
   pāhi pāhi dātāra hare.

2. Jaya rāmeśvara, jaya nāgeśvara,
   vaidyanātha kedāra hare,
   Mallikārjuna, somanātha jaya,
   mahākāla oṅkāra hare,
   Tryambakeśvara, jaya ghuśmeśvara,
   bhīmeśvara jagatāra hare,
   Kāśīpati, śrī viśvanātha jaya,
   maṅgalamaya, agha hāra hare,

Nīlakaṇṭha jaya, bhūtanātha jaya,
mṛtyuñjaya avikāra hare,
Pāravatī pati, hara hara śambho,
pāhi pāhi dātāra hare.

3. Jaya maheśa, jaya jaya bhaveśa,
jaya ādi deva, mahādeva vibho,
Kisa mukha se he guṇātīta prabhu,
tava apāra guṇa varṇana ho,
Jaya bhavakāraka, tāraka, hāraka,
pātaka-dāraka, śiva śambho,
Dīna duḥkhahara, sarva sukhākara,
prema sudhākara dayā karo,
Pāra lagā do bhavasāgara se,
banakara karṇādhāra hare,
Pāravatī pati, hara hara śambho,
pāhi pāhi dātāra hare.

4. Jaya mana bhāvana, jaya atipāvana,
śoka naśāvana śiva śambho,
Vipada vidārana, adhama ubārana,
satya sanātana śiva śambho,
Sahaja vachana hara, jalaja nayana vara,
dhavala varana tana śiva śambho,
Madana kadana kara pāpa harana hara,
charana manana dhana śiva śambho,
Vivasana, viśvarūpa, pralayaṅkara,
jaga ke mūlādhāra hare,
Pāravatī pati, hara hara śambho,
pāhi pāhi dātāra hare.

Om śāntiḥ śāntiḥ śāntiḥ. Hariḥ om